# THE BIG BANG
# THEORY
## AND
# PHILOSOPHY

# The Blackwell Philosophy and Pop Culture Series
Series Editor: William Irwin

# THE BIG BANG THEORY

## AND

# PHILOSOPHY

## ROCK, PAPER, SCISSORS, ARISTOTLE, LOCKE

Edited by Dean A. Kowalski

John Wiley & Sons, Inc.

Copyright © 2012 by John Wiley & Sons. All rights reserved

Published by John Wiley & Sons, Inc., Hoboken, New Jersey

Published simultaneously in Canada

For general information about our other products and services, please contact our Customer Care Department within the United States at (800) 762-2974, outside the United States at (317) 572-3993 or fax (317) 572-4002.

Wiley also publishes its books in a variety of electronic formats and by print-on-demand. Some content that appears in standard print versions of this book may not be available in other formats. For more information about Wiley products, visit us at www.wiley.com.

*Library of Congress Cataloging-in-Publication Data*

The big bang theory and philosophy: rock, paper, scissors, Aristotle, Locke / edited by Dean A. Kowalski.
    pages cm.—(The Blackwell philosophy and pop culture series; 44)
    Includes bibliographical references and index.
    ISBN 978-1-118-07455-8 (pbk.); ISBN 978-1-118-22252-2 (ebk.);
    ISBN 978-1-118-23641-3 (ebk.); ISBN 978-1-118-26137-8 (ebk.)
    1. Big bang theory (Television program)  2. Philosophy—Miscellanea.
I. Kowalski, Dean A., editor of compilation.
PN1992.77.B485B54  2012
791.45'72—dc23
                                                                    2011043333

Printed in the United States of America

# CONTENTS

# ACKNOWLEDGMENTS

When I Write My Memoirs, You Can Expect a Very
Effusive Footnote—and Perhaps a Signed Copy
—Dr. Sheldon Cooper, "The Electric Can Opener
Fluctuation"

I would like to thank all of the contributing authors. Each was a pleasure to work with, and many of them participated in voluminous e-mail exchanges and provided multiple drafts. Not one of them called me a giant "dic-tator," even though I may have come close to deserving that Sheldon-esque moniker on occasion. I would also like to thank my wife, Patricia, for indulging me in yet one more philosophy and pop culture book. Her patience knows no bounds. I must note Nicholas and Cassie; although they interrupted their dad's "research" numerous times, they also inspired me (and now flawlessly use the term *Bazinga*). And Joseph Foy continues to inspire me as a colleague and a (complete) friend.

I am especially indebted to series editor Bill Irwin. Working on a book with him was one of my professional goals, and he was incredibly gracious to make it just that—a collaborative effort. He gives generously of his time, enthusiasm, and expertise to make these books the best they can be. In fact, the whole Wiley team is deserving of recognition, especially Connie Santisteban.

As I was composing this volume, I was often reminded of the countless hours I had spent with my siblings in front of the television, giggling at shows like *The Big Bang Theory*. I dedicate this book to them and all the happy memories we shared as kids:

*To Amber, Beth, and Corey*

# INTRODUCTION
## "Unraveling the Mysteries"

*Dean A. Kowalski*

It took nearly fourteen billion years, but you finally hold in your hands *The Big Bang Theory and Philosophy*. Other bookstore browsers are perusing volumes such as *Bernie Bunny Has Two Daddies Now* or *Jerry the Gerbil and the Bullies on the Bus*, but they lack the basic social skills that you and I take for granted. Those dumbasses will probably buy a different book. But not you. You'll buy this one because you sit at the cool table—fo' shizzle. With receipt in hand, you'll run home like the Flash, pour your favorite bowl of cereal (with a quarter cup of milk), and find *your* favorite spot on the couch.

There are books that debate math, science, and history; there are books that help you build walls or even pyramids; there are even books that discuss Neanderthals with tools and autotrophs that drool. This book discusses philosophy, but you

1

don't need an IQ of 187 to enjoy it. I swear to cow! As you'll see, the philosophy is theoretical, but the fun is real.

Philosophers ponder the "big questions" about what is "really real," how we ought to behave, and whether we know anything at all. Philosophers tend to reexamine what intellectual greats of the past have said about such "big questions." Yet not quite like this. In this book, you'll have the chance to ponder what Aristotle might say about the life Sheldon leads, why Thomas Hobbes would applaud the roommate agreement, and whom Immanuel Kant would treat with haughty derision for weaving "un-unravelable webs."

Yes, some philosophy books attempt to explain the nature of science and why it's so important to study, but, inexplicably, they do so without references to Darth Vader Force-chokes, spherical chicken jokes, or oompa-loompas. Go figure. Rarely do philosophy books explore whether comic book–wielding geeks can lead the good life, or whether they can know enough science to tear the mask off nature and stare at the face of God. Rarer still are explorations into how socially awkward, Superhero-loving brainiacs meaningfully interact with down-to-earth beauties from India or the Cheesecake Factory. I know of none that investigate the evilness of Wil Wheaton. This book is a Saturnalia miracle!

No, I am not sassing you in Eskimo talk. Begin turning pages to see what I mean. As you continue to explore your new favorite philosophy book, you'll learn that regardless of our differences and Sheldon-like idiosyncrasies, we are not merely atoms randomly banging into one another. We are persons, none of us perfect, who seek meaningful relationships with others, even if doing so doesn't always make perfect scientific sense. (No, Sheldon, that's not sarcasm—even *you* cannot completely avoid the "inexplicable need for human contact.")

Okay, I admit that there are some things this book won't do for you. It won't help you clone your own Leonard Nimoy, build a "Kwipke Kwipplah," or single-handedly win a Physics

Bowl. It may not help you pick up Summer Glau on a train or make you forget the betrayal you still feel over FOX canceling *Firefly*. But it will make you laugh. Just as important, it will help you begin to unravel some of life's most profound mysteries—as you bask in the comforting glow of your luminescent fish nightlight.

So, what's your hesitation? Pull that fifty dollar bill you have stashed in Green Lantern's firm buttocks and start reading! Oh, wait—the humanities. Please donate the remainder of your fifty dollars to the National Endowment for the Humanities. Bazinga!

# PART ONE

# "IT ALL BEGAN ON A WARM SUMMER'S EVENING IN GREECE": ARISTOTELIAN INSIGHTS

# ARISTOTLE ON SHELDON COOPER: ANCIENT GREEK MEETS MODERN GEEK

*Greg Littmann*

If I may be permitted to speak again, Doctor Sheldon Cooper for the win.

—Dr. Sheldon Cooper, "The White Asparagus
Triangulation"

Should you live like Sheldon Cooper? Think hard, because you don't have the luxury of not making a choice. Fourteen billion years after the Big Bang, evolution has finally produced a type of animal, human beings, that must choose how it will live. As Sheldon himself points out in "The Cooper-Hofstadter Polarization," "We have to take in nourishment, expel waste, and inhale enough oxygen to keep our cells from dying. Everything else is optional." Should we devote ourselves to learning more about the world around us? Is it alright to spend vast amounts of time reading comics or watching television? Would it be better to neglect our social lives so that we can spare more time for other things? The geeky life of a Sheldon may be a new option in human history, but the question of how we should live is a very ancient one.

In this chapter, we'll examine the question of how we should live by asking how the life of Sheldon stacks up against the ideal set forth by the ancient Greek philosopher Aristotle, one of the most influential thinkers of all times. The interesting thing about looking at Sheldon from Aristotle's perspective is the degree to which this ancient conception of living well is fulfilled by a very modern geek such as Sheldon. The goal here is not to take Aristotle as a guru whose answers must be accepted, but to cast light on our condition to help us consider for ourselves the most important question we face: "How should we live?" Before we bring on Aristotle, though, we had better start with the question "What is it to live the life of Sheldon?"

## The Life of the Mind

> Bernadette: Sheldon, when was the last time you got any sleep?
> Sheldon: I don't know. Two, three days. Not important. I don't need sleep, I need answers. I need to determine where in this swamp of unbalanced formulas squateth the toad of truth.[1]

If there is one thing that sets Sheldon apart, it is that he has given his life over almost entirely to mental activity. He not only *works* with his mind, but when he isn't working, he finds recreation in imagination and puzzle-solving. The idea of losing his intelligence frightens Sheldon more than the idea of losing his life. When Amy suggests in "The Thespian Catalyst" that he burn the memories of bad student evaluations from his brain with a laser, he refuses on the grounds that "One slip of the hand and suddenly I'm sitting in the Engineering Department building doodads with Wolowitz."

In fact, Sheldon doesn't identify with his body at all. He would as happily alter it as he would upgrade any machine. In "The Financial Permeability," he reveals his hope that scientists will soon "develop an affordable technology to fuse my skeleton with adamantium like Wolverine." By choice, he would abandon his body altogether. In "The Cruciferous Vegetable Amplification," he looks forward to "the singularity . . . when man will be able to transfer his consciousness into machines and achieve immortality." Furthermore, he's flattered to be told that he resembles C3PO, and one of his goals is to be a thinking satellite in geostationary orbit. Compare this to Raj's attitude—although Raj would also be happy to upgrade to a different body, his ideal is not a body built for pure thought, but for pure pleasure. In "The Monopolar Expedition," he muses, "My religion teaches that if we suffer in this life, we are rewarded in the next. Three months at the North Pole with Sheldon and I'm reborn as a well-hung billionaire with wings."

Sheldon is largely happy to forgo mere bodily pleasures. It is true, he's *fussy* about the condition of his body—his food must be exactly right, the temperature must be exactly right, he must be sitting on *his* cushion in *his* place on the couch. Yet his body is a distracting source of discontent, rather than a source of pleasure. Sex is particularly uninteresting to him. As he derisively notes in "The Dumpling Paradox," all sex has to offer is "nudity, orgasms, and human contact." In "The Cooper-Nowitzki Theorem," Penny asks Leonard, "What's his deal? Is it girls? Guys? Sockpuppets?" and Leonard confesses, "Honestly, we've been operating under the assumption that he has no deal." In this regard, Sheldon thinks that the rest of us should be more like him. In "The Financial Permeability," he says of Leonard, "My theory is that his lack of focus [on work] stems from an overdeveloped sex drive." Sheldon holds the very idea of sex in such contempt that in "The Desperation Emanation," he follows his offer to make love to Amy with a cry of "Bazinga!" Conversely, Leonard, Raj, and Howard see value in the pleasures of sex. Howard arguably regards his interest in sex as an essential feature of himself. In "The Nerdvana Annihilation," when Penny tells Leonard, "It is the things you love that make you who you are," Howard interjects, "I guess that makes me large breasts."

## The Ancient Greek and the Modern Geek

Sheldon: I'm a physicist. I have a working knowledge of
   the entire universe and everything it contains.
Penny: Who's Radiohead?
Sheldon: I have a working knowledge of the *important*
   things.[2]

Is Sheldon right that the best life for a human being is a life of the intellect? Socrates (470–399 BCE), Plato (428–348 BCE), and Aristotle (384–322 BCE), just to tag ancient Greek philosophy's "big three," all stressed the importance of intellectual development and activity over indulging the body. The same is true of prominent ancient philosophical sects such as the Cynics, the Epicureans, and the Stoics.

Aristotle believed that you can tell the function of something from what it does best. A DVD player is the best thing for playing DVDs—that's the function of a DVD player. A screwdriver is the best thing for unscrewing screws from the back of your TiVo to install a larger hard drive—screwing and unscrewing is the function of a screwdriver. A fish is the best at swimming, so it is the function of a fish to swim. A horse is the best at galloping, so galloping is the function of a horse.

Looked at from this perspective, humanity doesn't seem to be good for much. Compared to the most capable animals in each category, we humans are slow, weak, clumsy, and oblivious—a slab of fresh, fatty meat on two useless little legs. What humans *are* relatively good at, though, is *thinking*. In fact, we are better at thinking than anything else in existence (yet, as far as we know). So our function is to think, and a life of thinking well habitually is the best life for a human being. Aristotle wasn't suggesting that we should never exercise, never have sex, or otherwise refrain from bodily activity. Given the sort of creatures we are, that simply wouldn't be practical. The body is there, however, to support a life of mental activity—it is *mental activity* that is the entire *point* of being human. Aristotle wrote "that which is proper to each thing is by nature best and most pleasant for each thing; for man, therefore, the life according to reason is best and pleasantest, since reason more than anything else is man."[3] Indeed, Aristotle thought that the *ideal* sort of existence would consist in nothing *but* pure thought, a life of uninterrupted Godlike contemplation.[4] This sounds not so very different from Sheldon's fantasy of being a mechanical satellite, thinking away in space. So, would Aristotle advise us to be like Sheldon? Is this the best life for a human being? The rise of geek culture has received too little attention from scholars of Aristotle, because the appearance and proliferation of geeky intellectuals such as Sheldon, Leonard, Raj, and Howard pose significant new problems for the Aristotelian account of living well. Geeks, after all, devote their intellectual activity to the *weirdest things*.

Some geeky obsessions, Aristotle would definitely applaud. Aristotle stressed the importance of observing and theorizing to learn more about the universe, and he wrote widely to spread his observations and theories about the world and the cosmos, contributing to biology, botany, logic, mathematics, and medicine. Enormously influential in the history of thought, he has as good a claim as anyone to being the father of science.

Aristotle said that the difference between the educated and the uneducated is as great as that between the living and the dead.[5] So Sheldon's and Leonard's work in physics and Raj's work in astronomy would impress Aristotle enormously, and he would respect Howard's somewhat lesser Ph.D.-less education.

Aristotle would even approve of many of Sheldon's obsessions that might seem the most ridiculous to someone without a curious mind. A discussion about "the scientific foundations of interstellar flight on a silver surf board," as conducted in "The Excelsior Acquisition," is an examination of the laws of physics, even if the motivation is unusual. Lectures on the correct undergarments for a medieval knight or what medieval bosoms would say if they could speak, as presented in "The Codpiece Topology," rest on a mastery of history—a subject that Aristotle held in high regard. Even turning lights in China on and off over the Internet, as performed in "The Cooper-Hofstadter Polarization," is a scientific experiment of sorts, exploring the limits of new technology. Arguments over whether the Terminator can be part of a causal loop when time traveling, as discussed in "The Terminator Decoupling," or whether *Star Trek*-style teleportation would constitute death, as considered in "The Jerusalem Duality," concern very real and very important *philosophical* issues. It's just that they use examples drawn from popular culture. Greek philosophers did that sort of thing all of the time, though. Aristotle, for instance, used Hector from the *Iliad* to investigate courage and Neoptolemus from Sophocles' play *Philoctetes* to investigate self-mastery.

## The Joy of Geekdom

> Penny: My God! You are grown men. How can you waste your lives with these stupid toys and costumes and comic books?[6]

Admittedly, some of Sheldon's obsessions seem both intellectually demanding and utterly *trivial*. For starters, he's knowledgeable about subjects that arguably just don't matter that much. He is an expert on the history of the X-Men, for instance, and has an expansive Klingon vocabulary. He devotes himself to challenging puzzles that resolve no real-world issues. He's a master of 3D chess and old text adventure games such as *Zork* and, as we saw in "The Hamburger Postulate," will painstakingly recreate the Battle of Gettysburg with condiments just to see what would have happened if the North had been reinforced by Sauron's Orcs and the South by superheroes and Indian gods. He has also clearly spent much time and effort mastering the strategies of popular games such as the MMORPGs *World of Warcraft* and *Age of Conan* and the *Magic: The Gathering*–like card game *Mystic Warlords of Ka-'a*. Sheldon will attend to problems in popular culture that have no bearing on real-world issues just as quickly as he will attend to problems that do. For example, he carefully considers the questions of how zombies eat and vampires shave in "The Benefactor Factor" and how Superman can clean his costume when it gets dirty in "The Bath Item Gift Hypothesis."

Similarly, Sheldon is passionate about art, but not the sort of art that is traditionally accorded status among intellectuals. He's a connoisseur of television, being devoted to *Battlestar Galactica*, *Doctor Who*, *Firefly*, *Star Gate*, *Star Trek* in all of its incarnations, and more (but *not Babylon 5*!). His love of cinema is so great that he can't stand the thought of being late to a screening of *Raiders of the Lost Ark* with twenty-one seconds of unseen footage, and he is willing to lose his friends rather than part with a genuine ring prop from *The Lord of the Rings* trilogy. His greatest artistic passion is literature and, in particular, comic books. The mere smell of them can send him into rapture, and he collects and dresses up in anything associated with his comic book heroes. Aristotle thought that pleasure is good in itself, but it must be pleasure gained from a worthy activity. Is such frivolity really a worthy activity for a sharp mind?

What makes a mental activity worthy, though? For Aristotle, the mere fact that a mental activity deals with fiction does not make it trivial. Indeed, he claimed that "Poetry . . . is a more philosophical and a higher thing than history: for poetry tends to express the universal, history the particular."[7] That is, poetry is more philosophical and significant than history, because history deals only with what *has* happened, while poetry explores what *could* happen and so has a far more universal scope. In his *Politics*, Aristotle stressed the essential importance of poetry and literature in education, and he wrote a great deal about what makes for good art in his *Poetics*.[8]

Aristotle saw art as serving two legitimate goals beyond offering mere relaxation. First, art can educate us; second, art can improve us as human beings. Art educates us by allowing us to explore the human condition and so learn more about ourselves. By examining theoretical situations, such as what happens to four friends who each crave a prop ring from *The Lord of the Rings*, we can learn more about human nature than if we had only examined actual cases of human behavior. Theater edifies us by allowing us to purge our negative emotions. Tragedy, for instance, edifies us through catharsis, through feeling negative emotions such as fear and pity on behalf of fictional characters. Music edifies us in a similar manner, rousing our emotions and so allowing us to get them out of our systems. What about comedy? Aristotle also wrote about comedy, but unfortunately, the second book of the *Poetics*, containing these writings, has been lost. We'll just have to continue watching *The Big Bang Theory* and consider the matter for ourselves.

## Geeky Fun and the Purpose of Life

Leonard: [Sheldon]'s asking if we can come as anyone from science fiction, fantasy . . .

Penny: Sure.

Sheldon: What about comic books . . . anime . . . TV, film, D&D, manga, Greek gods, Roman gods, Norse gods?[9]

Even Sheldon would accept that his preferred art forms are of dubious educational value. There is very little to be learned about *science* from watching *Battlestar Galactica* or *Star Trek* and less still from the surreal tales of *Star Wars* or *Doctor Who*. Similarly, it's unlikely that anyone will improve his or her scientific understanding by reading comic books devoted to the adventures of Batman, Flash, Green Lantern, Hulk, or the X-Men. Could such artworks instead teach us about *humanity*, as Aristotle desired? They might have something to teach Sheldon, given his disconnection from the human race, but that doesn't address the issue of what *we* should do. Is it alright for *us* to kick back and read a "graphic novel" about a costumed crime fighter with weird powers, or is it a shameful waste of our intellectual potential? To be honest, I don't think that there is *much* to be learned directly about human nature from the sort of art that Sheldon enjoys, particularly when you consider that unlike Aristotle's options, our available alternatives include well-researched nonfiction books about human psychology and culture.

On the other hand, works of the imagination can be extremely useful as food for thought. As we know, Sheldon uses franchises such as *Silver Surfer*, *The Terminator*, and *Star Trek* as inspiration for questions about physics, time and causation, and personal identity. Such fantasies, often *because* of the highly unusual situations that arise in them, can be very handy for exploring such issues, as well as issues relating to human nature, morality, or . . . just about anything, really. This very book you hold, *The Big Bang Theory and Philosophy*, is devoted to using the fictional world of *The Big Bang Theory* to explore important philosophical questions—questions such as "What sort of life is best for a human being?" Similar books explore important philosophical questions by relating them to superheroes and supervillains, computer games like *World of Warcraft*; science fiction programs like *Battlestar Galactica*, *Doctor Who*, and *Star Trek*; and fantasy works like *The Lord of the Rings.* If Aristotle held that poetry is more philosophical than history because poetry allows us to explore hypothetical situations, then perhaps outlandish literature is the most philosophical of all, because the range of hypothetical situations that arises is so great. So the issue for us isn't whether it's alright to kick back with a graphic novel (or a sci-fi movie or a computer game) per se, but whether we will be passive recipients of art or instead *use* it to help us think about humanity and the universe.

What about the use of art as a source of catharsis? It seems likely that Sheldon's preferred forms of entertainment can perform this function, if any art does. Sheldon's preferred genre might be described as "amazing adventure." Though he nitpicks plausibility, he'll suspend his disbelief for the sake of a thrilling fantasy. So what if Green Lantern's ring makes no sense, given the laws of physics? Swallowing the absurdity is a small price for Sheldon to pay for the fun of seeing a man with a ring that can do *anything* go up against an endless queue of supervillains. If tragedy allows us to purge our fear by experiencing it on behalf of others, then adventure presumably purges both our fear and our restless excitement. If an adventure truly grips us, then there is a sense of release when it is resolved, a shrugging off of the tension we carry.

Given that Aristotle justified art in terms of its educational and edificatory value, then he might approve both of Sheldon's art *and* his games. Aristotle, in his defense of the importance of music in education, stated, "It is clear . . . that there are branches of learning and education which we must study merely with a view to leisure spent in intellectual activity, and these are to be valued for their own sake."[10] If Sheldon's games exercise his mental muscles, and his art gives him food for thought and emotional catharsis, then perhaps Aristotle could allow for the usefulness of both, even if they often revolve around themes of no importance in themselves, such as whether an imaginary hobbit will manage to toss an imaginary ring into an imaginary volcano.

## Trial of a Nerd

Wil Wheaton: What is wrong with him?
Stuart: Everyone has a different theory.[11]

So much for the intellectual activities that Sheldon *does* engage in. How would Aristotle feel about the intellectual activities that Sheldon *doesn't* engage in? Despite his knowledge of history and tendency to philosophize, he's contemptuous of the Humanities in general. So great is his disdain that in "The Benefactor Factor," Sheldon's main motivation for ensuring that a large donation goes to the Physics Department is that otherwise, it will go to the *humanities*. Amy horrifies him with the thought of "millions of dollars being showered on poets, literary theories, and students of gender studies." Conversely, Aristotle held poetry in high esteem, wrote extensively on literary theory, and theorized about the nature of masculinity and femininity. Indeed, Aristotle regarded the study of human nature, culture, and politics to be every bit as important as the study of the natural world.

More damning yet from Aristotle's perspective is that Sheldon is lacking in the virtues of character, which Aristotle regarded as essential for a life lived well. Let it be said in Sheldon's defense, he's not *completely* without virtue. He's hard-working, dedicating himself, as he states in "The Benefactor Factor," to "tearing off the mask of nature and staring at the face of God." He's temperate in his bodily indulgences, neither stuffing himself with food nor getting drunk nor even drinking coffee. He's also open-handed when lending money, as Penny learns in "The Financial Permeability." On the other hand, Sheldon is extraordinarily arrogant, so much so that Raj concludes in "The Hot Troll Deviation" that "If you were a superhero your name would be Captain Arrogant. And do you know what your super power would be? Arrogance!" Sheldon is so lacking in fortitude that the slightest checking of his desires is intolerable to him. He *must* sit in exactly the right place on the couch, on the "0–0–0–0" point where temperature and position relative to the television are ideal. Sheldon is so rash in the face of artistic greatness that, as we learn in "The Excelsior Acquisition," he has earned a restraining order from both Leonard Nimoy and Stan Lee. Above all, though, Sheldon is incredibly self-centered. He is so selfish that in "The Creepy Candy Coating Corollary," he can't spare Leonard a napkin, though he has *four*; so selfish that in "The Cooper-Hofstadter Polarization," he would rather deny Leonard a chance to present their joint research than let Leonard present it without him, even though he intends *never* to present it himself.

Aristotle believed that friendship is crucial to human flourishing, while Sheldon clearly struggles with friendship. In "The Hamburger Postulate," for instance, he informs Leonard that he just doesn't care about his relationship problems. Similarly, in "The Bad Fish Paradigm," Howard confronts Sheldon over the fact that Sheldon doesn't look out for his interests—"How could you just sit there and let them spy on me?" he demands. Sheldon replies, "They were very smart! They used my complete lack of interest in what you are doing."[12]

## The Aristotle-Cooper Evaluation

Sheldon: Why are you crying?
Penny: Because I'm stupid.
Sheldon: Well, that's no reason to cry. One cries because one is sad. For example, I cry because others are stupid, and that makes me sad.[13]

Aristotle would have given Sheldon a mixed report card, then. He wouldn't have rated the life of Sheldon as highly as Sheldon does, but neither would he have joined mainstream society in dismissing Sheldon as a weird little loser, too wrapped up in unimportant things to grow up and get on with life. What is particularly interesting is the degree to which Sheldon is getting it *right*, on an Aristotelian model.

We all appreciate that Sheldon is, in many ways, dysfunctional, and it would be a flaw in Aristotle's model if it rated Sheldon as the epitome of what a human being should be like. Nevertheless, Aristotle would appreciate that Sheldon understands a few things about life that most people don't *get*. Sheldon cares more about understanding the universe than he does about stockpiling money. Sheldon realizes that a human being's most valuable possession is his or her own mind and that when a mind remains underdeveloped, a human life has not been fulfilled. Sheldon does not turn to the life of the mind out of a masochistic or puritanical desire to deny the body. He turns to the life of the mind with wonder and delight because he knows something of the fulfillment that mental life can bring. Even his geekiest of pleasures involves intellectual gymnastics and frequently consideration of important real-world issues.

It seems to me that the modern geek should find comfort in the degree of approval with which Aristotle would (probably) have judged Sheldon Cooper. Geekdom is something of a new social phenomenon, and like all new social phenomena, it is regarded in many quarters with a fair amount of suspicion and derision. Yet it may be that for all of the pomposity, pedantry, and obsessive behavior that geek culture is prey to, geekdom is *not* without its positive side. It may even be that the art and the games beloved by geeks can serve useful purposes. It would be grossly overstating the case to suggest that the rise of the modern geek fulfills Aristotle's dream of the intellectual citizen. On the other hand, I do suspect that the grand old man of philosophy would not have been entirely displeased with this new development in human culture.

## NOTES

1. "The Einstein Approximation."
2. "The Work Song Nanocluster."

3. Aristotle, *Nicomachean Ethics*, in J. Barnes, ed., *The Complete Works of Aristotle* (Princeton, NJ: Princeton University Press, 1984), Book X.

4. Ibid.

5. Diogenes Laërtius, *Lives of Eminent Philosophers*, trans. R. D. Hicks (Cambridge, MA: Harvard University Press, 1925), Book XI.

6. "The Nerdvana Annihilation."

7. Aristotle, *Poetics*, in J. Barnes, ed., *The Complete Works of Aristotle* (Princeton, NJ: Princeton University Press, 1984), Book IX.

8. Aristotle, *Politics*, in J. Barnes, ed., *The Complete Works of Aristotle* (Princeton, NJ: Princeton University Press, 1984), Book VIII.

9. "The Middle Earth Paradigm."

10. Aristotle, *Politics*, in J. Barnes, ed., *The Complete Works of Aristotle* (Princeton, NJ: Princeton University Press, 1984), Book VIII.

11. "The Creepy Candy Coating Corollary."

12. For more on assessing the relationships in *The Big Bang Theory* via Aristotle's ideas of friendship, please see chapter 2, "You're a Sucky, Sucky Friend": Seeking Aristotelian Friendship in *The Big Bang*, by Dean Kowalski in this volume. For a non-Aristotelian account of the friendship between Sheldon and Penny, please see chapter 16, "Penny, Sheldon, and Personal Growth through Difference," by Nicholas Evans, also in this volume.

13. "The Gorilla Experiment."

# "YOU'RE A SUCKY, SUCKY FRIEND": SEEKING ARISTOTELIAN FRIENDSHIP IN *THE BIG BANG THEORY*

*Dean A. Kowalski*

Why would philosophers worry about something as obvious as friendship? We certainly seem to know what friendship is, how to identify it, and how to judge its worthiness. For example, in *The Big Bang Theory*, it seems obvious that Sheldon, Leonard, and Raj act as worthy friends when they stay up all night to aid Howard in repairing and redesigning the space station zero-gravity toilet. It seems obvious, too, that Leonard, Howard, and Raj are not very good friends when they flee to the *Planet of the Apes* movie marathon, rather than care for a sick Sheldon. (Then again, what would "Soft Kitty" sound like coming from Wolowitz's mouth instead of Penny's?)

What does it mean when Amy Farrah Fowler claims that she and Penny are "besties"? Are there different kinds of friendship? And what kind of friendship is best, anyway? Cue the philosophers. Aristotle (384–322 BCE), for one, took a keen interest in the nature of friendship. So, in this chapter, we'll explore *The Big Bang Theory* to learn more about Aristotle's views of friendship and come to better appreciate his point about why true "besties" are so rare.

## "Do You Have Any Books about Making Friends?"

Aristotle wrote about friendship in books VIII and IX of his *Nicomachean Ethics*. He believed that friendship is indispensable to the human experience, saying, "Without friends, no one would choose to live, though he [or she] had all other goods."[1] This pertains even to socially reluctant people such as Sheldon. His time with Beverly Hofstadter, for instance, seems to be a boon to him, even though he typically doesn't feel comfortable around—well, anyone.

According to Aristotle, not only is friendship noble or good for its own sake, but it is good for you. The wealthy benefit because friends guard and preserve prosperity; the poor benefit because they can take refuge in their friends, if nothing else. The young benefit because friends keep them from error, and the elderly benefit because they can rely on those who minister to their needs and supplement their failing activities. Those in the prime of life benefit because it spurs them to become better. Good and just people require friendship, but friends have no need for justice. (Ever see the Superfriends bicker about whose turn it is to take out the garbage?)

Aristotle's account of friendship consisted of reciprocated goodwill and concern: "To be friends, then, they must be mutually recognized as bearing good will and wishing well to each other."[2] So, regardless of how much Sheldon admires his

Green Lantern lantern, how safe it makes him feel, or whether it helps him (unwittingly) pick up girls, he cannot be friends with it. After all, it's an inanimate object. Aristotle's point also means that Amy Farrah Fowler and Penny are not "besties" when Amy originally declares it exactly because Penny was unaware that they were friends—if only she had been keeping up with Amy's blog!

Even in cases where Aristotle's basic requirements for friendship are met, the underlying reasons for expressing mutual goodwill and concern can be varied. Aristotle believed that there are three kinds of friendship, corresponding to the three basic reasons for reciprocating goodwill. The first is for pleasure or what is pleasant, and the second is for utility or what is useful. Aristotle saw nothing inherently wrong or misguided about these two forms of friendship, but he distinguished them from the third and highest form: complete or perfect friendship. Perfect friendship obtains when the mutual care and concern are for the sake of the other. As Aristotle put it, "Those who wish well to their friends for their sake are most truly friends."[3]

## "Did You Ever Consider Making Friends by Being . . . Pleasant?"

Pleasure-based friendships are begun and sustained because they are fun or pleasant in some way. Yet there is nothing mercenary about such relationships. All of the parties involved are aware of the common goal: having fun. Our four young scientists often share this form of friendship. Their weekly Wednesday Halo nights and regular paintball weekends quickly come to mind. The former embodies their mutual love of technology and video games, and the latter facilitates stimulating outdoor recreation, tapping into their appreciation of role-playing games (and, yes, Sheldon, wearing contextually appropriate and historically accurate costumes).

Why did Aristotle deem pleasure-friendships a lower form? He didn't see anything inherently wrong with them, and he didn't believe that complete friendship should be without pleasant experiences. His position rested on two points.

First, he thought, probably rightly, that pleasure-friendships tend not to last. Once the fun is gone or replaced by something else more pleasurable, we tend to move on. Aristotle believed that this described many young people: "Friendship of young people seems to aim at pleasure; for they live under the guidance of emotion, and pursue above all what is pleasant to themselves and what is immediately before them."[4] This explains why Raj becomes so angry at Howard in "The Cornhusker Vortex" during their kite-fighting escapade in the park. String-burn or no, Howard agrees to be Raj's partner. Kites-ho! Howard knows the stakes: if they lose, Raj must surrender his prized Patang fighting kite (the one his brother sent him from New Delhi). When Raj calls for the "flying scissors" maneuver, Howard starts chasing after a female jogger. Raj screams, "What are you doing!? I can't scissors by myself!"

In the car on the way home, Raj is fuming. Howard tries to defend himself, "What was I supposed to do? She gave me that come-hither look." Raj interjects, "If it was any look at all, it was a you-suck look! You always do this. Ditch me for a woman you don't have a shot with." Howard adamantly replies, "I had a shot!" Raj: "With a woman you were chasing in the park? That's not a shot, it's a felony." Later in Raj's apartment, Howard tries to apologize—by buying Raj a pink Hello Kitty Kite. Raj, exasperated, points out, "Wow, you just don't get it do you? Buying me something pretty just isn't going to make our problem go away." Howard finally admits, "Look, I haven't always been the best friend I could be." Both Raj and Howard know that this kind of behavior falls short of true friendship.

The reason Raj is upset with Howard foreshadows Aristotle's second point about pleasure-friendships. Those who are friends for the sake of pleasure, he claimed, are "so for the sake of what is pleasant for *themselves*" but not for the sake of the other himself or herself.[5] A true friend doesn't ditch you at Radio Shack to go make eyes with the girl working behind the counter at Hot Dog on a Stick—especially when you are there to find one of those phones with the big numbers for *his* mother. That Howard is always ready to ditch Raj for the slightest chance of scoring with a girl speaks volumes. He likes Raj and enjoys spending time with him, but he is really out for himself. A true friend wouldn't be so quick to put his interests ahead of yours.[6]

## "Kripke! What'd You Say of the Idea of You and I Becoming Friends?"

Utility-based friendships are made and sustained because they are useful or profitable to us in some way. A more practical or pragmatic pursuit than pleasure is the goal. Aristotle wrote, "Those who pursue utility . . . sometimes . . . do not even find each other pleasant; therefore they do not need such companionship unless they are useful to each other; for they are pleasant to each other only in so far as they rouse in each other hopes of something good to come."[7] Again, there is nothing mercenary here. It's just that the primary motivation for being friends is that each of the parties somehow benefits in some way.

Perhaps this form of friendship best explains why the gang regularly orders take-out together. Doing so may be cheaper than ordering individually; plus, it saves each of them the chore of cooking and the loneliness of dining alone. (This way, Raj only needs to eat his fried chicken alone over the sink one day a year.) Sheldon's relationship with Leonard is utilitarian insofar as the latter regularly drives the former to work. Sheldon doesn't drive, and carpooling probably saves Leonard gas money. In fact, the relationship began out of utility. Leonard and Sheldon became roommates because Leonard was looking for a nice place to live, and Sheldon couldn't afford the rent all by himself. This also explains why Raj and Howard began hanging out with Sheldon. They like spending time with Leonard, but Leonard rooms with Sheldon.

Why did Aristotle deem utility-friendships a lower form of friendship? His reasoning was analogous to what he said about pleasure-friendships. Again, he didn't see anything inherently wrong with them, and he didn't believe that complete friendship should be without pragmatic benefits. His position rested on two familiar points.

First, he said that "the useful is not permanent but is always changing."[8] This is reason to think these kinds of friendships are (also) readily dissolved. Once the intended practical benefit ceases, so does the friendship. The most vivid excursion into utility-based friendship is Sheldon's decision to befriend Barry Kripke in "The Friendship Algorithm." (You know, the guy with the lisp who, on meeting Penny for the first time, said, "Yeah, it's not a vewy hot name. I'm gonna call you Woxanne. Ooh, pot stickers.")

Kripke is a fellow member of the Physics Department at the university, yet he lacks the social skills that Sheldon, Leonard, Raj, and Howard take for granted. (Imagine.) In fact, he is altogether unlikable. Recall his snarky lunchroom comment to Leonard: "Heard about your watest pwoton decay expewiment, twenty thousand data wuns and no statistically significant wesults. Vewy impwessive!" Howard reassures Leonard, "C'mon, don't let him get to you. It's Kripke," and Raj chimes in, "Yeah, he's a ginormous knob." Howard confirms, "That's why he eats by himself, instead of sitting here at the cool table." Raj testifies, "Fo' shizzle."

For all of that, Sheldon needs time on some laboratory equipment that Kripke apparently controls. Leonard wishes Sheldon luck, because "The only people he lets use it are his friends." Even though Sheldon doesn't like Kripke (at all), Sheldon quickly surmises, "The solution is simple—I shall befriend him." Of course, Kripke has no "intewest" in becoming Sheldon's "fwiend." What Sheldon gains by the pending friendship is clear, but Kripke sees no reason for entering into it. Sheldon tries to find common ground, mentioning hot beverages, recreational activities, and monkeys. Kripke counters with horseback riding, swimming, and ventriloquism. They finally agree on the least objectionable common interest: rock climbing—even though Sheldon is afraid of heights (or falling or both).

Sheldon stands before the rock wall. He looks up, admitting that it appears more "monolithic" that it did on his laptop. He looks around for "hominids learning to use bones as weapons." Sensing Sheldon's discomfort, Kripke asks, "You afwaid of heights, Cooper?" Sheldon tries to ignore him but replies, "What would you say is the minimum altitude I need to achieve to cement our new-found friendship?" Kripke goads him, "Come on, they have birthday parties here. Wittle kids climb this." (Little kid hominids, maybe.)

Up Sheldon goes, only to get stuck and pass out (after suffering a wee bit of incontinence.) Ironically, Sheldon later learns that Kripke doesn't control who gets access to the equipment after all. Because Sheldon doesn't find Kripke at all pleasant, the whole point of Sheldon striking up a friendship with him is nullified, leading Sheldon to conclude, "This entire endeavor seems to have been an exercise in futility."

The contrived nature of Sheldon's futile endeavor begins to capture Aristotle's second reason for classifying utility-based friendships as a lesser form of friendship. Again, the focus of the friendship is not the other person but what *you* get out of the relationship. As most people recognize, befriending someone simply for what the two of you get out of it is, at best, hollow. Consider the concept of "friends-with-benefits." This sounds like a good idea—and Howard and Leslie Winkle would no doubt agree. Yet we still feel for Howard when Leslie breaks it off; he was hoping for "something more." That something more is a deeper, more fulfilling relationship. Howard's hope paves the way to Aristotle's third form of friendship.

## "To Make Friends . . . Take an Interest in Their Lives"

Aristotle thought that the best friendships go beyond mere pleasure or utility. True friendship—what he called "complete" or "perfect" friendship—is a relationship between (morally) good people, each of whom recognizes the good character of the other, and each of whom desires to preserve and promote the other's virtue simply because it is good to do so. True friendship occurs between equals—a relationship in which one person is vastly superior to the other in distinctive ways is more likely a paternalistic relationship. As Aristotle said, "Perfect friendship is of [those] who are good, and alike in virtue; for these wish each other well alike to each other qua good, and they are good in themselves."[9] (Think of Kirk and Spock.)

Unlike pleasure and utility friendships, true friendships must involve genuine care for the well-being of the other person, not merely egoistic motives. Of course, that doesn't mean that one may not consider how the friendship affects one's own interests—Aristotle was not advocating slavishness or radical self-sacrifice. The idea is simply that one cares about the other person for his or her own sake and wants to see the other person flourish, regardless of any benefit that one might also receive as a result. (Think the *opposite* of David Underhill and Penny.) Yet Aristotle still held that as a matter of fact, true friendships are beneficial to those involved. In that way, true friendship involves a happy convergence of self-interest and altruism and, as such, results in an ideal kind of moral motivation.

So, for Aristotle, the highest form of friendship occurs between persons of equally good moral character (virtue), which is enhanced due to their interactions. Such friendships are admittedly rare; when they do obtain, it is because the friends spend a great deal of time together, developing a secure mutual trust. Their relationship is fostered by participating in joint ventures and engaging in activities that exercise their own virtues for the betterment of the other and the friendship. All of this is done primarily for the sake of the other person (and not for selfish purposes), even though their interests have grown so close together that it is difficult to separate them. Consequently, complete friendship results in a sort of second self, a true partner.[10]

## "That's Insane on the Face of It"

Aristotle's vision of true friendship is noble but perhaps idealistic. Let's see if we can find any traces of it in *The Big Bang Theory*.

The most obvious place to look is the relationship between Leonard and Sheldon (arguably the Kirk and Spock of the show), because they are roughly equals in terms of intellectual ability and moral virtue. In addition, they spend a great deal of time together, sharing many common interests and helping each other out. Sheldon memorably helped Leonard with the rocket fuel fiasco of 2002. (The elevator took the brunt of that one.) For his part, Leonard is tolerant of Sheldon's various idiosyncrasies and often drives Sheldon to work.

So, should Sheldon and Leonard be interpreted as complete friends? After all, in "The Electronic Can Opener Fluctuation," Sheldon asserts, "Leonard you are my best friend in the world." Yet he repeatedly sees their relationship in the context of the friendship rider of the roommate agreement. In "The Cornhusker Vortex," Leonard desperately seeks Sheldon's help in learning the vagaries of college football to better fit in with Penny's friends. Leonard is flabbergasted that Sheldon knows football in the first place. (Quidditch, sure. But football?) Nevertheless, he's desperate: "Please, I'm asking you as a friend." Sheldon woodenly replies, "Are you making this a tier-one friendship request?" Taking what he can get, Leonard shrewdly replies, "Yes." Sheldon (sighing): "Fine." When Leonard expresses his appreciation, Sheldon responds, "Yeah, yeah."

The wrinkle is obvious: Sheldon has difficulty with any sort of meaningful relationship. In "The Jerusalem Duality," and in the context of Dennis Kim "falling prey to the inexplicable need for human contact," Sheldon flatly states, "Social relationships will continue to baffle and repulse me." Even if we assume that this was uttered by an embittered Sheldon—after all, he is no longer the youngest winner of the Stevenson Award—he remains rather clueless about friendship. In "The Bad Fish Paradigm," he is completely caught off guard by Penny's contention that "friendship contains within it an inherent obligation to maintain confidences." He is even more baffled that they had become friends at all. When Sheldon considers befriending Kripke in "The Friendship Algorithm," his immediate reaction is to end one of his current friendships "because maintaining five friendships promises to be a Herculean task."

This doesn't mean that Sheldon has no understanding of friendship, only that he has great difficulty moving past utility-based friendships. Recall in "The Large Hadron Collision" that Leonard is chosen to visit the CERN supercollider in Switzerland. This is an awesome professional opportunity, and he is allowed to bring a guest. Sheldon runs home to immediately start packing, but, because Valentine's Day falls during the trip, Leonard wants to bring Penny. Sheldon will have none of this: "I call your attention to the Friendship Rider in Appendix C, Future Commitments. Number 37, in the event one friend is ever invited to visit the Large Hadron Collider, now under construction in Switzerland, he shall invite the other friend to accompany him." (Of course, Appendix C also stipulates that Leonard cannot kill Sheldon if he turns into a zombie.) Leonard begs Sheldon not to enforce this, but Sheldon adamantly replies, "I've lived up to all my commitments under the agreement. At least once a day I ask how you are, even though I simply don't care." Yet Leonard remains firm. He's taking Penny. Sheldon feels betrayed and likens his so-called best friend to Benedict Arnold, Judas, and Rupert Murdoch (the man ultimately responsible for canceling *Firefly*).

Sheldon soon has a change of heart, though, or so it seems. He wakes Leonard up with the soothing sounds of a wooden flute, which he plays himself. He further surprises Leonard, announcing, "I've made you breakfast. Juice, coffee, and pancakes in the shape of some of your favorite fictional characters. See, here's Frodo. . . . I can keep them warm with this beret that I thoroughly laundered and pressed into service as a pancake cosy." Smiling, Leonard asks why Sheldon is doing all of this. Sheldon humbly answers, "It's by way of an apology for my recent behavior. I've had some time to reflect and I've come to realize that friendship is not an aggregation of written agreements. It's a result of two people respecting and caring for each other." Sheldon further suggests that after Leonard finishes breakfast, they should spend the day watching *Babylon 5* together—even though "it fails as drama, science fiction, and it's hopelessly derivative"—simply because Leonard is his friend.

Aha! Is this the friendship-breakthrough we've been looking for? Alas, Leonard coyly adds, "Great. Still not taking you to Switzerland." Without missing a beat, Sheldon says, "Drat. No Frodo for you," removing the breakfast tray from Leonard's bed and unceremoniously leaving the room. Sheldon is happy to act as if he is Leonard's complete friend, but only if Leonard takes him to Switzerland. Sheldon seemingly knows what true friendship entails, but he simply cannot bring himself to act on that knowledge. He prefers relationships grounded in contractual agreements and will uphold his end of the friendship bargain if Leonard upholds his. All of this, at best, amounts to little more than utility-friendship.[11]

## "There Is No Algorithm for Making Friends!"

So, perhaps we should look elsewhere in *The Big Bang Theory* for Aristotelian friendship. The next most likely place to find it is probably between Leonard and Penny. Neither is completely baffled or repulsed by social relationships. It's not clear, though, whether Leonard and Penny are intellectual equals. Recall that this was the stressor the first time they dated. In "The Bad Fish Paradigm," Penny asks Sheldon whether Leonard has dated "regular girls" before. On clarifying that she didn't mean digestive regularity—he's "come to learn that such inquiries are inappropriate"—Sheldon confesses that Leonard hasn't dated very many "non-brainiacs" (except maybe that French literature Ph.D. from France). Penny then hesitantly asks, "Do you think he'll eventually get bored with me?" Sheldon replies, "That depends. Do you have a working knowledge of quantum physics? Do you speak Klingon?" Penny interrupts, "I get it. Leonard has no business being involved with a waitress-slash-actress who felt so insecure that she lied to him about finishing community college."

Perhaps Howard and Raj fare better? They spend a great deal of time together and have many common interests; however, given Howard's propensity for self-absorption, it's unclear whether he is a good candidate for complete friendship—with anyone. Unlike Sheldon, Howard doesn't find the need for human contact—especially some kinds of contact—at all inexplicable. In fact, he lives for it (and if that makes him creepy—then, fine, he's creepy). Yet perhaps Bernadette can turn him around. Leonard and Priya seemed like good candidates, but with her pending return to India, this has become unclear; their time together is growing short, dimming their prospects for complete friendship. Maybe Raj and Leonard? Perhaps, but they don't spend a great deal of time together. Worse, Raj's unforeseen tryst with Penny at the end of season 4 may jeopardize their friendship altogether.

For all of that, it certainly seems as if the characters of *The Big Bang Theory*—especially Leonard and Penny—have become good friends. Even though their romantic relationship failed, Leonard and Penny can still depend on each other. Yet Aristotle would no doubt have said that none of the characters are true friends, reminding us just how rare complete friendship is.

Should we conclude that Aristotle's account of friendship is too idealistic or perhaps outmoded (or both)? Aristotle certainly seems correct that there are different levels of friendship and that true friendship requires genuine care and concern for the other, but perhaps we don't need to be that much alike to become truly good friends with someone? If we break with Aristotle about this, then what does true friendship require?

Friendship, like love, may be among those things that are difficult to define clearly. Yet we know when someone is "a sucky, sucky friend." Maybe that's all we need to know? Beyond that, perhaps the only way to know what makes someone a true friend is to have one and be one.[12]

## NOTES

1. Aristotle, *Nicomachean Ethics*, trans. W. D. Ross, in Richard McKeon, ed., *The Basic Works of Aristotle* (New York: Random House, 1941), 1058. Hereafter citations of Aristotle's *Nicomachean Ethics* will appear via the standard margin number signaled by "*NE*." The margin number for this quote is 1155a5–1155a6.

2. *NE*, 1156a3–1156a5.

3. *NE*, 1156b9–1156b10.

4. *NE*, 1156a32–1156a33.

5. *NE*, 1156a15–1156a17, emphasis in the original.

6. Aristotle seems to have Howard pegged: "Young people are amorous too; . . . this is why they fall in love and quickly fall out of love, changing often within the same day" (*NE*, 1156a35–1156a36).

7. *NE*, 1156a27–1156a30.

8. *NE*, 1156a23.

9. *NE*, 1156b7–1156b9.

10. See *NE*, 1156b24–1156b28, 1157b33–1157b36, and 1166a29–1166a32.

11. Perhaps it might be argued that Sheldon's being baffled and repulsed by human relationships is a substantive moral defect in his character. If so, perhaps he and Leonard are not sufficiently similar for the comparison in the first place. It also follows, then, that Sheldon isn't a good candidate for Aristotelian friendship with anyone.

12. My thanks to the webmaster at <http://bigbangtrans.wordpress.com> for episode dialogue. Each section title is taken from "The Friendship Algorithm."

# THE BIG BANG THEORY ON THE USE AND ABUSE OF MODERN TECHNOLOGY

*Kenneth Wayne Sayles III*

After enjoying an episode of *The Big Bang Theory*, I often have two sobering thoughts: (1) I may have too much in common with Leonard, Sheldon, Howard, and Raj; and (2) I wonder if the show accurately depicts how technology is used in our modern age. As a computer scientist, I'm comfortable with using technology and know the benefits of the Internet and mobile computing. Yet it seems to me that modern society is quick to embrace new technologies because of their ease, appearance, or novelty, without due consideration of possible consequences. Don't get me wrong: I don't think technology is inherently good or bad. I just know there are always costs and benefits in using technology, and we generally do not give due consideration to the costs because we focus only on the benefits. For example, how much are we willing to give up for the sake of convenience? Consider items such as the match, the lighter, the stove, and the oven. Before their development, knowing how to build a fire was an essential skill. That skill is no longer common because it isn't crucial for everyday living anymore. This situation may be fine, but is society travel-ing along a similar path with modern computer use and the Internet? If so, what key skills are we sacrificing?

We have all benefited from the Internet, but with heavy computer use are we now also seeing a decline in social skills? *The Big Bang Theory* offers valuable insight on this issue by showing us healthy and unhealthy uses of technology. Healthy use of technology makes technology a supplement to normal living, whereas unhealthy use makes technology the focus of living and leads to imbalances in one's life and social skills. In the end, I think moderation is the answer to properly balancing technology and life. The characters in *The Big Bang Theory* humorously show us the pitfalls of unbalanced use.[1]

## Some Healthy Webcam-ing

In our modern digital age, it's very easy to interact with one another without actually inhabiting the same physical space, but such interaction can be healthy or unhealthy. Rajesh ("Raj") Koothrappali routinely converses with his parents in India via webcam, telling them about his life, "walking" them around his world, and introducing them to his friends. This is a healthy form of virtual interaction. Raj's parents could move to America, but, based on how they'd like Raj to move back to India, this doesn't seem likely. Raj could move back to India, but he loves living in the United States too much. In "The Pirate Solution," after alerting his friends about his possible deportation, Raj emotionally proclaims, "I don't want to go back to India. It's hot and loud, and there's *so* many people. You have no idea, they're everywhere."[2] Later, he tiredly proclaims, "Oh, beef, I'm going to miss you so much. Do you know, at the Mumbai McDonald's, you can't get a Big Mac? All you can get is a Chicken Maharaja Mac. And the special sauce, curry, which, in India, believe you me, is really not that special." The thought of moving back to India is so distasteful to him that Raj decides to work *for*—not with—Sheldon, and we all know how easy that becomes!

Instead of webcam-ing, Raj or his parents could travel between the United States and India on a regular basis. Obviously, though, the costs for such travel would be quite high. While Raj could call his parents or write, the webcam has the added advantage of allowing Raj and his parents to see one another in "real-time." They would not be able to see one another's expressions or reactions through the phone, but with the webcam, Raj and his parents have the opportunity to regularly converse with one another in an economical way, as they would in person. Furthermore, if Raj wishes to be alone, he can shut off the webcam. Although he can connect with his parents and show them his part of the world, he can also have the independence of an adult. Raj's use of the webcam with his parents is both reasonable and healthy because it does not hinder his growth as an individual, even with his "selective mutism."

In season 4, Sheldon Cooper and Amy Farrah Fowler use the webcam. Although no great distance separates them, I would argue that this virtual interaction is healthy. Their virtual interaction is more of a supplement to their relationship, not a substitution for physical interaction. They are free to develop their relationship in their own way, both inside and outside of the "virtual" world. Considering how Sheldon and Amy do not often interact with others socially, the webcam allows them to have a personal, "real-time" interaction that is more comfortable for them. The webcam also allows their relationship to develop without interrupting their lives, as they often multitask during these interactions. Because work and other activities are more important to them than social graces, the webcam becomes a useful tool to help them do both.

For Raj and his parents, as well as for Sheldon and Amy, the virtual interaction is healthy because it doesn't hinder the social development of the people involved or their relationships with others. In some ways, it even helps them develop and maintain those relationships.

## Unhealthy Interactions

Of course, *The Big Bang Theory* also shows us unhealthy virtual interactions. Consider "The Codpiece Topology," in which Sheldon resorts to playing on his laptop in the stairwell with an extension cord, rather than going out on his own after Leonard brings home a date. In fact, when Penny suggests that he go out, he doesn't see the point and rebuts every claim she makes. Penny suggests going to the movies or a coffee shop, to which Sheldon responds with "What if I choke on my popcorn . . ." and "I don't drink coffee." Here, Sheldon is clearly placing more importance on having solo virtual interactions with a video game than in indulging in social activities in the physical world.

Interestingly, Penny exhibits similar behavior in the subsequent episode "The Barbarian Sublimation." Penny becomes obsessed with the online multiplayer video game *Age of Conan*, and her life quickly spirals downward. She stops washing her hair and changing her clothes, and she becomes completely unproductive, even calling in sick to work so that she can continue playing the game. Penny doesn't realize how far down the rabbit hole she has gone until she finds herself attracted to Howard Wolowitz's avatar. After rather mindlessly agreeing to quest with Howard and meet him at a "virtual" tavern, an exhausted and haggard Penny suddenly regains her senses and exclaims, "Oh my God, I need help," as she tosses her laptop aside and covers it with a pillow!

The most extreme example of unhealthy virtual interaction, though, is Sheldon's behavior in "The Cruciferous Vegetable Amplification." Due to his dreams and thoughts about future cyborgs, he decides to use a computer monitor to interact with the world and forgo all physical contact. Through the computer screen, Sheldon announces:

> I am a mobile virtual presence device. Recent events have demonstrated to me that my body is too fragile to endure the vicissitudes of the world. Until such time as I am able to transfer my consciousness, I shall remain in a secure location and interact with the world in this manner.

In these three examples of unhealthy use of technology, the common link is that the virtual interaction becomes a substitute for healthy physical interaction. In fact, even physical concerns such as healthy eating and good hygiene become secondary. Because the technology is used *unreflectively*, without any consideration for possible consequences, the characters' lives are, or become, imbalanced and abnormal.

Penny's case illustrates this point rather well. Her behavior in "The Barbarian Sublimation" is in clear contrast to her previous gaming behavior and attitudes. In the "Pilot" episode, Howard, in a feeble attempt to woo her, informs Penny about his "virtual" pet tiger and a "virtual" tavern he likes to visit in a video game. He tells her, "Anyway, if you had your own game character we could hang out, maybe go on a quest." Penny unenthusiastically replies, "Uh, sounds interesting." Later in "The Dumpling Paradox," Penny uses playing Halo with the guys as a means to avoid a visiting friend from Nebraska, the "whore of Omaha," who is cozying up to Wolowitz in her apartment. Yet when Leonard says, "You know, Penny, we make such a good team, maybe we could enter a couple of Halo tournaments sometime," Penny replies with "Or we could just have a life." When you take these earlier episodes into context, it is easier to see how unbalanced Penny's life becomes when she shifts to excessive gaming. If this obsessive behavior is any indication of where society is headed, we must seriously question whether the benefits of modern computer use are worth the risk of such a sharp and continuing decline in our social skills and ability to interact in the physical world.

## Virtual Vengeance

The most obvious cases of imbalance involve extreme behaviors such as "virtual vengeance," in which some type of virtual interaction is used to take revenge on someone without having to confront that person directly in the physical world. The first example of this is in "The Panty Piñata Polarization." Sheldon and Penny butt heads over Penny's callous lack of concern for Sheldon's house rules, which include not touching his food. Penny spitefully breaks this same rule later with Sheldon's hamburger when the guys are at the Cheesecake Factory. In response, Sheldon blocks Penny from using his and Leonard's wireless network and uses a recorded video to describe his intentions:

> Greetings, hamburger toucher. You are probably wondering why you cannot IM with your little friends about how much you heart various things. Well, this recorded message is alerting you that I am putting an end to your parasitic piggybacking upon our WiFi. If you want to remedy the situation you can contact the phone company, set up your own WiFi and pay for it—or you may apologize to me.

Sheldon employs a similar technique in the episode aptly titled "The Vengeance Formulation." When Barry Kripke sabotages Sheldon's NPR phone interview by pumping helium gas into Sheldon's office, making him sound like a little person following the Yellow Brick Road, Sheldon vows revenge.

After setting an elaborate prank in the lab that dumps foam on Kripke (and, unfortunately, on the president of the university and the Board of Directors), Sheldon's recorded video states,

> Hello, Kripke. This classic prank comes to you from the malevolent mind of Sheldon Cooper. If you'd like to see the look on your stupid face, this video is being instantly uploaded to YouTube.

(An added level of humorous *virtuality* is that Sheldon, Leonard, and Raj watch Sheldon's prank and recorded video via webcam from Sheldon and Leonard's apartment!)

Yet virtual vengeance may be healthy or unhealthy behavior, depending on how it is used. On one hand, Sheldon is not confronting his targets directly. He sets up triggered videos that allow him to indirectly control the situation. This is unhealthy behavior because Sheldon is not dealing with his conflict directly, and he is not affording his targets the opportunity to address the situation with him. By keeping the interaction one-sided, he is not learning how to constructively deal with people when he has a problem with them. What if he has to confront someone directly without a computer? Dealing with people when you are angry or disappointed with them is an important social skill that Sheldon is not developing. On the other hand, not everyone is even-tempered, and some confrontations can quickly get out of hand. So, maybe virtual confrontation is a safer and more controlled alternative to direct confrontation.

A clear example of direct confrontation gone wrong is in the episode "The Zarnecki Incursion," when Sheldon is not successful at retrieving his stolen virtual *World of Warcraft* items directly from Mr. Todd Zarnecki. Although Leonard, Sheldon, Howard, and Raj are successful at finding Zarnecki via "virtual" techniques, they are at a complete loss as to how to effectively confront him face-to-face. In fact, Sheldon ends up also losing his Klingon bat'leth to Zarnecki. Penny, however, seems well-suited for direct confrontation when she kicks Zarnecki in the groin to get Sheldon's things back, after having politely said, "Give my friend his stuff back." This direct confrontation was certainly not healthy for Zarnecki, and the other guys will definitely think twice before crossing Penny in the future!

In the end, virtual interaction and virtual vengeance seem to be double-edged swords. When they are employed as supplements to healthy physical interaction, they can be useful tools to interact with others in a healthy way, such as Raj's "virtual" relationship with his parents. Yet when they are employed as substitutes for physical interaction or direct constructive confrontation, they result in a clearly unbalanced life, such as Penny's lack of hygiene or Sheldon's shunning of the physical world. Moderation seems to be the key to a healthy use of technology.

## Aristotle's Mean

Aristotle's (384–322 BCE) ethical system is grounded in character development and self-improvement.[3] In other words, Aristotle wanted the individual to learn to become the best person he could possibly be without following hard-and-fast rules. One of Aristotle's guiding principles was that people had to learn moderation between the extremes of excess and deficiency to develop proper virtues. Aristotle stated that "Excess and deficiency are characteristic of vice, hitting the mean is characteristic of virtue."[4]

When Aristotle spoke of virtue, he was not addressing purity (or the like), as much as he meant a way for humans to improve themselves toward excellence by developing desirable character traits. For example, the virtue of courage is the result of finding the mean between the vices of cowardliness, on one hand, and rashness, on the other. A person develops true bravery by understanding how not to run away and also how not to rush in foolishly. Aristotle defined the mean as what lay about evenly between excess and deficiency, especially as it pertains to the person and the situation he or she currently faces. As Aristotle defined, "The mean relative to us I understand as that which is neither too much nor too little for us; and this is not one and the same for all."[5] Aristotle was referring to a balance between extremes but not a mathematical mean. Unfortunately, finding the relative mean is not as simple as finding a midpoint between extremes. Aristotle used a simple example with food to illustrate this point:

> If ten pounds of food is too much for a given man to eat, and two pounds too little, it does not follow that the trainer will order him six pounds: for that also may perhaps be too much for the man in question, or too little.[6]

Aristotle's point is that you can't simply find the exact middle between extremes to obtain the virtue, or excellence, in some characteristic or endeavor. Instead, a certain amount of experimentation is needed to find the mean relative to a person.

For Aristotle, the key to reaching human excellence is to constantly moderate between extremes until you find that right mean, or golden mean. Although you can maintain that mean throughout your life, you may find through continued balancing and moderation that the relative mean will change. In a practical way, while excellence may not be achievable all of the time in everything, this moderating behavior is an improving behavior in itself because it allows an individual to approach excellence. As Aristotle stated, "The proper excellence or virtue of man will be the habit or trained faculty that makes a man good."[7] In other words, excellence takes practice!

While Aristotle used the concept of the mean and moderation to illustrate how one can develop virtues, the concept applies equally well in determining a healthy balance between using computers and technology and living in the "real" world. As Aristotle stated, "We do not regard a man as an individual leading a solitary life, but we also take account of parents, children, wife, and, in short, friends and fellow-citizens generally, since man is naturally a social being."[8] So an individual can find balance in his life, but we cannot ignore that the individual also interacts with a community. Consequently, the virtues an individual develops should improve his or her ability to interact with others in the community.

So Aristotle would tell us that not all technology will lead to degraded social skills, but not all technology helps social skills, either. Each individual will have a different relative mean in this regard, but each individual technology user should maintain good social skills.

## Aristotle in Television

Raj and his parents already exercise Aristotelian moderation. Their "virtual" talks seem to be a healthy mean when compared to the extremes of either Raj or his parents moving to another country, excessive and expensive plane trips between India and the United States, or no personal interaction between Raj and his parents at all.

Applying Aristotle further, reconsider how Penny transitioned from rarely playing video games to obsessively playing video games to the near exclusion of all other concerns. An Aristotelian moderation might be that Penny plays video games occasionally without sacrificing the other aspects of her life, such as hygiene and sleep. This practice certainly benefited her when she hid from her friend (and Howard) in "The Dumpling Paradox!"

In the realm of virtual vengeance, an Aristotelian mean might be that Sheldon cannot always resort to virtual vengeance and should also make an effort to handle things directly. Sheldon should probably start by learning how to confront his close friends, such as Penny, when he has problems with them, without having to resort to any kind of virtual vengeance. In the spirit of moderation Sheldon might also use two-sided virtual confrontation, such as his conversations with Amy, so that he learns to confront others more directly when he has issues. Maybe it's still fine, however, for Sheldon to use one-sided virtual vengeance with Kripke, because Kripke is clearly not a close friend.

In any case, as the characters in *The Big Bang Theory* demonstrate, we can benefit from Aristotle's insights when balancing computer and technology use so that other aspects of life, especially social skills, do not suffer. As Aristotle stated, "We may say generally that a master in any art avoids what is too much and what is too little, and seeks for the mean and chooses it—not the absolute but the relative mean."[9] As such, a person must work to find the proper mean in using technology so that it becomes the relative mean that pushes the person toward excellence.

## Bright and Shiny Penny

Perhaps surprisingly, Penny and Amy Farrah Fowler are the two characters who most consistently illustrate Aristotelian moderation regarding technology. To be fair, Leonard, Sheldon, Howard, Raj, and Amy cannot help that their careers require heavy technology use, whereas Penny doesn't use much technology as a waitress and a bartender. Yet what happens after work? Leonard, Sheldon, Howard, and Raj are typically found playing video games, building a robot, or doing something else that involves technology in some way. Going out to clubs and other social activities become humorous adventures due to their continued awkwardness and lack of social skills.

Consider Penny. Excepting her brief misadventure with *Age of Conan*, Penny knows how to play games, surf the Internet, and shop online without missing out on the rest of life. Penny goes out to dance, drink, and be with other people. She seems to have found the right balance of technology in her life, allowing her to continue developing in other ways. The guys, by contrast, never develop proper social skills. Sure, Leonard and Howard have relationships, but they are still awkward in their relationships, and although Sheldon's relationship with Amy works because of their similar personalities, he is still socially inept.

Incredibly, Amy also seems to have found the right balance of technology in her life. Although she definitely uses technology more than Penny does, she is willing to go out and have fun with her "bestie!" Sure, her social activities are usually an experiment for her, but she is still putting herself out in the physical world with other people and enjoying herself. She has even gotten drunk on occasion! And she is able to educate Sheldon in social concerns. While the guys, and Sheldon especially, are still awkward in social activities after four seasons, Amy is getting better and more comfortable the more she hangs out with Penny in different situations. So, actually, maybe Penny is the show's supreme role model in balancing technology and life à la Aristotle!

## Where Do We Go?

As the Internet has become more prevalent and mobile computing and social networking have continued to expand, it helps to see characters show us in interesting and funny ways how some of those things can become imbalanced in our lives and how quickly things can get out of control. In the show, we can learn how to move from Penny's adventures in sloth and Sheldon's strictly virtual presence to healthy virtual relationships, such as the one Raj has with his parents, and healthy virtual confrontation, such as Sheldon uses against his nonfriend Kripke. We can also see clear differences in living a well-rounded life, such as Penny's or Amy's, as opposed to lives that revolve too much around technology, such as those of the guys. In some ways, the show can teach us how to apply Aristotle's moderation in using technology so that we don't lead unbalanced lives by sacrificing social skills through overusing computers and technology. Of course, to learn that lesson from the show, we need to watch television, another engagement with technology that should concern us—but that's the subject for another discussion.[10]

## NOTES

1. I have a minor disclaimer. I don't plan to debate about which came first: poor social skills or heavy computer and technology use. I think it's a debate that could go on endlessly, and I'm sure that there are legitimate arguments on both sides. I also don't want to debate about which technologies, if any, have no unhealthy side effects. I don't want to get into these arguments because I'm more interested in the phenomenon that if you use computers and other technology heavily in your life, you tend to have a poor understanding of social protocols.

2. My thanks to the webmaster of "Big Bang Theory Transcripts" at <http://bigbangtrans.wordpress.com> for all episode dialogue used in this essay.

3. Aristotle, *Nicomachean Ethics*, trans. F. H. Peters (New York: Barnes & Noble, 2004), xi–xii. Hereafter, all references to the *Nicomachean Ethics* will be cited as *NE*.

4. *NE*, 31, 1107a–1107b.

5. *NE*, 30, 1106a–1106b.

6. *NE*, 30, 1106a–1107a.

7. *NE*, 29, 1106a–1106b. Aristotle used the male pronoun rather exclusively, and his views on women are rather notorious. Later Aristotelians make a point of explaining how his views about moderation and excellence apply equally to women, as the subsequent discussions of Penny will show.

8. *NE*, 9, 1097b–1098a.

9. *NE*, 30, 1106b–1107a.

10. I would like to thank Dean Kowalski, Adon, Brenda, Erika, Nora, and Richard for commenting on earlier drafts of this essay. Special thanks to Bill Irwin for encouraging me to contribute.

# PART TWO

# "IS IT WRONG TO SAY I LOVE OUR KILLER ROBOT?": ETHICS AND VIRTUE

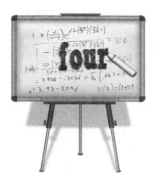

# FEELING BAD ABOUT FEELING GOOD: IS IT MORALLY WRONG TO LAUGH AT SHELDON?

*W. Scott Clifton*

In "The Bozeman Reaction" (among other episodes), Sheldon Cooper asserts, "I'm not crazy—my mother had me tested." He makes no further comment about what kind of test was administered, but it's reasonable to infer that it was for a *cognitive* disorder. The word *crazy* in this context was likely intended to refer to developmental deficits in learning. The negative results thus showed that he had no cognitive impairment, which should come as no surprise to anyone familiar with the show—Sheldon is *brilliant*. . . . But he is also unusual.

It's safe to say that much of *The Big Bang Theory*'s appeal involves our enjoyment of Sheldon's idiosyncrasies. Yet here is our philosophical problem: We value the show, in large part, because of Sheldon's humorous and strikingly unusual behavior, but the best explanation of this behavior is that Sheldon has a social disorder. Many viewers pick up on the fact that some of Sheldon's characteristics are those typically found in people with autism. If Sheldon has autism, however, and it's his having this condition that makes his behavior so entertaining, then it appears as if we are laughing at a character's disability. What is more problematic, morally speaking, is that we value the show based on our laughter. Are we moral monsters for laughing at a character's disability? And if we are, does this mean that we cannot both value the show and maintain our moral integrity?

I am going to argue that we are not moral monsters, in part, because Sheldon doesn't really have a disability, but what could actually be called an *en*ability. He may have some symptoms associated with autism, but these symptoms don't constitute a disadvantage within the life he has created for himself.

## Lorre and Prady on Sheldon Cooper

When asked by a reader of *Time* magazine about how he prepared to play a character with autism, Jim Parsons answered that the writers had informed him that Sheldon doesn't, in fact, have the condition.[1] If this is true, then our problem goes away—no disorder, no disability. And if there's no disability, then we should have no qualms, on the grounds presented previously, about laughing at his behavior.

Yet why should the writers' statement about Sheldon settle the issue? There are several reasons we might not want to take the statement as conclusive evidence that Sheldon has no disorder. It's possible that the writers aren't being completely honest, either for Parsons's sake, because he might start to play Sheldon differently, given the new knowledge, or for the audience's sake, because viewers might start to expect more paradigmatically autistic behavior. Even if the writers are being forthright and genuinely don't intend Sheldon to have the condition, our own determination might legitimately overrule their stated intention. Perhaps the writers aren't sufficiently familiar with the condition and its symptoms.

This issue harkens back to the ideas of William Wimsatt and Monroe Beardsley, two literary theorists and aestheticians. They famously declared it a fallacy to investigate the intentions of the creator of an artwork in order to construct an interpretation.[2] Since then, most theorists have decided that this is too strong a condition. Wimsatt and Beardsley should have focused criticism on the *prioritizing* of authorial intention over the judgment of the audience. When they argued that authorial intention is irrelevant to the meaning of a work, they overreached, ending up with an implausible conclusion. We can grant that an author's intentions shouldn't be the only, or even a central, factor involved in rendering a work of art meaningful and still hold that the author's intentions shouldn't be dismissed as irrelevant, either. It's one piece of evidence among many and shouldn't be considered either supremely important or totally worthless.

So, we should take into account the stated intentions of the writers of *The Big Bang Theory* but also feel free to investigate for ourselves whether there is evidence that Sheldon exhibits symptoms of autism. We can think of ourselves as amateur psychologists, diagnosing a patient from video representations of his behavior.

### Diagnosing Sheldon I: Cognitive Impairment

In making a diagnosis, we have to keep in mind that autism comes in degrees. It's considered a *spectrum disorder*, with intensely adverse cases on one end of the spectrum and less adverse cases on the other. One variant of autism located on the less adverse end of the spectrum is called Asperger's syndrome. People with this condition exhibit a subset of the family of symptoms characteristic of autism but are still able to live fully functional and autonomous lives. Sheldon is fairly independent, so if he is autistic at all, it's likely that he has Asperger's, rather than a more serious form of autism.

We can diagnose Sheldon by using the *Diagnostic and Statistical Manual of Mental Disorders* (*DSM*), which is the standardized source of diagnosis of disorders used by mental health professionals.[3] The manual, a primary resource for healthcare providers diagnosing patients who display certain sets of symptoms, classifies disorders and conditions by symptoms and pathologies. Thus, a person exhibiting a set of symptoms matching those classified under disorder X in the manual can be diagnosed by the physician as having disorder X. The most recent version of the *DSM* specifies that individuals with Asperger's syndrome should satisfy the following criteria:

> No evidence of developmental delay in language or cognition, exhibiting a "qualitative impairment in social interaction," exhibiting "restricted repetitive and stereotyped patterns of behavior, interests, and activities," and, finally, the symptoms resulting in disturbance causing "clinically significant impairment in social, occupational, or other important areas of functioning."

To what degree or extent, if any, does Sheldon meet these criteria?

It's clear that there's no evidence that Sheldon showed any linguistic or cognitive delay in growing up. Just the opposite. Sheldon was a precocious child, entering college at eleven, graduating at fourteen, and getting his Ph.D. at sixteen. He was also quite creative. In "The Luminous Fish Effect," Mary Cooper tells us that Sheldon's attempt to construct a nuclear reactor at the tender age of thirteen was motivated by the hope of securing free electricity for the whole town. After he tried to procure yellowcake uranium to fuel the reactor, a government official paid him a visit that was intended to get him to stop.

Having been reprimanded, he built a sonic death ray, which, his mother tells us, didn't "even slow down the neighbor kids" but "pissed off our dog to no end."

## Diagnosing Sheldon II: Sociability

In order to establish that Sheldon exhibits impairment in social interaction, we would have to show that at least two of the following must be true: that he fails to develop appropriate peer relationships, or that he has trouble reading and using physical gestures in social interactions, or that he finds it difficult expressing reciprocal social feelings and/or emotions toward those with whom he interacts. Sheldon does have the ability to develop appropriate peer relationships. He has functional friendships with Leonard, Howard, and Raj—though probably functional more because of *their* efforts, rather than his own. He also has what seems to be a (mostly) healthy, adversarial relationship with Barry Kripke. There might be some question about whether his other adversaries, Leslie Winkle and (especially pre-season 5) Wil Wheaton, provide him with abnormal grief, but we'll leave that question unaddressed here.

We do have evidence, however, that he has difficulty reading and using body language in social interactions. For example, in "The Big Bran Hypothesis," he demonstrates a fundamental inability to pick up on several instances of sarcasm. This reaches a crescendo when Penny bursts into the apartment, livid because, while she slept, Sheldon and Leonard had cleaned her apartment the night before. After Sheldon suggests she see an "otolaryngologist" for her snoring, which is, he explains, a "throat doctor," she responds, "And what kind of doctor removes shoes from asses?" Her facial expression, body posture, and head movement all indicate to anyone capable of reading body language that she doesn't intend her question as a sincere request for information. Yet Sheldon, not picking up on any subtext, answers, "Depending on the depth, that's either a . . . proctologist or a general surgeon." It's only when Leonard holds a placard up behind Penny's back with the word *Sarcasm* written on it that Sheldon gets it, saying, "Oh." This instance is representative of a whole set of episodes in which Sheldon's ability to read body language is shown to be seriously impaired, even getting him jailed in "The Excelsior Acquisition."

Similarly, there is evidence that Sheldon has difficulty with the experience and expression of reciprocal social feelings and emotions. In the episode "The Bath Item Gift Hypothesis," he agonizes about what to do when he hears that Penny has a Christmas or, as he calls it, "Saturnalia," present for him. He knows that he is *expected* to respond to her gesture appropriately, saying, "The essence of the custom is that I now have to go out and purchase for you a gift of commensurate value and representing the same perceived level of friendship as that represented by the gift you've given me." His problem is that he has no idea what is appropriate. For most people, the solution to this problem would be to reflect on the friendship itself and try to anticipate what gift Penny will give, all based on an intuitive grasp of the emotional valence of the relationship. Sheldon's solution, however, is to hedge his bets.

He goes to a store in the mall specializing in bath items and buys several different sizes of gift baskets. His plan is to keep them all in his bedroom and, after he has unwrapped Penny's gift and has judged what the commensurate return gift would be, to feign "digestive distress" and leave the room to retrieve the most appropriate gift in return. Note here that his decision will be based on his estimate of the monetary value of her gift—not on the underlying sentiment. This is presumably the reason he has to adopt the hedged-bet approach—because he cannot gauge the emotional valence of Penny's behavior toward him.

It's informative to recall how he responds when he has finally been presented with Penny's gift: a napkin signed by

Leonard Nimoy. This elates him, but there's more—it's a napkin Nimoy used to wipe his mouth. Thus, Sheldon has not only the signed napkin but "the DNA of Leonard Nimoy!" The reason this thrills Sheldon is that he can now clone his own Leonard Nimoy, if only he had access to a healthy ovum. Worried, Penny is quick to point out that she is only providing him with the napkin.

Now, which size basket should Sheldon give in return for such a perfect gift? For most people, the appropriate one would probably be the biggest basket, or perhaps scrapping the basket idea altogether. Sheldon's decision, however, is to give her *all* of the baskets, because the nonmonetary value of the napkin outstrips the monetary value of the biggest basket. Yet it also outstrips the monetary value of all of the baskets combined. He has nothing else to give which is of value to him, but he recognizes that he can give Penny something that is valuable to her. So he hugs her—but he hugs her in such a manner that it's obvious his sentiment, while genuine, isn't motivating the hug. Leonard declares the event a Saturnalia miracle. Thus, these examples indeed seem to provide evidence of Sheldon's experiencing impairment in social interactions.

Let's turn our attention to the next symptom set—restricted repetitive and stereotyped patterns of behavior, interests, and activities—the satisfaction of which requires at least one of the following be true of Sheldon: encompassing preoccupation with one or more stereotyped patterns of interest, or an apparent inflexible adherence to nonfunctional routines, or repetitive movements of the body or preoccupation with parts of objects. The first two seem particularly relevant.

Our challenge in determining whether Sheldon shows an unusual preoccupation with a pattern of interest is that the entire group—Sheldon, Leonard, Howard, and Raj—could be said to demonstrate such a preoccupation. Consider their discussion of Kryptonian laundry. In "The Bath Item Gift

Hypothesis," Sheldon comments that Superman "cleans his uniform by flying into Earth's yellow sun, which incinerates any contaminate matter and leaves the invulnerable Kryptonian fabric unharmed and daisy fresh." Leonard counters with the insightful reminder that Superman's sweat is Kryptonian. Superman's *pit stains* would not be cleaned via the sun incinerator method of uniform laundering, leading Raj to eventually exclaim, "Booya!" True, Sheldon is often portrayed as abnormal within the group—that is, abnormal within an abnormal group—and would be more than deviant: super-deviant, perhaps. Because it's unclear what measure we should use for abnormality here, I recommend reserving judgment about whether Sheldon satisfies this criterion.

## Diagnosing Sheldon III: Functionality

Accordingly, let's see whether Sheldon exhibits an inflexible adherence to specific nonfunctional routines. Before we do, however, we should distinguish functional, nonfunctional, and once functional/now nonfunctional routines. Functional routines are those that serve a purpose—one that, at any given time, the person adhering to the routine would give as a reason.[4] Nonfunctional routines are those that have no, or only arbitrary, reasons underlying them. Finally, once functional/now nonfunctional routines are those that persist, but not because of any purpose, though they once did fulfill a function. We can trace the emergence of the pattern to a set of reasons, even if those reasons no longer motivate the preservation of the routine. Note that the second and third kinds of routines are still nonfunctional, irrespective of how they have developed.

Now let's ask whether Sheldon's routines—to which he resolutely clings—are functional or nonfunctional. His weekly schedule has been revealed to be the following:

Monday: Oatmeal for breakfast; takeout Thai for dinner.

Tuesday: Dinner at the Cheesecake Factory. Barbecue bacon cheeseburger, barbecue, bacon and cheese on the side.

Wednesday: *Halo* night; comic book day.

Thursday: Takeout pizza from Giacomo's—sausage, mushrooms, light olives.

Friday: Chinese food for dinner and vintage game night.

Saturday: Bowl of cereal with 1/4 of a cup of 2% milk for breakfast while watching *Doctor Who* on BBC America; laundry night at 8:15.[5]

Every week is the same, and this is how Sheldon likes it. When a change is proposed, Sheldon resists, returning again and again to the fact that certain days/nights are scheduled for certain events. Now, some of these events might be assigned to their days for functional reasons, in which case there would be a good reason not to change the schedule. For example, comic book day is Wednesday because that is the day on which new issues come out. This is a good reason, but it's a good reason only for making Wednesdays *generally* comic book day. If one were occasionally compelled to put off visiting the comic book store until Thursday, little harm would be done. Yet as we see in "The Euclid Alternative," Sheldon has no flexibility in this matter, not even for exigent circumstances, such as when Sheldon has to bum rides from others because Leonard is working nights. Sheldon presses the point that he must go to the comic book store on Wednesday, even though he is already imposing on others for rides. One gets the impression that his motivating reason isn't the new issues awaiting him but the mere fact that Wednesday is comic book day, and today is Wednesday.

Some of the events are mentioned with no reference to any function. Saturday nights are for laundry, but it's not clear why. Nonetheless, when Penny prevents him from doing laundry on Saturday, he lashes out, throwing her "unmentionables" on the power lines outside. For no obvious reason, he always gives a series of three knocks, three times on someone's door. (The iconic: knock-knock-knock, Penny . . . knock-knock-knock, Penny . . . knock-knock-knock, Penny.) Even if the person answers before the third series of knocks, he insists on completing the cycle.

This lack of attention to purpose is starker when Sheldon maintains his routines and rituals even in the face of *dysfunctionality*—that is, when the routine event causes a marked disadvantage for him. An instance of this can be found in "The Gothowitz Deviation." Penny has cooked French toast for Leonard and Sheldon on a Monday morning—but Monday mornings are for oatmeal. Penny tries to get Sheldon to deviate from the routine but finally gives up, leaving him holding a plate full of French toast. When he's alone, he says, "Boy that does smell good. . . . Too bad it's Monday," and tosses the French toast into the trash can.

Of course, most of Sheldon's routines are functional, based on good reasons, but we see that even these routines are clung to less for the good reasons and more because of the fact that they are routines. This is evident when we see how upset he becomes when his plans are thwarted, such as when someone sits in his place on the sofa, or opens the door before the third set of knocks, or when he is unable to do his laundry on Saturday night. Thus, he exhibits an inflexible adherence to nonfunctional routines, which is evidence that he exhibits restricted repetitive and stereotyped patterns of behavior, interests, and activities.

## What Is a Disability?

One criterion relevant to judging whether Sheldon has Asperger's syndrome remains: that the disturbance causes clinically significant impairment in social, occupational, or other important areas of functioning. This is what classifies

Asperger's syndrome as a *disability*, and this is the point at which we determine whether we are moral monsters for laughing at Sheldon. If Sheldon has a disability and we are laughing at behavior caused by his disability, then we are, I think, moral monsters. So everything rides, not on whether Sheldon has the behavioral traits characteristic of Asperger's, but on whether these traits constitute a disability. To answer this question, we have to consider the recent discussion in bioethics of how to define the term *disability*.

The most common way that "disability" has been defined is, first, to define "health" as something such as *species-typical normal functioning* and, second, to define "disability" as any characteristic, innate or adventitious, falling outside that range.[6] This approach takes evolved human traits as fixed and objective, and then treats any traits falling outside that fixed range as disadvantageous and disabling.

There is, of course, the challenge of determining what constitutes "species-typical normal functioning." Once we are able to do this, the argument runs, we can then determine how to help those with disabilities. This "medical model" of disability holds that the appropriate way to help the disabled is what is called "leveling"—that is, ameliorating the effects of the disability in the individual. Take, for example, Raj's selective mutism. Raj is unable to speak to women (apart from his mother and sister) in any context except that in which he has consumed, or believes he has consumed, alcohol. The way Raj would be treated according to the medical model is through the prescription of certain antianxiety drugs. Of course, Raj self-medicates, through the use of alcohol, but because this has undesirable side effects—such as hangovers—it wouldn't be pragmatic to adopt this course long term.

Some bioethicists, such as Anita Silvers, have objected that this way of addressing the issue of disability is not leveling so much as *normalizing*.[7] The end goal of normalizing isn't to remove disadvantages of the disabled, but to make the disabled more similar to the typical human being. This way of dealing with the issue, however, is harmful to the disabled, because it sends the message that there is something inferior about them as individuals, making them less worthy than the so-called normals.

A different conception of disability has been suggested in opposition to the medical model—the "social constructivist model." In this view, disability doesn't lie completely within the individual. There is a social component that is also partly constitutive of the disability. It's the failure of fit between the individual's traits and the environment in which she lives that constitutes the disability. Thus, we should seek to repair the fit, which would require addressing the features of the environment, as much as of the individual.

In this model, Raj's selective mutism is considered a disability in American culture, where men who can talk to women are preferred over those who can't, but it wouldn't be a disability in other contexts. If Raj were, say, a monk who had taken a vow of silence, his mutism might be an asset. Or, if Raj lived in his own native, patriarchal culture of India, in which marriages are often arranged and men are not tasked with wooing prospective brides, his mutism would be neither an advantage nor a disadvantage.

In the social constructivist view, then, disabilities exist when two pieces of the puzzle are both present—a certain physiological, cognitive, or behavioral condition *and* an environment in which that condition is not favorable for success. Thus, Raj in America has a disability; Raj in a monastery or in the patriarchy of India doesn't. Yet in both environments he has the same condition.

We can't get into a long defense of the social constructivist view here, but I hope it's clear why we might be tempted to adopt it for our purposes. If Sheldon has Asperger's syndrome or all of the behavioral symptoms of Asperger's, but the symptoms aren't disabling in his prevailing environment, then we should have no qualms about laughing at his behavior. It's not a moral problem to laugh at characters whose behavior stems from nondisabling traits. After all, we're not worried about laughing at the travails of Leonard, Howard, and Raj, who suffer from especially high IQs, or at how difficult it is for Penny, who is so (conventionally) attractive that people often fail to take her seriously.

So, do Sheldon's traits constitute a disadvantage for him? Consider that he has distinguished himself in a career that relies very little on social interaction and rewards the ability to engage with inanimate matter or, in the theoretical physicist's case, ideas and equations representing inanimate matter. Sheldon has set up his personal life in such a way that he spends most of his spare time at home, with friends who have agreed to accommodate his eccentric desires. When he does go out, he is accompanied by friends (we hardly ever see him eat in public alone) or frequents places where there are others very similar to him (the comic book store, run by Stuart and frequented by customers such as Captain Sweatpants). In other words, Sheldon has intentionally designed his life so that conditions are hospitable to the traits that result from his Asperger's. More than this, he has actually succeeded in making these very traits *benefit* him. His success as a physicist derives from his having Asperger's, and he emerges as a kind of leader in his pack—the "alpha nerd"—as a result of his rigid and rigorous attention to subtle details. Thus, in contrast to the suggestion that Asperger's is a *dis*ability for Sheldon, we should actually say that it's an *en*ability, because it has made him more (and not less) able to succeed—both professionally and personally.

We shouldn't feel bad about laughing at Sheldon, any more than we feel bad about laughing at intelligent people because of their intelligence or wealthy people because of their wealth. We shouldn't feel bad about feeling good. So laugh on![8]

# NOTES

1. "10 Questions for Jim Parsons," *Time*, February 21, 2011.

2. W. K. Wimsatt Jr. and Monroe C. Beardsley, "The Intentional Fallacy," in *The Verbal Icon: Studies in the Meaning of Poetry* (Lexington: University Press of Kentucky, 1954), 3–18.

3. *Diagnostic and Statistical Manual of Mental Disorders : DSM-IV-TR* (Washington, DC: American Psychiatric Association, 2000).

4. Think of the checklist that air crews go through pre-flight. There is a good reason for having a routine in place—guarding against human error.

5. See <http://wiki.the-big-bang-theory.com/index.php/Schedule>.

6. Norman Daniels, *Just Health Care* (New York: Cambridge University Press, 1985).

7. "A Fatal Attraction to Normalizing: Treating Disabilities as Deviations from 'Species-Typical' Functioning," in Erik Parens, ed., *Enhancing Human Traits: Ethical and Social Implications* (Washington, DC: Georgetown University Press, 1998).

8. My thanks to the webmaster at <http://bigbangtrans.wordpress.com> for episode dialogue.

# ...BUT IS WIL WHEATON EVIL?

*Donna Marie Smith*

Well, well, well. If it isn't Wil Wheaton, the Green Goblin to my Spider-Man.

> —Dr. Sheldon Cooper, "The Wheaton Recurrence"

Portraying a "delightfully evil version" of himself on *The Big Bang Theory* gives Wil Wheaton a chance to play a character much different from his role in *Stand by Me* or his stint on *Star Trek: The Next Generation* as Ensign Wesley Crusher.[1] With geeky aplomb, Wheaton transforms into one of Sheldon's most formidable enemies after only three encounters. Sheldon accordingly bestows on him the moniker "Evil Wil." Yet what exactly makes Wil, or anyone, evil in the first place? Is he inherently evil? Is anyone? Questions such as these have long interested philosophers. By examining some of the more noteworthy attempts at dealing with evil, perhaps we'll even help Sheldon come to terms with his nemesis "Evil Wil."

## The Wheaton Occurrences

In "The Creepy Candy Coating Corollary"—the episode in which Wheaton first appears—Sheldon provides the back story behind this rivalry. As a young boy, he idolized Ensign Crusher; they shared a love of science and an eidetic memory. Sheldon, wearing a Starfleet Academy uniform, traveled for ten hours on a bus filled with strangers from his home in East Texas to Jackson, Mississippi, to attend the 1995 Dixie Trek Convention. The trip was arduous, forcing Sheldon to "twice violate his personal rule about not relieving himself on a moving vehicle." Despite this great personal discomfort, he was determined to meet his idol and have Wil autograph his mint-in-package Wesley Crusher action-figure. Wil, though, skipped the convention. Sheldon felt personally betrayed by this and vowed revenge on the actor, who is ranked in sixth place on his "All-Time Enemies List," right between Joel Schumacher, "who nearly destroyed the Batman movie franchise," and Billy Sparks, "who lived down the street and put dog poop on the handles of his bicycle." When Stuart informs Sheldon that Wil is competing in a *Mystic Warlords of Ka'a* tournament he is hosting at the comic book store, revenge becomes imminent! Sheldon teams up with Raj to destroy Wil Wheaton.

The tournament initially goes well, as Sheldon and Raj effortlessly dismantle the competition. After thrashing Lonely Larry and Captain Sweatpants in the semifinals, Sheldon barks, "Fetch me Wil Wheaton!" The finals begin equally well. As Sheldon is about to "finish off" his enemy, he recounts the horror of the 1995 Dixie Trek. Wheaton is initially confused but soon apologizes to Sheldon for missing the convention and disappointing him. Wheaton's "grandmother had just died," and he "had to go to her funeral." Because Sheldon dearly loves his own grandmother—his "mee-maw," who sweetly calls him her "Moon Pie"—he now recognizes Wil as a kindred spirit. Taking pity on his opponent, Sheldon plays his Enchanted Bunny card. ("Everything beats Enchanted Bunny . . . unless you have the Carrot of Power.") Yet Wil lied! His "nana" is alive and well. Wil taunts Sheldon, triumphantly and sarcastically proclaiming, "Game over, Moon Pie!" Sheldon howls, "Wheaton! . . . Wheaton!"

In "The Wheaton Recurrence," Wil again enters a contest against Sheldon and the gang by becoming an unannounced member of Stuart's bowling team. Wheaton now lives in Sheldon's head "rent free," vexing Sheldon and misleading him about how the bowler on the right always rolls first ("It's a custom, not a rule," after all). Wheaton's main target this time, however, is Penny. Fortuitously overhearing that Leonard has disquieted Penny by prematurely dropping the "L-bomb," Wil deviously but nonchalantly weaves a tale of woe about a girl he loved. She never returned his "I love you," strung him along, and broke up with him two years later. Making the connection to her romance with Leonard, Penny storms out of the bowling alley. The gang loses the match. Consequently, they appear—in full garb—as female superheroes in Stuart's store the next day.

Wil makes a third appearance in "The 21 Second Excitation," in which Sheldon and the guys make plans to see a midnight special edition of *Raiders of the Lost Ark* (because it includes "21 seconds of additional, previously unseen footage"). Much to Sheldon's chagrin, they arrive late to the theater. Raj surmises they "might not even get seats," and Sheldon's mood sours further when his nemesis Wil Wheaton appears with some pals and is let into the theater by a staff person who recognizes the *Star Trek* celebrity. Sheldon fumes at the unfairness of the situation: "This affront to justice and decency cannot go unanswered. As Captain Jean-Luc Picard once said, 'The line must be drawn here! This far, no farther.'" Sheldon yet again vows revenge against the dastardly "Evil Wil."

## The Theodicy Corollary

Of course, the history of evil long predates sitcoms. For most of human history, ruminations about evil primarily fell under the purview of religion. Sheldon is probably an agnostic, given the question he asks during "The Zarnecki Incursion": "Why hast thou forsaken me, O deity whose existence I doubt?" With Sheldon having been raised in a religious home, perhaps we can imagine him calling his mother and asking for her guidance about "Evil Wil." Thus, turning to philosophers and theologians for help is not out of the question. We don't, however, want to discuss the *entire* history of evil—recall Sheldon's debacle teaching physics to Penny—so we're going to limit our exploration to thinkers influenced by Christian and Jewish traditions. (Sorry, Raj.)

With the advent of the scientific revolution, many thinkers, without abdicating their religious commitments, changed their approach to God, religion, and evil. One notable attempt was made by Gottfried Leibniz (1646–1716) in his book *Theodicy*. The term *theodicy* has since come to be synonymous with any attempt to explain the existence of evil in a world created by God. Leibniz argued that the very nature of God, his perfect power, knowledge, and goodness, dictates that God creates the best of all possible worlds. Yet any created thing is inherently imperfect, to some degree. Creation is bound to contain instances of evil, especially if rational creatures are left free to make their own decisions. In turn, the best of all possible worlds very well may contain wars, plagues, and even Sheldon being bested at *Mystic Warlords of Ka'a* by Wil Wheaton's deception. The created world, though, as Leibniz argued, contains the best overall balance of goodness over evil, thereby solidifying its status as the best of all possible worlds.[2]

Voltaire (1694–1778), one of Leibniz's most vociferous dissenters, satirized Leibniz's optimistic naïveté in his novel *Candide*. The young narrator, Candide, has been taught that he lives in the best possible world by his mentor Doctor Pangloss, Voltaire's stand-in for Leibniz. Yet after experiencing an earthquake, being whipped, and facing other horrible travails, Candide proclaims, "If this is the best possible world, what must the others be like?"[3] Sheldon, as naïve as Candide, might pose a similar question. If the best of all possible worlds contains Wil Wheaton's failing to appear at a fan convention and besting Sheldon twice via duplicitous means, what must the other possible worlds be like?

Leibniz's is not the only theodicy.[4] A more recent but still influential attempt was offered by Martin Buber (1878–1965).[5] Buber, who studied stories of the Old Testament, such as that of the fall of man after Adam and Eve ate from the Tree of Knowledge, discussed how people, who have God-given free will, can use their will to oppose God's way. If Buber were present at Stuart's comic book store to witness the exchange between Sheldon and Wil, he would say that Wheaton's dishonesty was wicked. Buber held that "the lie is the specific evil which man has introduced into nature."[6] He explained, through close reading of biblical scripture, specifically Psalm 73 of the Old Testament, that one who deceives does harm to his neighbor and his community.[7] Therefore, by choosing to lie to Sheldon—his neighbor—Wil abuses his free will for a wicked purpose, his own selfish gain.

True, Wil's lie seems rather benign—it's only a card game, after all. Still, it introduces evil into Sheldon's world, just as Adam and Eve brought evil into the world at large. Sheldon, who has difficulty empathizing with people in the first place, deliberately loses the card game out of concern for Wil. Sheldon's attempt at finding common emotional ground with another person by sharing his feelings about his mee-maw was met not only with disdain but with blatant disregard and disrespect. In fact, lies such as these are, as journalist William Hart points out, what "the world's greatest thinkers" considered to be the most "foul and deadly form of evil that eats away at human goodness."[8] Sheldon was a victim of Wil's lies and manipulation. Wil wins a game that he by rights should have lost, harming Sheldon with his deceitful actions.

Sheldon seems to be struck particularly by Wil's callous disregard for him. Note that Sheldon on other occasions is willing to practice dishonesty. In "The Loobenfeld Decay," he works to make Leonard's lie to Penny "un-unravelable." Similarly, when Sheldon wants to break up with Amy Farrah Fowler in "The Vengeance Formulation," he asks Leonard to lie for him and goes so far as to say, "You'll have to devise a scenario that plausibly explains my absence, keeping in mind that the key to a good lie lies in the details." In neither case, however, does Sheldon purposely try to hurt anyone.

As William Hart notes, "Cutting in line is bad, as are littering, auto theft, and slander; but if we deem these evil, what do we call genocide?"[9] In light of something as incomprehensively horrible as the Holocaust, lying or exploiting someone's emotions to win a fantasy card tournament seems relatively harmless and probably not evil. Consider the case of Adolf Eichmann, who was brought up on trial in 1961 for his war crimes and crimes against humanity. Reporting on this historic trial for the *New Yorker*, Hannah Arendt (1906–1975) had an opportunity to see and hear the man responsible for the horrific "Final Solution of the Jewish Question." She was struck by the fact that Eichmann seemed to be a normal person with no apparent psychiatric problems, who didn't exhibit any outright anti-Semitism. To Arendt, he appeared to be merely a high-ranking official of average intelligence in Hitler's government who considered what he did to be following orders. With mechanized efficiency, this nondescript bureaucrat ordered the slaughter of Jews and other "undesirables," such as gays and gypsies, without thinking anything other than that it was his job. Eichmann showed a thoughtless disregard to what he was doing; he didn't consider the consequences of his actions. Arendt summed up Eichmann's lack of reflection in blindly following orders to commit these seemingly pointless evil acts as "banal" evil.

There are two relevant insights to be gleaned from this discussion of theodicy. First, the banal types of evil, especially those that are seemingly pointless, will forever make it difficult for philosophers to construct a completely persuasive theodicy. Second, and more to the *Big Bang Theory* point, we need to distinguish between evil acts and bad moral choices. We need to understand the difference between Eichmann deciding to carry out an order to slaughter people enmasse versus Wil choosing to play mind games or cut in line. In Sheldon's case, the next time he takes offense at Wil's taunts, he should think about the millions of people who were murdered during the Nazi regime. If the highly intelligent physicist would take a moment to compare what Wil did to what Eichmann did, he would be able to put things into better perspective. So, considering these two points together, we might say that *the* problem of evil is significantly different from Sheldon's "problem" with evil. Even though learning about theodicies provides important background, we must look elsewhere to understand Sheldon's take on "Evil Wil."

## Beyond Good and Evil Wil—or, the Wrath of Sheldon

During "The Wheaton Recurrence," Wil chooses an action that allows him to keep the upper hand on Sheldon, to be master over his rival. According to Friedrich Nietzsche (1844– 1900), "Exploitation" . . . is part of the *fundamental nature* of living things, as its fundamental organic function; it is a consequence of the true will to power, which is simply the will to life."[10] He called this inherent function, this self-development, the "Will to Power," where the individual strives to be the best he can be, no matter what.

Nietzsche looked at the concept of good and evil in ways that contradict the religious and democratic ideologies and values familiar to many of us. Unlike Sheldon, Nietzsche would probably have approved of Wil and his seemingly wicked ways. In fact, he might have seen Evil Wil as approaching his ideal of the *Übermensch*—often translated as "Overman"—that which goes beyond man, beyond human nature.[11] Nietzsche specifically targeted the guiding principles of the Judeo-Christian tradition and the democratic societies that were flourishing in America and France. Whereas these societies stressed the equality of all individuals for the good of society, Nietzsche's morality focused on the good of the individual. He believed that a person should strive to perfect himself, no matter what the cost to others or to society as a whole.

Sheldon compares the Dixie Trek horror he suffered to the wrong suffered by Khan Noonien Singh at the irresponsible hands of Captain James T. Kirk. As we know, Khan seeks revenge against Kirk at any cost. His vengeance consumes him, calling to mind Khan's passionate recitation of the famous "He tasks me" quote from *Moby Dick*. Sheldon echoes Khan, revealing his vengeful side, and vows "eternal hatred for Wil Wheaton." When he and Raj are playing an early round of the fantasy card tournament, Sheldon declares—in fluent Klingon, no less—"revenge is a dish best served cold." Sheldon therefore appropriates Khan's Captain Ahab persona by becoming completely fixated on his target. He proclaims his desire to destroy Wheaton—become what he later terms a "Wesley Crusher"—in the final round of the tournament by barking, "Now fetch me Wil Wheaton!"

The lengths Kahn goes to exact revenge against Kirk far exceed anything Sheldon is capable of (well, except that failed childhood attempt at constructing a sonic death ray). Nevertheless, it's tempting to argue that both characters are morally blameworthy for seeking it, because seeking revenge is morally undesirable and ultimately self-destructive, as in the way it consumed Khan. Nietzsche, however, would likely have disagreed with this assessment. He would probably have encouraged both Sheldon's and Khan's quests for revenge, though he would have disapproved of their feelings of resentment. He would especially have admired Khan with his superhuman strength and intelligence. In *Thus Spoke Zarathustra*, Nietzsche even suggested that vengeance was a favorable use of one's will to achieve personal growth: "A little revenge is more human than no revenge."[12]

Accordingly, Khan is a plausible candidate for being Nietzsche's ideal Overman. As such, Nietzsche wouldn't have labeled Kahn evil. Likewise, although the analogy is far from perfect, it seems that Nietzsche wouldn't have labeled Wil evil for his exploitation of Sheldon and the rest of the gang. Perhaps Sheldon should do as Wil suggests and "embrace the dark side" (even though that "phrase isn't from his franchise.")

Nietzsche would have argued that Sheldon is simply misapplying the term *evil*. Yet neither Sheldon nor the writers of *The Big Bang Theory* would be likely to accept this. Consider Dr. David Underhill, the MacArthur Genius Grant recipient whom we met in "The Bath Item Gift Hypothesis." If ever there was a Khan-type Nietzschean "Overman," it's him, never mind that he does something morally wrong in cheating on his wife with Penny. What is more, Sheldon doesn't seem to accept Nietzsche's implicit view of ethics anyway, as he literally sings Leonard's praises for "having right on his side" when bravely confronting "Kurt the Giant" to retrieve the money he owes Penny in "The Financial Permeability." So, a Nietzschean solution to Sheldon's problem doesn't get us very far, either.

## The Name-Calling and Line-Cutting Topologies

Wil Wheaton is not the only person in Sheldon's social circle he considers evil. Barry Kripke, a physicist at the university, likes to play practical jokes on Sheldon, some of which go beyond teasing. In "The Vengeance Formulation," Sheldon is interviewed on NPR (National Public Radio) via phone. Kripke sabotages the interview by pumping helium into Sheldon's office, causing Sheldon to have a high-pitched voice—as Raj quips, just like the *Wizard of Oz*'s Lollipop Guild.

Sheldon also declares Leslie Winkle, another physicist at the university, to be his "arch enemy." After she and Leonard start hooking up, she is added to Sheldon's "All-Time Enemies List." In "The Codpiece Topology," we find out that Leslie is always mean to Sheldon. He explains to Penny that Leslie calls him "dummy" and "dumbass" and often mocks his research into string theory. Penny isn't sure that this qualifies as an "arch enemy," but Sheldon persists.

> Sheldon: Yes, the Doctor Doom to my Mr. Fantastic. The Doctor Octopus to my Spiderman. The Doctor Sivana to my Captain Marvel.
> Penny: Okay, I get it, I get it, I get it.

Labeling Leslie evil is misguided. Calling Sheldon names and making fun of his research does not harm him or anyone else. Certainly, those actions aren't nice, but neither are they willfully harmful or manipulative, as Sheldon believes Wil's lies and exploitation are. If this behavior counted as evil, then Sheldon's always insulting Penny's community college education and Howard's master's degree would also be evil. For that matter, Sheldon has often made fun of Leslie's work, saying that her research in supersymmetry physics is silly. Yet he doesn't consider his observations to be insults; he thinks he is merely stating the "facts." Although Leslie vexes Sheldon with her comments, much as Sheldon annoys Penny and Howard, she does not intend to hurt him. She has no underlying motivation in what she does, unlike Wil, who takes malicious delight in other people's misfortunes. Saying that someone with a high IQ such as Sheldon is "dumb" is different than saying someone with a learning or mental disability is "dumb." Being mean to a colleague in the spirit of competition is not the same as being mean to a person with Down syndrome, where such name-calling could cause irreparable damage.

Distinguishing between being "not nice" and being "evil" in this context becomes surprisingly important. We can't fully grasp what makes someone or something evil, if, like Sheldon, we think that what Leslie Winkle says to him is evil. Even Wil Wheaton is not always evil in his interactions with Sheldon and the gang. Certainly, he wasn't evil in accepting admittance to the special showing of *Raiders*. Yes, he acted a bit smugly, and cutting in line is generally discouraged, but recall Hart's claim about line cutting. If we call cutting in movie theater lines evil, then what do we call things such as the Holocaust? Being a celebrity and getting "perks" such as "the best seats in the house," even if it includes "complimentary popcorn," simply does not make a person evil.[13] So, why is Sheldon so quick to label his adversaries evil?

## The Comic Book Paradigm

Sheldon is obviously familiar with the world of comics. Every Wednesday he visits Stuart at the comic book store. Comic book stories, of course, offer rather clear-cut distinctions between good and evil and superheroes and villains. Coupled with his social insecurities and trouble discerning the nuances of human emotions, Sheldon has constructed his own way of coping with the world and understanding interpersonal relationships: by using what we'll call the paradigm of the Comic Book World. This is especially true when he thinks that someone has wronged him. In "The Excelsior Acquisition," Sheldon tells Penny that she is "responsible for all the evil that has befallen [him]" because he got a traffic ticket, had to go to court, and thus did not get to meet famed comic book creator Stan Lee at the comic store.

Sheldon's Comic Book World paradigm allows him to neatly categorize people. His friends are the "good guys," and people such as Wil, Leslie, and Barry are the "bad guys." This ordering provides him with a sense of security and a framework from which to interact with others. That he relies on such frameworks is not surprising. After all, he designated the left side of the couch as his, and he instituted a detailed emergency escape plan for the apartment. He maps out his weekly meals and activities around a fixed schedule. Just as Batman has the Bat Cave and Gotham, Sheldon has his apartment, his research lab, and the comic book store. We even learn that he thinks he can be Batman—as long as he has "enough tech support and start-up capital." He understands the world in the context of science, comic books, games, and sci-fi television shows and movies. Thus, it is not surprising that he utilizes a Comic Book World paradigm to make sense of good and evil.

As we have seen, Sheldon uses good-evil analogies—"the Green Goblin to my Spider-Man"—to compare others to himself, especially to those on his "All-Time Enemies List." He sees people and situations in black and white and often doesn't catch the nuances of interpersonal relationships or the shades of gray within people's emotions. Recall in "The Large Hadron Collision" that Leonard chooses Penny and not Sheldon to accompany him to Switzerland to visit the Large Hadron Collider. Sheldon perfunctorily deems Leonard a traitor. (Who cares if the trip falls over Valentine's Day!) Sheldon compares the "heinousness of his betrayal" to that of Darth Vader or Rupert Murdoch because he holds the latter ultimately responsible for FOX canceling "Joss Whedon's brilliant new show *Firefly.*" Surely, Leonard is not evil for wanting to take his girlfriend on a romantic getaway to Switzerland? So, even though Wil does bad things, Barry and Leslie are sometimes mean, and FOX executives make ill-advised decisions, none of this makes them evil people—even if Sheldon elevates them to the supervillian category.

Rejecting traditional theories of evil, Paul Ricoeur (1913–2005) argued that evil could be understood through myths and symbols, claiming that "theodicies and their mad project of justifying God" are all bound to fail in the face of senseless, Job-like suffering.[14] Even so, Ricoeur maintained that evil occurs as a result of free will that could be used for bad, as well as for good. By studying the symbols found in the creation myths and stories of Judeo-Christian and other cultures, one can learn about right and wrong actions and about good and evil. Thus, when Sheldon quotes lines from *Star Trek: The Wrath of Khan*, he is using a framework of myths to cope with a perceived wrong. He incorporates the *Star Trek* mythology into his life, much as a religious person would Bible stories. He uses Khan as a construct of how to act when faced with what he thinks is a similar situation, and thus he imitates Khan's speech when responding to Wil's lies and taunts. He doesn't understand why Wil would trick him into thinking his meemaw died or why he instigated the break-up of Leonard and Penny at the bowling alley. Yet Ricoeur didn't suggest that evil is a myth. All of the interactions Sheldon has with Wil are real, and the lies that Wil tells Sheldon are real. By thinking about the world of *Star Trek* or comic books, Sheldon is better equipped to try to make sense of how people act and why they might choose to do bad things or be evil.

With Sheldon's limited way of understanding people and with his limited ways of viewing and coping with the world, he sees the world in black and white or perhaps in the flat, two-dimensional colors of comic books. Living within his Comic Book world paradigm, Sheldon fails to see the world in Technicolor, with all of its vibrant joys, saturated levels of meaning, and big-screen flaws.[15]

## The Inscrutability Factor

Despite all of the lies, the mind games, and the insults, Wil is probably not a thoroughly bad person. It remains unclear whether he is truly deserving of the "Evil Wil" label Sheldon placed on him with his handy label maker (which, itself, is labeled "label maker"). Is his character simply beyond the pale? Such character assessments are difficult to make. Think of a person who might have said mean things to you or played a practical joke on you, or who lied to you to get what he wanted. Are such persons truly evil? Probably not. Instead, they might be described as selfish, inconsiderate, or self-serving. The nature of evil remains rather impenetrable. No theory of theodicy can fully capture all of the nuances. Yet even if the problem of evil remains, perhaps we have gone some way in making sense of Sheldon's problem with evil.

## NOTES

1. For more from Wil Wheaton's experiences as a guest star on *The Big Bang Theory*, see <http://wilwheaton.typepad.com/wwdnbackup/2009/10/the-creepy-coating-corollary.html>.

2. For more on this topic, see Michael Murray, "Leibniz on the Problem of Evil," in *The Stanford Encyclopedia of Philosophy*, http://plato.stanford.edu/archives/spr2011/entries/leibniz-evil/.

3. Voltaire, *Candide* (New York: Barnes & Noble, 2003), 29.

4. For an overview of various responses to the existence of evil, see William Hart, *Evil: A Primer: A History of a Bad Idea from Beelzebub to Bin Laden* (New York: MJF Books, 2004), 130–131.

5. Martin Buber, *Good and Evil* (Upper Saddle River, NJ: Prentice-Hall 1997), 60.

6. Ibid., 7.

7. Ibid., 10.

8. Hart, *Evil: A Primer*, 130–131.

9. Ibid., 21.

10. Friedrich Nietzsche, *Beyond Good and Evil: Prelude to a Philosophy of the Future*, trans. and ed. Marion Faber (Oxford: Oxford University Press, 1998), 153.

11. Some have translated the word *Übermensch* as "Superman." Can you imagine how annoyed Sheldon would be if Evil Wil was thought to be "Superman," or the "good" guy, in Nietzsche's opinion?

12. Friedrich Nietzsche, *The Portable Nietzsche*, trans. Walter Kaufmann (New York: Penguin Books, 1977), 180.

13. Arguably, Sheldon is far more blameworthy for his deeds in this episode. He convinces the guys to steal the film reels, because if he "can't see it, no one can," especially his enemy. This is a case where Sheldon, and not Wil, is acting selfishly.

14. Paul Ricoeur, *The Conflict of Interpretations* (Evanston, IL: Northwestern University Press, 1974), 281.

15. The season 5 episode "The Russian Rocket Reaction," which aired after writing this chapter, happily confirms this interpretation of Sheldon. In that episode, Wil provides Sheldon with his last original in-the-package Wesley Crusher action figure. Wil signed it: "To Sheldon, sorry this took so long. Your friend, Wil Wheaton." This immediately takes Wil off Sheldon's mortal enemy list. Sheldon announces, "Look, everyone. Wil Wheaton is my friend!" But when Brent Spiner (a.k.a. Mr. Data) proceeds to rip open the package, he instantaneously takes Wil's place on the list (keeping its membership at 61).

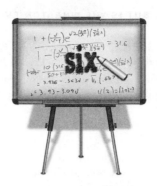

# DO WE NEED A ROOMMATE AGREEMENT?: PLEASURE, SELFISHNESS, AND VIRTUE IN *THE BIG BANG THEORY*

*Gregory L. Bock and Jeffrey L. Bock*

What is the good life? What is the right thing to do? What kind of person should I become? Despite their shared interests in science and comic books, Howard, Sheldon, and Leonard exemplify very different answers to these big questions. By putting our favorite nerds under the philosophical microscope, we'll consider whether the life of pleasure, selfishness, or virtue is best. As a bonus, we'll be in a better position to determine whether the gang "ruined Dennis Kim's life."

## The Giant "Hedon" Collider

One answer to the question of the good life immediately presents itself: hedonism, the life of pleasure. The philosopher Jeremy Bentham (1748–1832) provided a classical expression of hedonism: "Nature has placed mankind under the governance of two sovereign masters, *pain* and *pleasure*. It is for them alone to point out what we ought to do, as well as to determine what we shall do."[1] The hedonist, then, interprets the good life to consist of successfully pursuing the life of pleasure and avoiding pain.

Howard Wolowitz exemplifies hedonism. He will go to great lengths in trying to obtain pleasure—just think of all of the work he put into finding the various "future Mrs. Wolowitzes" living in *America's Top Model* house. And he seeks pleasure in unusual ways. Recall his announcement from "The Work Song Nanocluster": "Hey! You know what'd be a great idea: we get some girls over here and play laser-obstacle-strip-chess." Persistent in his pursuit, in "The Gothowitz Deviation" Howard dons fake tattoo sleeves to scam Goth girls, and in "The Adhesive Duck Deficiency" he scours the desert to hook up with "not unattractive middle school teachers who reek of desperation."

Howard is drawn to loose women as Sheldon is to new comic books. Never mind the actual prostitute from "The Las Vegas Renormalization." Instead, consider Penny's friend Christy—the "whore of Omaha." In "The Dumpling Paradox," after a morning session of "exfoliating Christy's brains out," Howard triumphantly enters Leonard and Sheldon's apartment, declaring, "When they perfect cloning, I'm gonna order twelve of those"—that is, Christies. When Leonard cautions him about getting used, Howard replies, "Who cares? Last night she pulled off her blouse and I wept." But Penny warns, "Howard, I know her. She'll have sex with anyone as long as they keep buying her things."

Howard: "Yay! If you'll excuse me, I have some bar mitzvah bonds to cash."

Aristippus (435–356 BCE), a lesser-known follower of Socrates (470–399 BCE), effectively captures Howard's brand of sensual hedonism. Aristippus practiced immediate sensual gratification without regard to social standards. When rebuked for sleeping with a courtesan, he argued that there was no important difference between "sailing on a ship in which many people have sailed and none." Anticipating the Wolowitzian school of thought, he concluded, "It likewise makes no difference whether the woman you sleep with has been with many people or none."[2]

Yet it seems implausible to hold that Wolowitz's brand of hedonism is sufficient for leading the good life. This sort of naïve hedonism looks like a doctrine "worthy only of swine," to paraphrase the classic objection. Penny seems to agree; in "The Robot Instability," she calls Howard "a pig" and warns that he will "grow old and die alone" if he doesn't change his ways. John Stuart Mill (1806–1873), a student of Bentham, tried to defend hedonism against "piggish" objections leveled against it by distinguishing between higher and lower pleasures. The higher pleasures are associated with our intellectual abilities: listening to classical music, writing poetry, and doing philosophy (and presumably physics, of course). The lower pleasures are associated with our baser, animalistic drives—our desires for food, drink, and sex. Mill argued that the happiness derived from the higher pleasures is more valuable than happiness derived from lower pleasures.

Wolowitz, of course, is not solely devoted to sensual pleasure. He values his mother's affections, still sleeping in the room where his bassinet was kept. In some sordid and contrived way, he must gain a kind of satisfaction from living under his mother's smothering care. Yet this kind of satisfaction still seems infantile. His aspirations toward a more adult relationship with Bernadette are more appropriate, but he continues to struggle with convoluted priorities. After Bernadette welcomes him with open arms in "The Cohabitation Formulation," proclaiming her love for him, he reciprocates but promptly asks, "So, what's for dinner?" After she admits that her cupboards are bare, he suggests that they go fool around in the bedroom but states, "And then you can go shopping." Bernadette rightly refuses to be Howard's mother, pandering to his every infantile need, so Howard is quickly back on his mother's porch, explaining to her that he's not a sex criminal trying to break in.

Howard redoubles his efforts to leave his baser and infantile desires behind in "The Herb Garden Germination," when he proposes to Bernadette. Because of his relationship with Bernadette, Howard is becoming less creepy and more admirable. It may not be as funny, but it would be better for him to outgrow his childish dependence on his mother's care and his adolescent obsession with carnal pleasure.

## The Egoism Polarization

Hedonism is a theory of the good, which is consistent with various theories of what we ought to do. As a utilitarian, Mill argued that we should take everyone's good into account before deciding to act; actions are morally right insofar as they produce the most happiness for everyone involved. By contrast, an ethical egoist would argue that only the agent's happiness matters.

The rudiments of ethical egoism go back at least as far as Plato's (428–348 BCE) *Republic*, in which the character Glaucon serves as the mouthpiece for an egoistic approach to ethics. Glaucon argues that people act justly only when it is in their best interests. Acting unjustly often has too many negative side effects, especially given the likelihood of getting caught.

Yet what if the negative side effects could be removed? Glaucon argues that if anyone had the magic ring of Gyges, which turns its wearer invisible, he or she would immediately act unjustly: "No man would keep his hands off what was not his own when he could safely take what he liked out of the market, or go into houses and lie with any one at his pleasure, or kill or release from prison whom he would, and in all respects be like a god among men. . . . For all men believe in their hearts that injustice is far more profitable to the individual than justice."[3] One can only imagine what Howard would do with Gyges's ring.

Moral theories spell out what agents ought to do. You ought to drive your injured neighbor to the hospital but not sneak into her apartment while she sleeps. Regardless of exactly what you ought or ought not to do, any such imperative must be grounded in good reasons for keeping it. If you ought to do something, then there are sufficiently good reasons for doing it—you have good reasons for upholding the obligation. Yet if *you* have good reasons for doing something, then doing it thereby serves (or satisfies) *your* personal interests. Therefore, if you morally ought to do something, then doing it thereby serves your interests.[4] This is what the ethical egoist believes. According to ethical egoism, you are morally required to engage only in those behaviors that serve your best interest.

Ethical egoists may choose to help others, but they are morally required to do so only if it's in their own best interest. Howard again serves as a vivid example. He enjoys the time he spends with the guys, but he often takes an egoistic approach to his friendships, thinking primarily of himself. Recall the exchange in "The Pirate Solution" when it appears that Raj will be deported to India:

> Howard: I'm really going to miss you.
> Raj: Will you come visit me in India?
> Howard: Gee, that's like a seventeen hour flight. How about I meet you halfway?
> Raj: Halfway is 600 miles off the coast of Japan.
> Howard: "Tell you what—we'll Skype."

The future of their relationship hinges on how it benefits or inconveniences Howard. Because the inconvenience of traveling to India is considerable, Howard decides to curtail the relationship. If curtailing the relationship is in Howard's best interests, then, according to egoism, this is what he is morally obligated to do.

Ethical egoism doesn't have a wide following among philosophers because it's difficult to defend the view that only the agent's interests matter. Furthermore, if someone is your friend merely because of what he or she gets out of the deal, he or she is no real friend. It is difficult to have an intimate relationship with anyone if the interests of only one of the partners matter. Why do Howard's interests matter over Raj's (or Bernadette's)? What if Howard's and Raj's interests collide? What should they do? Are there any nonarbitrary ways to answer these questions? If not, ethical egoism remains theoretically dubious.

## The Social Contract Instability

The philosopher Thomas Hobbes (1588–1679) was a proponent of psychological egoism, according to which it is psychologically impossible for a person to act contrary to his or her (perceived) best interest. No matter what people decide to do, it is necessarily done out of self-interested motives. Psychological egoism is a descriptive theory, not prescriptive. It asserts something about how human beings do (necessarily) act, not how we ought to act. The psychological egoist affirms that all human action is done either to gain some personal benefit or to avoid some personal harm.

Hobbes asked us to envision a time before governments kept societies stable. In those conditions, how do psychological egoists behave? What happens when egoists compete for the same good? Hobbes answered, "If any two men desire the same thing, which nevertheless they cannot both enjoy, they become enemies; and in the way to their end . . . endeavor to destroy, or subdue one another."[5] We laugh when Sheldon employs Darth Vader's "Force-choke" or tries to make Leonard's head explode, as on *Scanners*. Yet Hobbes was quite serious. He called our pregovernmental egoistic existence the "state of nature."

In the state of nature, there is competition for limited resources, pitting one person against another in a state of war, in which the two, if necessary, will fight to the death. This kind of life is bleak. Hobbes wrote:

> In such a condition, there is no place for industry; because the fruit thereof is uncertain: and consequently no culture of the earth . . . ; no commodious [suitable] building . . . ; no knowledge of the face of the earth; no account of time; no arts; no letters; no society, and which is worst of all, continual fear and danger of violent death; and the life of man, solitary, poor, nasty, brutish, and short.[6]

Hobbes thought that rational persons would naturally want to avoid such a state of nature, exactly because we seek our own best interests. Eventually, then, we make agreements with one another to avoid threatening behaviors in exchange for peace and prosperity.

The contractual agreements we make with other peace-seekers are the beginnings of moral rules. Once a government is established that is powerful enough to suppress violating the rules, Hobbes believed that the contracts we make are morally binding. It is wrong to break a contract. This is Hobbes's version of social contract theory.

As we know, Sheldon Cooper is very concerned about social contracts. In "The Classified Materials Turbulence," Stuart phones Leonard. Because Leonard believes Stuart is looking for advice about dating Penny, he doesn't answer and allows the call to go to voice mail. When Leonard doesn't promptly check his messages, Sheldon becomes unnerved, declaring, "You have to check your messages!" Sheldon elaborates, "Leaving a message is one half of a social contract, which is completed by the checking of the message. If that contract breaks down, then all social contracts break down. And we descend into anarchy." Hobbes would probably have smiled.

No wonder, then, that Sheldon requires Leonard to sign an extensive contract-based roommate agreement before they begin cohabitating. In "The Vartabedian Conundrum," we learn just how detailed the agreement is. Once Leonard and Dr. Stephanie become serious, Sheldon invokes "Article One, Section Three," of their roommate agreement to call an emergency meeting. (Leonard moves that the meeting not occur, but because no one seconds it, his motion fails.) Sheldon congratulates Leonard on his relationship with Dr. Stephanie but goes on to enact the "cohabitation rider" of the roommate agreement because Leonard and Stephanie are now living together. Confused, Leonard replies, "We're not living together." Sheldon disagrees and reads from the agreement, "A girlfriend shall be deemed, quote, 'living with' Leonard 'when she has stayed over A) ten consecutive nights or B) more than nine nights in a three week period, or C) all the weekends of a given month plus three weeknights.'" Leonard: "That's absurd." Sheldon: "Really? You initialed it. See?" In protest, Leonard explains, "And I initialed another clause naming you my sidekick if I get superpowers."

Sheldon's provisos don't stop at defining girlfriends and sidekicks. They include more mundane regulations: for example, at what temperature to set the thermostat (72 degrees), the times at which the apartment may be vacuumed, and what television shows will be watched on which nights (*Firefly* on Fridays).

It seems that no matter what the circumstances, Sheldon can appeal to the roommate agreement. In "The Cooper-Nowitzki Theorem," Sheldon gets his ego stroked by a perky young grad student named Ramona Nowitzki, who soon commandeers his life to keep him focused on work. When he has to give up *Halo* night and paintball weekends, Sheldon quickly and literally cries out to Leonard for help.

> Sheldon: I'm invoking the Skynet Clause . . .
> Leonard: That only applies if you need me to destroy an artificial intelligence you created that's taking over the Earth.
> Sheldon: Come on, don't nitpick.
> Leonard: Good night!
> Sheldon: Alright, I'm invoking our body snatcher's clause.
> Leonard: The body snatcher's clause requires me to help you destroy someone we know who's been replaced with an alien pod.
> Sheldon: Yes, she's in the living room. Go. I'll wait here.[7]

The agreement is surprisingly detailed, including provisions for outlandish eventualities, but it's all in the hopes of avoiding "apartment anarchy," where the roommates suffer a "nasty, brutish, and short" existence.

Hobbes believed that powerful governmental control—in the form of a sovereign—must oversee all contracts if they are to be binding. Only then do the terms *just* and *unjust* truly apply. Yet note that the roommate agreement lacks a Hobbesian sovereign. What forces compliance? Sheldon can be unpleasant to live with if Leonard fails to abide by his agreements, but he falls short of being a Hobbesian sovereign. Furthermore, what if Leonard invents time travel, but his first stop isn't their original agreement-signing meeting?

Consider "The Staircase Implementation." After a squabble about watching *Babylon 5*, Sheldon invokes the "all ties will be settled by me" proviso of the roommate agreement. Leonard reminds him, "But I said no to that." Sheldon quickly replies, "And I said yes. And I settle all ties." This smacks of a kind of arbitrariness that Hobbes wanted to avoid. Perhaps the sovereign was supposed to "settle all ties" in his system. Yet it does raise an interesting question: in the absence of a Hobbesian-type sovereign, what should we do in the case of contractual disagreement? In turn, this makes us wonder whether all of ethics can simply be a matter of making agreements with others. After all, how detailed would a Sheldon-like roommate agreement have to be to cover any and every situation that may arise? Even a brainiac such as Sheldon may fail to anticipate one of the roommates coming to own a full-scale replica of a time machine.[8] The pending worry here only intensifies as we try to imagine what kind of agreement would be necessary for all of us to live by.

The problem with social contract theory, in general, is that it offers a rather thin conception of ethics. There is more to living well than just following a set of rules. Consider a football example: To be an excellent football player, you need to know and follow the rules of the game, but this is not sufficient for being an excellent player. You also need to have talent, to train, and to show judgment on the field. In the same way, being a good person requires more than simply rule following; to be excellent at life, you must have the virtues of the good life.

## The Aristotelian Virtue Vortex

According to Aristotle (384–322 BCE), the good life is attained only through a life of virtue, a well-balanced life that avoids the extremes of "too little" and "too much." For example, a person who has the virtue of courage is one who is neither cowardly nor rash but one who hits on the middle ground, the mean between both extremes.

Acting virtuously requires practical wisdom. By this, Aristotle meant something different than, or perhaps in addition to, intelligence. Sheldon is incredibly intelligent, but he doesn't know what to do in an astounding number of situations. Aristotle said that morally appropriate behavior was "as a man of practical wisdom would determine it."[9] A person of practical wisdom is someone who is a moral role model, someone we want to emulate because he knows the right thing to do and he acts for the right reasons. The virtuous person also has the appropriate emotions. Aristotle explained that a virtuous person feels the emotions "at the right times, with reference to the right objects, towards the right people, with the right motive, and in the right way . . . and this is characteristic of virtue."[10]

Aristotle would have faulted Howard for overemphasizing sensual pleasures. Aristotle wasn't a prude, but he did advocate temperance. He called those who overemphasized pleasurable experiences "vulgar," being slavishly led by their appetites like "grazing animals." Aristotle wasn't sure how to characterize those at the other extreme, those who are "deficient in pleasures." He claimed that people who "enjoy them less than is right are not often found."[11] Sheldon, though, comes uncomfortably close to being the kind of person who underemphasizes pleasurable experiences. In any event, Aristotle would have us aim somewhere between Howard and Sheldon regarding attitudes toward pleasure.

In "The Justice League Recombination," Sheldon repeatedly insists on authenticity in the group's costumed portrayal of the various members of the comic book team the Justice League of America. For example, as soon as he dons the Flash costume, he speeds up his ordinary routine, saying, "This is how the Flash paces." Likewise, he criticizes Penny: "I'm sorry. But in what universe is Wonder Woman blonde?" Sheldon's call for authenticity omits the Justice League's most important quality, however: justice. After happening upon a group of guys breaking into a car, does the team step in and save the day? No. Sheldon says, "We're the Justice League of America. There's only one thing we can do. Turn around and slowly walk away." The obvious disconnect here is evidence that

Sheldon knows what the Justice League would do, but he cannot bring himself to follow their example. At the very least, Sheldon-dressed-as-the-Flash should have the courage to call the police, but he seems overcome with fear. Sheldon's flaws here are nicely contrasted with the virtues of his heroes. We should act more like Flash and less like Sheldon-as-Flash.

Leonard has more practical wisdom than Howard or Sheldon has. When compared to Howard's hedonistic ways, Leonard's quest to find a true romantic mate is almost saintly. He doesn't yearn for a merely physical fling but instead seeks out solid relationships that will benefit him emotionally, as well as physically. In the pilot episode, Leonard immediately falls for Penny and shows the early signs of infatuation. Sheldon assumes that this interest in the new neighbor is strictly carnal, but Leonard assures him that his interest in Penny is neighborly, even though thoughts of it being more aren't completely out of the question.

> Leonard: That's not to say that if a carnal relationship were to develop that I wouldn't participate. However briefly.
>
> Sheldon: Do you think this possibility will be helped or hindered when she discovers your Luke Skywalker no-more-tears shampoo?
>
> Leonard: It's Darth Vader shampoo. Luke Skywalker's the conditioner.

Although his relationship with Penny will grow into something more in the coming seasons, Leonard respects her boundaries and doesn't overtly pursue his interest in her. This action alone is decidedly un-Howard-like.

Of course, Leonard does have some hedonistic tendencies. Take his liaison with Leslie Winkle in the first season. In "The Hamburger Postulate," Leslie invites Leonard to practice his cello with her string quartet. Immediately afterward, she comes on to him, and they quickly find themselves in the throes of passion, signaling their escapade with the standard necktie around a doorknob. Although Leonard starts to develop feelings for Leslie (no doubt, this is naturally a side effect of coitus), she quickly quashes those feelings and insists that it must be nothing more than physical. At first, he's put off by the idea of casual sex, but he doesn't seem too upset when Leslie offers it up once again in the second season's "The Codpiece Topology."

Leonard's ability to deal appropriately in trying situations, including those involving Sheldon, is aptly displayed in "The Terminator Decoupling." Recall the TiVo conundrum.

> Sheldon: Stop. We can't do this; it's not right.
>
> Raj: Sheldon, you have two choices. Either you let him put a bigger hard drive in the TiVo, or you delete stuff before we go out of town.
>
> Sheldon: But once you open the box, you've voided the warranty. The warranty is a sacred covenant we've entered into with the manufacturer. He offers to stand by his equipment, and we in return agree not to violate the integrity of the internal hardware. This little orange sticker is all that stands between us and anarchy.
>
> Leonard: Okay, then we won't touch the hard drive. We'll just erase the first season of *Battlestar*.
>
> Sheldon (*ripping off sticker*): There. We're outlaws.

We've already seen Sheldon's propensity to seek social contracts, be they implicit or explicit. Yet here again, we see how trying to shape one's life completely around them seems implausible. As Howard is slavish about his hedonism, Sheldon is slavish about his rules. Leonard, on the other hand, lives on the basis of discernment and judgment. It's not that rules or agreements don't matter, but that one must approach and apply them in thoughtful ways.

Leonard, despite his flaws, is the most well-balanced character on the show and, hence, the closest thing to a person of practical wisdom. In fact, he is a leader. As Amy Farrah Fowler explains in "The Toast Derivation": "Sheldon . . . I think it's time to face the fact that Leonard is the nucleus of your social group. Where he goes, the group goes. . . . Your group is Leonard-centric. If it were a town, it would be Leonardville. If it were an Islamic nation—Leonardstan. If it were the birthplace of motion pictures, we'd all be singing, 'Hurray for Leonardwood!'"

Towards the end of the fourth season, Leonard seems to have reached his ideal good-life scenario. He's found love with Raj's sister Priya and moved on from his relationship with Penny (though he still shows some feelings for her). He's become more confident in his day-to-day interactions. It's as if his relationship with Priya (the addition of that final social aspect of the good life that he was missing) has instilled in him a confidence that he's never had before. He's changing his image, standing up to bullies, and more vociferously challenging Sheldon's roommate agreement. Although he and Priya are on the rocks at the end of season 4, Leonard has come a long way from being the nerd whose pants were stolen by Penny's ex in the pilot episode.

## The Dennis Kim Conundrum

In "The Jerusalem Duality," Dr. Gablehauser introduces fifteen year-old Dennis Kim to Sheldon and Leonard, informing them that Dennis is a "highly sought-after doctoral candidate" touring the university. Sheldon is impressed, sharing with Dennis that he started graduate school at fourteen. Dennis politely explains, "Well, I lost a year while my family was tunneling out of North Korea." Gablehauser hopes that Sheldon and Leonard will show Dennis around, letting him see that they're the best physics research facility in the country. Dennis not so politely explains that he already knows they're not but nevertheless ultimately accepts Gablehauser's invitation to attend the university.

Sheldon immediately senses "a disturbance in the Force." Dennis is the youngest winner of the prestigious Stevenson Award, supplanting Sheldon by six months. Dennis calls Sheldon's research a "dead end" and begins to explain why. Sheldon calls Dennis "The One" and asks him if he can see the Matrix. He was certain that the next person to be smarter than he is would be a cyborg. Sheldon's despair makes him unbearable (just imagine) and the rest of the gang miserable.

Leonard, Raj, and Howard agree to take action. Raj asks, "What if something were to happen to [Dennis] so he was no longer a threat to Sheldon?" Howard: "Then our problem would be solved." Leonard cautions, "Hang on, are we talking about murdering Dennis Kim? [*beat*] I'm not saying no." Howard: "We don't have to go that far. There are other means available." Raj promptly complains that they can't send him back to North Korea ("he knows how to get out"). Instead, they concoct a plan to get Dennis a girlfriend and thus distract him from physics. Marching over to Penny's apartment, they lament, "We need a hot fifteen year old Asian girl with a thing for smart guys." She slams the door on them.

When the department has a welcome reception for Dennis, the guys arrange a phony bring your (fourteen to sixteen) year-old daughter to work day. Dennis meets Emma, and he promptly leaves so that he can go to the mall with her. We next see Dennis, with Emma, drinking cheap wine from a paper bag in the park. Raj admits, "I kind of feel bad about what we did to him." Dennis and Emma start making out. Leonard, more than a little sarcastically, "Yeah, we really ruined his life." Sheldon: "Screw him. He was weak."

Did the gang ruin Dennis's life? Did the gang act selfishly, considering only their interests and not Dennis's? Did they break some social contract? Did Dennis ruin his own life? Is a life spent pursuing carnal pleasures less desirable than one dedicated to unlocking secrets of the universe? Beyond the comedy and the cosmology, these are the big questions *The Big Bang Theory* leaves us to ponder.

## NOTES

1. Jeremy Bentham, *An Introduction to the Principles of Morals and Legislation*, ed. J. H. Burns and H. L. A. Hart (Oxford: Clarendon Press, 1970), 11.

2. Tim O'Keefe, "Hedonism," Internet Encyclopedia of Philosophy, <www.iep.utm.edu/aristip/>.

3. Plato, *Republic*, Book 2 (Mineola, NY: Dover, 2000), 32–33.

4. This argument is adapted from Russ Shafer-Landau, *The Fundamentals of Ethics* (New York: Oxford University Press, 2010), 106–108.

5. We have modernized the spelling in this quote from Thomas Hobbes, *Leviathan* (New York: E. P. Dutton and Company, 1950), chap. 13, 102.

6. Ibid., 104.

7. Our thanks to the webmaster at <http://bigbangtrans.wordpress.com> for episode dialogue.

8. Also, the agreement itself seems to cause only discord in their relationship, culminating in the situation that arises in "The Agreement Dissection," where Priya almost successfully nullifies the contract through legal arguments. Only through Sheldon's blackmailing of her is he allowed to keep the agreement with updated amendments that remove loopholes.

9. Aristotle, *Nicomachean Ethics*, trans. W. D. Ross, in Richard McKeon, ed., *The Basic Works of Aristotle* (New York: Random House, 1941), 959. References to Aristotle hereafter will be given by margin number signaled by "*NE*." The current quote can be found at 1107a1–1107a2.

10. *NE*, 1106b21.

11. See *NE*, 1095b14–1095b 22 and 1119a1–1119a20.

# PART THREE

# "PERHAPS YOU MEAN A DIFFERENT THING THAN I DO WHEN YOU SAY 'SCIENCE'": SCIENCE, SCIENTISM, AND RELIGION

# GETTING FUNDAMENTAL ABOUT DOING PHYSICS IN *THE BIG BANG THEORY*

*Jonathan Lawhead*

You tell people I'm a rocket scientist?! . . . I'm a
theoretical physicist! . . . My God! Why don't you just
tell them I'm a toll-taker at the Golden Gate Bridge!
Rocket scientist! How humiliating!

—Sheldon Cooper, Ph.D.,
"The Pork Chop Indeterminacy"

As a theoretical physicist, Sheldon considers himself above
getting his hands dirty to experimentally validate his work—
unless it's dirt from the residue of a dry-erase marker. He
scoffs at the more applied work of Leonard and Raj, and he
finds Howard beneath contempt, a lowly oompa-loompa of
science. Still, Sheldon values engineers over social scientists.

Brain researcher Dr. Beverly Hofstadter echoes Sheldon's sentiments on the hierarchy of knowledge, when she explains that she and her cultural anthropologist husband once did papers on the same topic, and hers was the only one worth reading. And oh, the humanities! They simply do not deserve funding.

*Scientism* is the view that the scientific project occupies a privileged position among human endeavors, and *fundamentalist scientism*, the more specific position that Sheldon often expresses, is the view that all human endeavors form a kind of inverted pyramid, with fundamental physics as the load-bearing point on which everything else rests. Science, in this view, is the most important thing that humans have ever done, and fundamental physics is the most important part of science, justifying Sheldon's "haughty derision" of other disciplines.

Although *fundamentalist scientism* is tempting, it can and probably should be resisted without doing any damage to the structure of the scientific project. If only Sheldon could see this, he would be able to deal better with Amy, Leonard, Raj, and even Howard.

## Studies in Sheldonology

In what sense is fundamental physics *fundamental*? In "The Codpiece Topology," Sheldon and his nemesis Leslie Winkle argue over whether string theory or loop quantum gravity theory is correct. What, exactly, are they fighting about? On one level, they're arguing over who is the bigger "dumbass," but on a deeper level, they're arguing about which theory best describes the world as it actually is. Regardless of whether Sheldon or Leslie has the better of that debate, we cannot overlook the fact that these two scientists have the same goal.

That goal, not surprisingly, is tied to what scientists do. On a very general level, scientists make predictions about the world, specifically about how it behaves. Sheldon predicts the existence of magnetic monopoles. Leslie predicts that there are minute differences in the speed of light for different colors. Leonard predicts the existence of "supersolids," a previously unknown state of matter, at temperatures approaching absolute zero. Amy predicts that if she maps Penny's brain as she cries, she can make a monkey cry by exciting similar brain regions. Arguably, the deeper goal of science is to make predictions about what's going to happen in the world from *any* one moment to the next—to make predictions about how the world changes over time. Eventually, debates over which predictions most accurately describe the world will become rather general and abstract. So, we begin to see the nature of the debate between Sheldon and Leslie. In the most general, abstract, and fundamental sense, does the string theorist or the loop quantum gravity theorist make better predictions about the world and its behavior?

To better appreciate how scientists go about making their predictions, let's invent a novel field of scientific inquiry: "Sheldonology." Clearly, Leonard, Howard, and Raj are the leading experts—thus transforming Howard from an oompa-loompa to a "Willy Wonka" of science! Sheldonologists deal with the study and prediction of Sheldon's deeply unusual behavior; they specialize in predicting what Sheldon is going to do from one moment to another—where he's going to go, what he's going to say, what he's going to have for dinner, where he's going to sit, and so on. So, how might Sheldonologists go about achieving this goal?

Any aspiring Sheldonologist (such as Penny) will immediately note that her subject of study is—putting it rather mildly—a creature of habit: Sheldon has very particular routines and invariably becomes "disquieted" when those routines are disturbed. This fact is incredibly useful for Sheldonologists because it means that his behavior is consistently nonrandom; their job of *predicting* what he's going to do is made easier in virtue of this fact. Consider, for instance, that for every location where he spends any amount of time, Sheldon seems to have a particular "spot" where he prefers to sit, and he gets rather upset if he can't sit there: call this the *Sheldon Parking Principle* (SPP). In his and Leonard's apartment, Sheldon's spot is the edge of the couch. Given the SPP, we can make fairly reliable predictions about Sheldon's behavior across a wide variety of circumstances. For example, we know (with a high degree of certainty) that if a newcomer to the apartment sits on Sheldon's preferred cushion, Sheldon will ask him (or her) to move. This explains Leonard's warning to Penny in the pilot episode not to sit on the right end of the couch. Penny is a quick study, and in "The Gorilla Experiment," she shares her knowledge with Bernadette during her first visit. When Bernadette asks why Sheldon can't sit somewhere else, Penny articulates the SPP in great detail:

> Oh no, no, you see, in the winter, that seat is close enough to the radiator so that he's warm, yet not so close that he sweats. In the summer, it's directly in the path of a cross-breeze created by opening windows there and there. It faces the television at an angle that isn't direct, so he can still talk to everybody, yet not so wide that the picture looks distorted.[1]

Sheldon, mildly surprised, nods in approval, saying, "Perhaps there's hope for you after all."

With the SPP in hand, Sheldonologists can predict Sheldon's behavior in a wide variety of novel circumstances. They know that if there's some sort of *damage* to that spot—such as that caused by Penny (or anyone, really) accidentally firing a paintball gun at the cushion—Sheldon will be unable to comfortably sit *anywhere* in the apartment. Moreover, the SPP allows for predictions across a range of *unobserved* or *hypothetical* circumstances. When Sheldon first visits Penny's apartment in "The Tangerine Factor," he spends a long time deliberating about where to sit (outlining the SPP again to a bemused Penny—no wonder she learned it so well). Once he makes this decision, the SPP allows even amateur Sheldonologists to predict with very high confidence that he will return to that spot every time he visits Penny's apartment (which he does, of course). Generalizing on this instance allows us to predict that Sheldon would behave similarly in any new locale. In fact, if we think about it, we can tell a great deal about how the Sheldon-containing parts of the world are going to change from one moment to the next, given the SPP and a very small amount of information about the world (where Sheldon sits the first time he visits a location).

Of course, Sheldonology includes much more than just the SPP. In "The Cooper-Nowitzki Theorem," for example, Sheldon outlines his eating schedule day by day, explaining that he rotates through seven dinners from seven restaurants, one for each day of the week. Given this piece of information and an arbitrary date, Sheldonologists can predict (with great confidence!) what Sheldon will have for dinner on a given day. There are many other predictable scenarios as well: what happens when he attempts to drive a car, when he gets sick, and when he interacts with his mother. All predictions would be grounded in the observation that there are very stable patterns to be identified in Sheldon's behavior. So, the business of Sheldonology consists of three tasks: observing regions of the world that contain Sheldon, identifying patterns in how those regions change over time, and using those patterns to predict how *other* Sheldon-containing regions might change in various circumstances. This goes a long way toward describing how nonimaginary scientists do science.

## A Unified Theory of Sheldon?

Penny's description of the mechanics behind the SPP might seem to appeal to general psychological principles. Yet Sheldonologists are not psychologists specializing in Sheldon's unusual mind or trying to divine the underlying psychological *reasons* for his behavior. They're more like physicists. For Sheldonologists, then, Sheldon exists as a kind of basic atomic unit or particle. That's not to say that he's small or round or looks like a billiard ball, but only that he's an unanalyzed object in Sheldonologist theory, just as (say) electrons are in particle physics or *strings* are in Sheldon's own field of string theory. That is, Sheldonologists aren't concerned with what's going on inside Sheldon's mind as he makes his way through his day. Rather, they treat him as a *simple*—as an atomic unit—and just try to discern patterns in his (outward) behavior.

This insight begins to capture another important aspect of doing science: it is conducted in distinct domains. Think of the common experiment, conducted in many elementary school classrooms, to determine whether sugar cubes dissolve more quickly in warm or cold water. Here the basic atomic unit is the sugar cube, and water temperature is the variable. This is akin to Sheldonologists studying Sheldon in a new locale in which he sits. After some experimentation, fledgling scientists will be able to make reliable predictions about sugar cubes in water and Sheldon in new places. So, there are "sugarologists" and "Sheldonologists," and these represent distinct fields of inquiry. Distinct fields of scientific inquiry are often called the "special sciences" because each attempts predictions only about its subject matter (that is, *especially* about its topic).

Yet we could ask: what is going on inside sugar cubes or Sheldon that explains their respective behaviors? The former requires us to (rather literally) dig deeper into the nature of sugar. The latter requires us to (more metaphorically) dig deeper into Sheldon. Consequently, we no longer take sugar cubes or Sheldon as a basic unit; we begin to analyze our subject more deeply. This might occur to us once we have learned a great deal from our "sugarology" or "Sheldonology" endeavors. What explains why sugar dissolves the way it does? What explains why Sheldon acts the way he does? This, in turn, suggests that there is a scientific mode of inquiry that is more fundamental than "sugarology" or "Sheldonology" because it provides deeper or more profound information about the subject matter. This subsequent level of scientific inquiry—the next special science—would be more fundamental to explaining its subject matter. It seems "sugarologists" will eventually reach the special science of chemistry. Chemistry presumably can explain everything sugarologists study, but not vice versa. This is another way to understand how it is more fundamental, but also explains why scientists would probably say that chemistry is theoretically more general than "sugarology." It's tempting to argue that the special science of physics is more fundamental than chemistry. If so, then physics can explain everything chemistry can, but not vice versa. This explains why some scientists hold that physics is more general than chemistry; its scope includes more than only chemistry. Clearly, the most fundamental of the special sciences would also be the most general; its scope would include everything.

What about Sheldon, though? Where is the next stop for Sheldonologists? Some scholars might contend it's sociology or anthropology. From there, it's a short step to psychology. Yet if Dr. Beverly Hofstadter is correct, neurobiology is more fundamental to cognitive systems than is psychology. If so, then neurobiology explains everything psychology does but not vice versa. This makes neurobiology more general, because its scope includes more than only psychology. Amy Farrah Fowler would no doubt agree. But is there a field of inquiry about Sheldon (or anyone, I suppose) more fundamental than neurobiology? Biology, perhaps? It's tempting to argue that just as physics is more fundamental than chemistry, it is also more fundamental than neurobiology or biology. Sheldon Cooper (and Leslie Winkle) would agree. Sheldon holds that because the world is made of matter, physics is the most fundamental of the special sciences, and whatever is the most fundamental to physics would explain everything. In "The Zazzy Substitution," however, Amy staunchly disagrees with

Sheldon's assessment, signaling one of the more memorable "non-breakups" in sitcom history.

> Amy: Absolutely not. My colleagues and I are mapping the neurological substrates that subserve global information processing, which is required for all cognitive reasoning, including scientific inquiry, making my research *ipso facto* prior in the *ordo cognoscendi*. That means it's better than his research, and [to everyone else at the table] by extension, of course, yours.
>
> Sheldon: Excuse me, but a grand unified theory, insofar as it explains everything, will *ipso facto* explain neurobiology.
>
> Amy: Yes, but if I'm successful, I will be able to map and reproduce your thought processes in deriving a grand unified theory, and therefore, subsume your conclusions under my paradigm.

Sheldon accuses her of "rank pyschologism," and they nonacrimoniously agree to "terminate their non-relationship immediately," which mysteriously occasions Sheldon's becoming a cat lover.

In any event, Sheldon's quarrel with Amy harkens back to his spat with Leslie: what mode of scientific inquiry is most fundamental to understanding the world in terms of predicting its behavior from one moment to the next? Sheldon and Leslie agree that it's (fundamental) physics but disagree about which specific theory it is. Amy, though, disagrees with Sheldon, arguing that theoretical physics—even in its attempt at a grand unified theory—is not fundamental in the way Sheldon believes.

## Resolving a "Nonlovers" Quarrel (about Science)

Fundamental physics is the enterprise of identifying patterns that will predict the evolution of *any* system we might choose to consider, from Sheldons to dolphins, stars, cloned Leonard

Nimoys, check-engine lights, distant planets, subatomic particles, or "sweaty" stuffed animals (and, by extension, "whores of Omaha"). If successful, a grand unified theory would be fantastically important. No wonder Sheldon believes that there is a Nobel Prize in his future.

In his fight with Amy, Sheldon quite rightly notes that "a grand unified theory, insofar as it explains everything, will *ipso facto* explain neurobiology." There's a rather large nugget of truth here: Sheldon is certainly right that any system that can be studied by neurobiologists—any *cognitive* system—will also be subject to study by fundamental physicists. Any *patterns* identified by neurobiologists will *by definition* be patterns in systems that fundamental physicists are also concerned with; a grand unified theory is neither very grand nor much unified if it has nothing to say about (for instance) the human brain.

It's worth considering this point in greater detail, because this gets at the heart of the question we're concerned with: is Sheldon's arrogant attitude toward other modes of inquiry justified or not? Let's think more carefully about Amy's claim that if her research pans out, she will "be able to map and reproduce your thought processes in deriving a grand unified theory, and therefore, subsume your conclusions under my paradigm." Although Sheldon dismisses this as "rank psychologism," there's surely something to Amy's claim. If she succeeds in discerning *all* of the patterns underlying brains, then, given enough information about the state of a brain-containing system at a particular time, she should be able to predict what that system will be doing at a later time, right? We know, for instance, that Leonard's mother (also a neuroscientist) has a detailed scan of Sheldon's brain on hand from their "date" with the CAT scanner in "The Maternal Capacitance"; might not Amy and the elder Dr. Hofstadter put their heads together (no pun intended), figure out how brains work in general, and then predict every thought (about physics and otherwise) that Sheldon will have in the future?

Perhaps, but it's worth asking what they will have accomplished if they succeed at this task. Would a success here amount, as Amy argues, to "subsuming [Sheldon's] conclusions under [her] paradigm?" Does this prove that neuroscience is *more fundamental* than fundamental physics? Sorry, Amy, but not exactly. If Amy and Beverly were to succeed at cooking up the kind of Sheldon-simulation we've been talking about so far, they would have (in effect) built a system that can *do physics*. This would be a triumph for neuroscience, to be sure, but recognizing this fact still amounts to recognizing that a tremendous number of patterns are outside the purview of Amy's project. Simply put, there are physical things that don't do physics. This point is reminiscent of Sheldon's comment to Penny in "The Gorilla Experiment": "Physics encompasses the entire universe, from quantum particles to supernovas, from spinning electrons to spinning galaxies." Neuroscience cannot make this claim, nor can *any* of the special sciences: a biologist such as Bernadette has no more to say about supernovas than a neuroscientist such as Amy does. Only physicists can make the claim of ultimate generality, and *that's* the sense in which fundamental physics is fundamental.

Yet this falls short of justifying Sheldon's arrogance completely because fundamental physics is far from the *only* project worth pursuing. Although it's true that the patterns of fundamental physics must also apply to brains, the project of identifying patterns that hold *only* in brains might still be fantastically useful. The fact that these patterns hold only in a restricted set of systems might be considered a benefit, rather than a problem: if we're interested only in predicting the behavior of systems that contain brains, then we're allowed to ignore a tremendous amount of extraneous information about how systems that *don't* contain brains behave, especially if it makes our task easier! If we encounter brain-containing systems on a daily basis (as we do), then we have good reason to care a great deal about how those systems behave, even if, in identifying the relevant patterns, we ignore information about how (for instance) "spinning electrons and spinning galaxies" behave. The business of science is in identifying interesting systems and discerning patterns in how those systems change over time, and it's an inarguable fact that there are tremendously useful patterns to be found that don't hold everywhere in the universe. It is the business of the special sciences to identify those patterns, and Sheldon should recognize that this enterprise is a fantastically important one in its own right.

None of what we've said so far gives us a reason to prefer Sheldonology, neuroscience, microbiology, or fundamental physics *full stop*. It's certainly true that any Sheldon-containing system is *also* a brain-containing system (and thus that any system that can be studied by Sheldonologists can *also* be studied by neuroscientists). And any brain-containing system is *also* a living thing–containing system (and thus that any system that can be studied by neuroscientists can *also* be studied by biologists). Yet there might still be circumstances in which we'd prefer Sheldonology to neuroscience or neuroscience to biology. In particular, it might be the case that we have compelling reasons to *care* about patterns that hold only in Sheldon-containing systems more than we care about patterns that hold in *all* brain-containing systems (for example, if we encounter Sheldon far more than we encounter most other people).

That is, we might well be willing to trade the generality of neuroscience for the relative simplicity of Sheldonology, even if it means working with a special science that holds in a smaller set of possible systems. When Leonard and the gang attempt to work out the optimal restaurant/theater pairing at the beginning of "The Financial Permeability," they (quite reasonably) choose to do it in terms of Sheldonology. The relevant problem, as Leonard puts it, is finding "a Sheldon-approved restaurant proximate to a Sheldon-approved theater." It would be possible, of course, to work out this problem in terms of (say) fundamental physics—Sheldons, restaurants, and theaters are all within the province of fundamental physics. There's a far easier way to go about it, however. Given the principles of Sheldonology, the gang can hone in on *just* the relevant patterns (which contain facts about things such as Red Vines and Ice-ee machines) and exclude all of the irrelevant patterns about supernovas and galaxies. Expressing the problem as a problem in Sheldonology makes their lives *easier*, so why not go about things that way?

## The Pragmatics of the Special Sciences

This brings us to another important aspect of doing science, no less important than the others: in many cases, the choice of which special science to appeal to is a highly pragmatic one. That is, science contains a pragmatic element that sometimes gets overlooked. For instance, it makes little sense to object to Amy that in studying human brains she's wasting her time, because the patterns she identifies are ones that couldn't possibly hold in the interior of the sun. Why not? For exactly the same reason that Leonard might well specialize in Sheldonology, rather than in something more general: we encounter conditions such as the ones in which the generalizations of neurobiology hold far more often than we encounter conditions such as those of the interior of the sun. We have good reason to care about the patterns that neurobiologists identify, because there are a lot of systems displaying those patterns around here. If our goal is to predict the behavior of those systems, we don't necessarily care whether those predictions would break down in certain extreme conditions—that is, if there are possible systems in which the patterns identified by neurobiology wouldn't apply.

So, where does this leave Sheldon and his disdain for sciences other than fundamental physics? In some sense, he's correct in his belief that his project of finding the patterns that underlie everything is special. If he's successful, he'll be able to claim that he's succeeded in articulating a set of patterns that has a level of generality beyond those of any other science. In another sense, though, this isn't the only project worth pursuing.

It might also be useful to point out, in closing, that it isn't even clear that Sheldon actually *thinks* only science is worth pursuing. Though he claims to be humiliated when his sister implies he is a rocket scientist, rather than a theoretical physicist, he nevertheless shows what can only be described as loving reverence for Leonard's mother, a brain researcher, calling her a "remarkable woman." It's also worth noticing his dedication to physics isn't absolute. When Ramona Nowitzki takes over his life in "The Cooper-Nowitzki Theorem," he eventually tries to enlist Leonard's help to destroy her (invoking the "Skynet clause" of their friendship), despite the fact that she is pushing him toward greatness. Sheldon values things other than physics—Red Vines, *Halo*, comic books, good Thai food, and (perhaps) even Amy's companionship.[2] He values all of these things because they help him live the life he wants to live—he values them for *pragmatic* reasons. Ultimately, he should have a similar appreciation for biology, neuroscience, and the other special sciences.[3]

## NOTES

1. I offer my sincere thanks to the webmaster at <http://bigbangtrans.wordpress.com> for episode dialogue here and throughout.

2. This is confirmed by Sheldon's desire that Amy become his girlfriend and cease being merely his "girl-who-is-a-friend"—assuming she abides by the newly penned "girlfriend agreement!"

3. Thanks go to Dr. Dean Kowalski for his helpful feedback, comments, and editorial suggestions.

# SHELDON, LEONARD, AND LESLIE: THE THREE FACES OF QUANTUM GRAVITY

*Andrew Zimmerman Jones*

At the beginning of *The Big Bang Theory*'s second season, a romantic relationship ends abruptly, virtually before it begins. The relationship has the potential for some good laughs, but it fizzles after just one episode. No, I'm not talking about Leonard and Penny's romance (version 1.0), but instead the second episode of the season, "The Codpiece Topology," in which a rebounding Leonard begins to date his physicist colleague Leslie Winkle. Recall the heated debate between Leslie and Sheldon about loop quantum gravity and string theory. Leslie believes that loop quantum gravity best describes the universe, and Sheldon disagrees (strongly). Leonard is pulled into the fracas and diplomatically asserts, "Well, there's a lot of merit to both theories." Leslie will have none of it; she complains, "Well, I'm glad I found out the truth about you before this went any further." Leonard promptly responds, "What truth? We're talking about untested hypotheses. It's no big deal." Leslie presses, "Oh, it isn't, really? Tell me, Leonard, how would we raise the children? . . . I'm sorry. . . . This is a deal breaker."

Yet what is the "deal breaker," exactly? Her quarrel was (originally) with Sheldon. Did Leonard fail to defend her honor in some sufficiently chivalrous way? Sure, the apartment is bereft of strumming minstrels, but the relationship ends in a way that leaves many of us a bit perplexed. At the very least, it is more mysterious than the breakup Leonard experienced only one episode earlier in "The Bad Fish Paradigm": Penny was insecure about her lack of formal education, and Leonard was not sufficiently sensitive to it.

Believe it or not, we can better understand (and appreciate) the Leonard/Leslie breakup if we delve into the rudiments of science and how it is performed in our modern era. This will require encountering the thorny question of science's ultimate goal and what methods should be employed to reach it.

## The Methods of Science

The scientific method involves observing some behavior in nature, formulating a rule that would explain that behavior, and then constructing a test to see whether that rule holds up in a new, but relevantly similar, situation. What, though, is the "most important" part of this process? Is it the coming up with the rule (theoretical science) or the testing of that rule (experimental science)? What if each is about equally important?

Leonard and Howard are practical and hands-on about their scientific work, but Raj seems to be something of a mix between a theoretical and an experimental scientist. He is an astrophysicist who, at least in "The Pirate Solution," works *for* (and not with) Sheldon to explore "the string theory implications of gamma rays from dark matter annihilations." Yet in "The Griffin Equivalency," Raj is recognized in *People* magazine for discovering a planet-size object. Sheldon, of course, is firmly (and proudly) on the theoretical side of this divide. In "The Monopolar Expedition," he is awarded a prestigious grant from the National Science Foundation, but his acceptance requires him to take to the field—to the North Pole, nonetheless. He initially hesitates, explaining, "I'm a theoretical physicist, a career I chose in no small part because it's indoors." After accepting the NSF grant, Sheldon quickly displays his lack of practical experimental intuition by having *his* team practice setting up equipment in the Cheesecake Factory freezer. It takes Leonard only minutes to suggest they could set it up inside and then take their equipment outside.

These fictional scientists and their pending trek to the North Pole illustrate how science tends to unfold. Theoreticians build mathematical models and use them to make predictions that experimentalists then test against the real behavior of physical systems. Today's theories are often so elaborate that the skill sets involved are fundamentally different in many ways. Even so, we must be wary of the misperception that theoretical physicists alone drive scientific advancement, with the experimentalists along for the ride. The interplay between the theoretician and the experimentalist is much more subtle than that.

One of the key points about scientific ideas, at least according to the philosopher of science Karl Popper (1902–1994), is that they must be falsifiable. In other words, if there's no experiment that could be conducted (in principle, if not in actual practice) to show an idea to be mistaken, then you can't really say that the idea is scientific. For example, the idea of God is an idea that, according to most thinkers, can never be falsified and so doesn't qualify as a scientific idea.

Through this process of falsification, the experimentalists force the theorists to revise their failed theories. Once a theory is falsified, then its status as part of the current "scientific paradigm," is called into question.[1] The current paradigm represents a coherent way to systematize all incoming data; it provides a status quo for how science—and scientists—operate. If a theory fails to account for any new data, this upsets the scientific status quo. Yet theorists don't immediately abandon their theories wholesale just because of a few contradictions or failed predictions. In the words of philosopher of science Thomas Kuhn (1922–1996), "Normal science . . . often suppresses fundamental [data] novelties because they are necessarily subversive of its basic commitments."[2]

That is, scientists go about their business, perfectly happy with the status quo described by their existing paradigm. Occasionally, however, some contradictory or unexpected evidence comes along, disrupting the status quo. Scientists must then make a choice. Some are tempted by the new data, such as a hot new neighbor moving in across the hallway. These scientists are eager to jettison their old paradigm in the hope of breaking new ground, just as Leonard was keen to leave his geeky, lonely self behind to woo Penny. Such scientists are intent on looking for new theories that are "intelligent and beautiful." Yet just as Sheldon chides that Leonard's children with Penny will be imaginary, most scientists are not nearly as ready as Leonard to break out on a new path to follow the hot new neighbor—that is, the new, unexpected scientific evidence—wherever it leads. Many prefer to cling desperately to the status quo, refusing to acknowledge that any fundamental change has actually taken place. These scientists prefer attempts to explain the new, *seemingly* unexpected data under their current paradigm.

This latter strategy coheres with another of Kuhn's points about science. Regarding the accumulation of contrary evidence, he wrote, "Once it has achieved the status of paradigm, a scientific theory is declared invalid only if an alternate candidate is available to take its place."[3] This suggests that scientists are prone to hold on to a theory longer than they should. Even so, the very nature of science helps ensure that hidden flaws in a theory will be eventually uncovered by someone who is keen to establish a new scientific paradigm. Kuhn also grasps this propensity among scientists, as he wrote, "The scientist must . . . be concerned to understand the world and to extend the precision and scope with which it has been ordered."[4]

In "The Alien Parasite Hypothesis," Sheldon provides a humorous example of a scientist illicitly shying away from the force of countervailing data. He attempts to help his girl-who-is-a-friend Amy Farrah Fowler discover the cause of her irregular biological behaviors in the presence of Penny's ex-boyfriend Zack. Sheldon's working under the quasi-paradigm that Amy, like himself, has evolved past tawdry desires of the flesh. They are intellectual beings. Yet all of the data point to the conclusion that Amy is sexually aroused by Zack. Sheldon refuses to accept this, proffering instead the hypothesis that Amy has been infected by an alien parasite, creating biological reactions consistent with sexual arousal. This allows Sheldon to retain his paradigm, but because there is no evidence that Amy has encountered extraterrestrials, his preferred hypothesis also requires him to unduly twist the data. In the end, Sheldon is being unscientific.

Accordingly, consider another fundamental component of science: its skeptical and inquisitive nature. Science ultimately seeks answers *wherever* they may take us. Nobel Prize–winning physicist Richard Feynman (1918–1988) tersely explained this aspect of science:

> Science is a way to teach how something gets to be known, what is not known, to what extent things are known (for nothing is known absolutely), how to handle doubt and uncertainty, what the rules of evidence are, how to think about things so that judgments can be made, how to distinguish truth from fraud, and from show.[5]

From Feynman's viewpoint, although scientists are certainly not looking to refute the existing paradigm at every turn, they are also not running from contradictory evidence. Or, at least they shouldn't be.

Feynman more succinctly described science as "the organized skepticism in the reliability of expert opinion."[6] Again, Dr. Sheldon Cooper has difficulty embracing this sentiment, as evinced in the following exchange from "The Work Song Nanocluster":

Sheldon: I'm a physicist. I have a working knowledge of the entire universe and everything it contains.
Penny: [unimpressed] Who's Radiohead?
Sheldon: I have a working knowledge of the *important* things in the universe.

Sheldon doesn't know the answer to Penny's question, but instead of literally running away from the data as he did by quickly leaving Amy's office, here he simply fails to acknowledge the question. He responds not by attempting to expand his knowledge, but by staying comfortably within his existing paradigm. All that he needs to know is included in his current understanding of theoretical physics. If it appears that there might be any phenomenon that falls outside of it, he dismisses it as unimportant and not worth knowing or even exploring.

A vivid example of scientists *following* Popper's and Feynman's guidance is the discovery of "dark energy." In 1998, astrophysicists discovered that the expansion of the universe was accelerating. This discovery was unexpected, but the evidence was solid, so scientists modified their models. This is Popper's falsification at work, because the evidence clearly contradicted the idea of a universe with expansion slowing down or constant (the two prevailing thoughts prior to 1998). It's one of the clearest cases of experiments leading to new theoretical work. More than a decade later, physicists are still trying to figure out the exact nature of the "dark" (unseen) energy powering this acceleration, as well as its implications for the rest of physics . . . especially since evidence now suggests that about 75 percent of our universe is made up of this unobservable dark energy!

## Theoretical "Discoveries"

Physicists take physical properties of the universe and translate them into equations, which they can then use to predict or interpret other physical properties of the universe. For example, consider the current paradigm in physics, sometimes called "modern physics." This paradigm consists of Einstein's general relativity, which describes gravity, and a comprehensive model of everything else in nature, called the "standard model" of quantum physics. These two domains both grew out of experimental evidence that did not match up with the classical Newtonian physics, which was dominant for the three centuries prior to Einstein. Today, general relativity and quantum physics are the foundation for all of our understanding of the universe's workings.

Both general relativity and quantum physics take the form of mathematical equations. In fact, when physicists do any sort of science, they are typically working with equations. Even the experiments, really, are just a means to get the right numbers to plug into the equations. The variables in these equations represent the physical properties of the universe. Experiments set some of these values, but theoretical physicists often alter some parameters to see what results they get, in sort of a "What if the universe were like this?" scenario.

In fact, much of the theoretical work of physics is figuring out the correct equations to use to describe a given situation. These equations have to conform to the known experimental evidence, but the mathematical work can also constitute a sort of new discovery in itself. Consider the discovery of antimatter. Physicist Paul Dirac (1902–1984) was working with equations to describe the behavior of electrons and discovered that they allowed for electrons to be negatively or positively charged. This perplexed him because electrons had been observed only with a negative electrical charge. Because his equations seemed correct, Dirac was led to consider the existence of positively charged electrons: positrons. Did the universe contain "antimatter"—stuff exactly like ordinary matter but with an opposite charge? Indeed. Dirac's supposition was experimentally confirmed only a few years later by Carl David Anderson (1905–1991).[7]

It's easy to imagine this as a discovery that could have been triggered by experiment, instead of by theory. It's conceivable that physicists would have never considered antimatter until Anderson accidentally stumbled on these strange, positively charged electrons in his experimental work, thus forcing the theoreticians to revise their equations accordingly. Yet it's unclear whether Anderson would have found positrons had it not been for Dirac's equations. In any event, it does seem that Dirac's theoretical work led to the prediction before the experimentalists got to it.

The discovery of antimatter gives insight into the science that seemingly drives "The Monopolar Expedition." Sheldon seeks to confirm his theoretical work by experimentally detecting slow-moving monopoles at the magnetic North Pole. Monopoles are theoretical but not purely fictional. Theoretical physics equations have predicted that in the high energy levels of the very early universe, there would have been freestanding magnetic poles, called magnetic monopoles. They can be understood by contrasting them with a common magnet (including the Earth itself). Magnets have negatively and positively charged poles ("north pole" and "south pole"), but the problem is that these are always connected. If you take a magnet (or anything else that produces a magnetic field) and cut it in half, you don't end up with a north pole and a south pole separately; you end up with two smaller magnets, each of which has a north and a south pole. Monopoles, then, are tiny particles that consist of only a single north pole without any connected south pole (or vice versa).

All of Sheldon's (and actual) current science points to—predicts the existence of—monopoles. The math supports this prediction. If such things existed, there should still be a few of them floating around out there, or they'd come into existence in high-energy collisions in space. Presumably, the Earth's magnetic field would make them hard to detect normally, which is why a trip to the North Pole is required. If his experiments prove successful—even if it means including Raj, Howard, and Leonard—the ramifications would be great. In his own words: "If I'm able to detect slow-moving magnetic monopoles, I'll be the scientist who confirmed string theory. People will write books about me. Third graders will create macaroni art dioramas depicting scenes from my life." Alas, his hopes are dashed; he was not as fortunate as Dirac was about predicting antimatter. He must either revisit his equations or construct a different experiment.

Interestingly enough, Sheldon was correct about his predictions of supersolids in "The Cooper-Hofstadter Polarization." In this case, Leonard played the role of Carl David Anderson, experimentally verifying Sheldon's theories. Yet again, Sheldon's preference for theoretical science takes center stage. He is so certain that the math was correct that he sees no point in presenting their findings at a prestigious conference. Why should he "kow-tow to lesser minds?" Moreover, he forbids Leonard from presenting their findings without him. When Leonard decides to present them anyway, Sheldon attempts to sabotage the presentation (and Howard uploads the whole embarrassing spat to YouTube).

## The String Theory Paradigm

Attempts at explaining string theory in the presence of Dr. Sheldon Cooper are bound to provoke ridicule, if Sheldon's "probing" questions of Dr. Brian Greene in "The Herb Garden Germination" are any indication. . . . "Mua-ha-ha." Nevertheless, here goes. Recall that current theoretical physics consists of two separate theoretical frameworks. Quantum mechanics describes the ways fundamental particles interact through electromagnetic forces and also through the strong and weak nuclear interactions. There's a fourth type of interaction, gravity, but quantum theory doesn't actually cover it. Instead, it is covered by Einstein's theory of general relativity.

The problem is that predictions made in quantum theory don't really carry over into general relativity and vice versa. For most things, this isn't a problem, because the methods of approximation smooth everything over. So physicists can describe most behaviors without running into the conflicts, but they do occasionally creep up in exotic situations, for example, along the edge of a black hole.

Einstein spent the last half of his life trying to create a "unified field theory," a single equation and paradigm that would encompass all of the fundamental rules about how reality functions. He was unsuccessful at these attempts, though there's (evidently) some dispute as to why, as tantalizingly conveyed in the following exchange from "The Wildebeest Implementation":

Sheldon: I must say, ever since you started having regular intercourse, your mind has lost its keen edge. You should reflect on that.

Leonard: Excuse me, but Einstein had a pretty busy sex life.

Sheldon: Yes, and he never unified gravity with the other forces. If he hadn't been such a hound dog, we'd all have time machines.

(For the record, there is no evidence that Einstein's promiscuity hampered his work or our owning time machines.)

Eventually, the field of string theory came to prominence as a possible unified theory of quantum gravity. In "The Fuzzy Boots Corollary," Leonard references this point in passing during his first pseudo-date with Penny:

Penny: So, what's new in the world of physics?
Leonard: Nothing.
Penny: Really, nothing?
Leonard: Well, with the exception of string theory, not much has happened since the 1930s. And you can't prove string theory. At best you can say, "Hey, look, my idea has an internal logical consistency."
Penny: Well, I'm sure things will pick up.

In string theory, all matter is envisioned as tiny vibrating strings, orders of magnitude smaller than the tiniest particle we can now observe. They are so small, in fact, that most scientists who work on the theory don't believe there's any way to experimentally observe a string itself, only the consequences of the strings interacting. This, in part, explains Leonard's comment that "you can't prove string theory." He appreciates the math, but the experimentalist in him calls for discernible proof.

Yet there's more. It's not just matter that is made up of strings. In quantum mechanics, the forces—electromagnetics, the strong nuclear force, and the weak nuclear force—work only because there are special types of particles, called bosons, that bounce around and make them work. These bosons are also created by vibrating strings, so all matter *and* its various interactions are described as different types of vibrating strings. This realization led to a particularly amazing prediction that caused many scientists to abandon it. String theory works only if you set up the equations so that the universe has a total of twenty-six dimensions!

This tantalizing issue is raised in the "Pilot" episode, shrouded in the guys' initial attempt to impress Penny:

Leonard: At least I didn't have to invent 26 dimensions just to make the math come out.
Sheldon: I didn't have to invent them. They're there.
Leonard: In what universe?
Sheldon: In all of them. That's the point.

Again, we see the clash between the more experimental Leonard and the more theoretical Sheldon. Leonard requires testable predictions. Sheldon believes that the math, carefully done, speaks for itself. In part, this further explains their tiff in "The Cooper-Hofstadter Polarization." Leonard rhetorically asks Sheldon, "So, the whole scientific community is supposed to just take your word?" Sheldon confidently (but somewhat cryptically) replies, "They're not supposed to, but they should."

There's a complex undercurrent here, which will prove vital to understanding the Leonard/Leslie breakup. The *equations* of string theory demand extra dimensions, which is sufficient for Sheldon to be confident of their existence. Leonard, as an experimentalist, scoffs that the theory doesn't match up with our known *experience* (which suggests only four spacetime dimensions: up/down, left/right, front/back, and a dimension representing our movement through time). Furthermore, it is unclear whether string theory offers any testable predictions. So, is it science or not?

This brings us to the heart of the issue with string theory, the Leonard/Leslie breakup, and, really, all of theoretical science: how much trust should be put in the equations, absent experimental confirmation? Certainly, based on what we know so far, there's no real reason to put any faith in this crazy theory, but in the 1970s there was another fascinating discovery. Physicists had applied concepts from quantum mechanics to gravity and had predicted that if these two paradigms were unified, then there would need to be a boson explaining the force of gravity. They called this particle the graviton and predicted the properties that it would need to have.

Here's the fascinating discovery: the equations for string theory predict—in fact, demand—that boson particles with exactly these properties exist. Under string theory, gravitons have to exist and, therefore, gravity also has to exist. This is the linchpin for string theory as a theory of quantum gravity. It was created to explain particle interactions but seems to require that the universe it describes must have gravity. Thus, the prediction that string theory makes about gravitons is extremely powerful. If the math is correct, it would make great strides toward a unified theory.

## Hang-Ups, Breakups, and New Beginnings

There are still a lot of hang-ups with string theory (like all those extra dimensions), but it is clearly the most well-developed and influential theory of quantum gravity we have. Yet it is not the only one. By most standards, string theory's biggest competitor is the theory of loop quantum gravity, which is championed by Leslie Winkle in *The Big Bang Theory*. Loop quantum gravity is in much the same state that string theory was in the late 1970s. It's an interesting theory, but aside from a small cabal of dedicated theorists, most scientists think the equations don't do what is needed and see little merit in the approach.

In this theory, instead of the fundamental nature of matter and forces, scientists look at the fundamental nature of spacetime and view it in tiny quantum increments. It interacts in various "loops," which is where the field gets its name. Consequently, Leslie operates out of the mainstream, as illustrated by Sheldon's frequent attacks against her, explicitly in "The Codpiece Topology," which focus (mostly) on the quality of her scientific work, equating it to a game of "one potato, two potato." Moreover, he claims, "Her research methodology is sloppy, she's unjustifiably arrogant about loop quantum gravity, and, to make matters worse, she's often mean to me." For all of that, it's certainly easy for a viewer to believe that Sheldon's evaluation is driven more by emotion than by objectivity, which might be another key to better appreciating their professional clashes.[8]

To better understand how two seemingly intelligent scientists can be so certain in their opposing ways, let's consider what they're really doing. They're working with equations that purport to describe reality but that contain other bits of information, other parameters, which theoretical physicists have devised in a "what if" scenario. Within the current stage of our universe, at the sorts of energy levels we normally interact with, the two theories match up with our observations and also with general relativity and quantum physics.

It's the extra parameters, the exotic situations, that make things interesting. These can be used to predict how black holes behave, what the universe was like close to its beginning, and what sorts of results to expect in the high energies of the Large Hadron Collider. For most cases, these parameters have no impact on what we expect to see; it's only in the hypothetical world of theoretical extrapolation that one theory has an upper hand over the others.

This brings us back to the scene at the beginning of this chapter: the Winkle/Hofstadter breakup. It all focuses around the roles of string theory and loop quantum gravity—neither of which has any discernable experimental support—as the proper approach to unifying physics under a more comprehensive paradigm. Sheldon obviously prefers string theory. As is Sheldon, Leslie is motivated by a strong commitment to the equations and their consequences, but she is committed to a *different* set of equations. She is opposed to Sheldon's equations, but she plays every bit the part of a theoretical physicist as he does. Leonard is still holding out for more experimental proof and implicitly doubts Leslie's conclusions. Worse, he seems a bit sympathetic to string theory. This is too much for Leslie, signaling the "deal breaker." Yet might this be hubris on Leslie's part? After all, Sheldon sometimes allows nonrational factors to creep into his professional work. (How might we test for *that*?) In any event, Leonard is an experimental scientist, embracing Feynman's skeptical approach to science much more strongly than either Leslie or Sheldon does. He seeks not merely internal consistency of the mathematical equations; he wants to discover how the universe works by confirming those equations.[9] Can he be blamed for that?

Of course, Leonard also wants to put the necktie back on the doorknob, but revisiting that bit of semiotics will have to wait a few more episodes. Leslie has left the building. Although Leonard and Leslie seem to be ended—for good—it is my hope that this chapter spurs you to learn more about what science is and what scientists do (even if no one calls you a "magnificent beast" for doing so).

## NOTES

1. The term *scientific paradigm* is usually attributed to Thomas Kuhn. See his *The Structure of Scientific Revolutions*, 2nd ed. (Chicago: University of Chicago Press, 1970).

2. Ibid., 5.

3. Ibid., 77.

4. Ibid., 42.

5. Lawrence Krauss, *Quantum Man: Richard Feynman's Life in Science* (New York: W. W. Norton & Company, 2011), quoting Richard P. Feynman, 1.

6. Richard P. Feynman, "What Is Science?" *The Physics Teacher* (September 1969).

7. Based on his previous theoretical work, Dirac proposed the idea of antimatter particles in 1930. These particles are exactly like ordinary matter but with an opposite charge. In 1932, Carl David Anderson experimentally discovered the positron in cosmic rays in 1932. Dirac received the 1933 Nobel Prize in Physics (jointly with Erwin Schrodinger) "for the discovery of new productive forms of atomic theory," while in 1936 Anderson received it "for his discovery of the positron. For more on these scientists and their accomplishments, see <http://nobelprize.org/nobel_prizes/physics/laureates/1933/> and <http://nobelprize.org/nobel_prizes/physics/laureates/1936/>, respectively.

8. Nothing about Leslie suggests she is an inept scientist; in "The Cushion Saturation," we learn that her research is worthy enough to justify a trip to the CERN Large Hadron Collider in Geneva, Switzerland. Furthermore, unlike Sheldon, Leslie seems equally comfortable in both the experimental and the theoretical realms. When she's introduced, it's said that she works in the same lab as Leonard, and in her first appearance she is trying to use a laser to heat up a cup of noodles.

9. Due to the lack of discernable experiential evidence, it is tempting to interpret the debate between Sheldon and Leslie as if they were fundamentalists of different religions. This might explain why Leslie refers to "the children"; although the analogy is a bit loaded, many parents face the difficult issue of deciding in which religion their children should be raised. Leonard suggests a nonpartisan approach of allowing the children to choose for themselves, but Leslie suggests that they need more guidance. In any event, the analogy breaks down in the sense that if experimental evidence ever firmly contradicted string theory or loop quantum gravity, one would expect Sheldon or Leslie to eventually concede the point, which isn't typically a factor in religious partisanship.

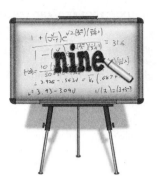

# THE ONE PARADIGM TO RULE THEM ALL: SCIENTISM AND *THE BIG BANG THEORY*

*Massimo Pigliucci*

Why is *The Big Bang Theory* so funny? Some fans think it's the writing; others, the acting; still others, the directing. Different aspects of the show no doubt work together on multiple levels. This chapter explores one way in which the various facets—writing, acting, directing—come together to make us laugh. The characters of Sheldon Cooper, Leonard Hofstadter, Howard Wolowitz, and Rajesh "Raj" Koothrappali are so funny (in part) due to their extremely "scientistic" worldviews, entirely framed by their practice of science. The humor manifests as their scientific approach unfolds in everyday life. They, of course, invariably fail at various mundane tasks, in sharp contrast with their nonintellectual but much more pragmatic neighbor Penny. In this way, art teaches us something about life. Through the lens of *The Big Bang Theory*, we can see how attempts to develop a thoroughgoing scientistic worldview are bound to fail, calling for more balanced approaches to understanding the world around us.

## The Data

In "The Hamburger Postulate," Leonard Hofstadter finally decides to ask his equally nerdy colleague, Leslie Winkle, to go out on a date:

> Leonard: Leslie, I would like to propose an experiment. . . . I was thinking of a bio-social exploration with a neuro-chemical overlay.
> Leslie: Wait, are you asking me out?
> Leonard: I was going to characterize it as a modification of our colleagues slash friendship paradigm with the addition of a date-like component, but we don't need to quibble over terminology.

Leslie suggests they simplify things a bit, as in any good scientific experiment, by skipping the actual date and going straight to the kissing stage. This will determine empirically what sort of neuro-chemical arousal they get from the experience and hence determine whether they wish, in fact, to begin dating. Leslie reports that Leonard's kiss produces absolutely no arousal in her, ending their experiment and Leonard's inquiry. Having agreed with the parameters, he quietly leaves the lab a bit wistful.

It's "Anything Can Happen Thursday Night" from "The Hofstadter Isotope," and the guys are—gasp—considering going out to a bar to pick up women. Leonard quickly comes back to Earth, muttering, "C'mon, Howard, the odds of us picking up girls in a bar are practically zero." Undaunted,

Wolowitz replies, "Oh, really? Are you familiar with the Drake equation?" Sheldon unflinchingly recites the formula for the Drake equation, used to calculate the odds of finding an extraterrestrial civilization with whom to communicate.[1] "Yeah, that one!" Howard quickly injects and continues:

> You can modify it to calculate our chances of having sex by changing the formula to use the number of single women in Los Angeles, the number of those who might find us attractive, and what I call the Wolowitz coefficient: Neediness, times Stress, squared. In crunching the numbers I came up with a conservative 5,812 potential sex partners within a 40 mile radius.

Leonard muses that he must be joking. Stone-faced, Howard replies, "I'm a horny engineer, Leonard, I never joke about math or sex."

In "The Friendship Algorithm," Sheldon endeavors to develop a scientific approach to acquiring friends. He proceeds to demonstrate the power of the algorithm over the phone, trying to convince the irksome Barry Kripke to spend time with him. Sheldon, however, soon gets stuck in an infinite loop caused by the structure of his own algorithm. Howard notices this and promptly strolls over to Sheldon's whiteboard to modify the procedure, thereby helping Sheldon achieve his goal. Placing his hand over the phone, Sheldon muses, "A loop counter, and an escape to the least objectionable activity. Howard, that's brilliant. I'm surprised you saw that." Slowly making his way back to his chair, Howard rhetorically and sarcastically asks, "Gee, why can't Sheldon make friends?"

These examples illustrate the attempt to reduce complex social skills to simple matters of logic, of the kind that might be implemented in a computer program. Once we are finished chuckling at Sheldon, Howard, Leonard, or Raj, the inevitable reaction is: dating or making friends simply isn't that cut and dried. This, in turn, leads us to ask: why even try to apply scientific methodologies to complex social interactions? Why think that science holds all of the answers?

## The Background

Science is indisputably the most effective way human beings have developed to understand—and even control, to a point—the natural world. It used to be a branch of philosophy, until the scientific revolution of the seventeenth century. Galileo and Newton thought of themselves as "natural philosophers," and the very term *scientist* was coined by the philosopher William Whewell as recently as 1834, in analogy with the word *artist*. The root of the term, however, is the Latin *scientia*, which means knowledge broadly construed, not only in the sense of what we today consider scientific knowledge.

Scientism is the idea that science can and should be expanded to every domain of human knowledge or interest, including the social sciences and the humanities, or alternatively the idea that the only kind of knowledge really worth having is that provided by the natural sciences. The appeal of scientism may derive from another important idea that is fundamental to the practice of science: reductionism. Reductionism is a basic and very successful approach common to the physical and biological sciences, articulated by René Descartes (1596–1650) in his *Meditations on First Philosophy*. Descartes was interested in establishing firm epistemic foundations for mathematics, philosophy, and science. To this end, he proffered four principles that he discovered on which to build a successful science. The second and third principles summarized the practice of reductionism:

> The second, to divide each of the difficulties under examination into as many parts as possible, and as might be necessary for its adequate solution. The third, to conduct my thoughts in such order that, by commencing with

objects the simplest and easiest to know, I might ascend by little and little, and, as it were, step by step, to the knowledge of the more complex; assigning in thought a certain order even to those objects which in their own nature do not stand in a relation of antecedence and sequence.[2]

The "divide and conquer" strategy (second principle), coupled with the "building from the bottom up" (third principle) approach, are exactly how physics has been able to subsume the entire domain of chemistry, and why molecular biology has been such a successful science since the discovery of the structure of DNA as recently as 1953. It is this triumph of the Cartesian method that has made reductionism a staple of the way science is done today.

Moreover, there is an intuitive appeal to reductionism and, by extension, to scientism, because of the common acknowledgment—among both scientists and philosophers—that the world is made of the same kind of basic stuff, be it quarks or superstrings. From this, it is tempting to conclude that a complete understanding of the world can be arrived at by simply studying the basic stuff of the universe carefully. Of course, science—particularly physics—is the discipline that studies the basic stuff of the universe. Perhaps this kind of thinking fuels the heated discussion between Leslie and Sheldon about string theory and loop quantum gravity in "The Codpiece Topology." If a complete understanding of everything depends on exploring the basic stuff of the universe, it is very important that you are studying the correct basic stuff.

## The Controversy

Do real scientists actually engage in scientism, though? Well, there are some data to consider. Note physicist Steven Weinberg's notorious essay "Against Philosophy."[3] And note the more recent bold (and unfounded) declaration by another physicist, Stephen Hawking, that philosophy is dead.[4]

One of the more ambitious examples of scientism, however, has come from biologist Edward O. Wilson.[5] In the (unwittingly) ironically titled *Consilience: The Unity of Knowledge*, Wilson attempts to subsume the humanities and the social sciences under biology on the somewhat flimsy epistemological ground that anything human beings do must eventually come down to their biology.[6] In a trivial sense, of course, Wilson is correct: human beings are biological entities, and everything we do is made possible (and constrained) by our physical bodies, our senses, and our brains. It simply doesn't follow, however, that biological explanations—though perhaps a necessary part of the picture—are sufficient or even our best bet when it comes to the complexities of human culture, such as dating or making friends. Yes, we date (in part) because we want sex, and we want sex (in part) because we are programmed by our genes to reproduce. Yet if anyone seriously thinks that human courtship and relationships can be accounted for solely (or even largely) on those terms, that person deserves the kind of "haughty derision" Sheldon and the guys regularly elicit from Penny for their absurd science-dominated take on the world.

More recently, neuroscientist Sam Harris has approached scientism by challenging (and dismissing out of hand) the entire field of ethics, a classical province of philosophy.[7] He claims that moral "facts" are of the same type as scientific facts, and that science—and particularly his own field of neurobiology—is therefore better poised than philosophy (or religion) to investigate them. Harris rejects the standard distinction between facts and values that was made famous by David Hume (1711–1776) in his *Treatise of Human Nature*. For Hume, empirical facts—such as those that science deals with—were of a very different nature from ethical judgments, the stuff that moral philosophy is interested in, and one could not simply slide without argument from facts to values.

Harris will have none of it, pointing out, for instance, that brain scans show that when people accept the truth of a mathematical proposition (as in "2 + 6 + 8 = 16"), they activate the same brain region (the medial prefrontal cortex) that is engaged when we accept the truth of a moral proposition ("it is good to let your children know that you love them"), from which Harris deduces that "the physiology of belief may be the same regardless of a proposition's content [which] also suggests that the division between facts and values does not make much sense in terms of underlying brain function."[8] That may very well be, but it has nothing whatsoever to do with the question of whether moral truths are of the same kind as scientific or mathematical truths. To convince yourself of this, simply reflect on the well-known neurobiological fact that your brain engages the same circuitry when you have sex in the real world and when you *think* of having sex. Hopefully, this will not lead you to believe that the two kinds of experience are even remotely the same, just as Howard and Raj found out at the end of "The Gothowitz Deviation," where we find them reimagining how their evening went, or at least what they intend to tell their friends about how the evening went. After their night of scamming chicks at a Goth club fails, they invent a story about group sex and hot tubs. Raj goes so far as to include the (imaginary) detail of how their female conquests smelled of jasmine. Yet it becomes immediately and painfully clear that there are all-too-important differences between imagining having had sex and actually having done the deed, which no doubt explains the plans to visit a country bar the next night.

Perhaps surprisingly, it isn't only scientists who engage in scientism; some philosophers are guilty of it, too! For instance, Paul and Patricia Churchland have endorsed a position in philosophy of mind known as eliminative materialism, the idea that talk of subjective experience should be eliminated and substituted with the more precise language of neurobiology.

So, for instance, "I am in pain" *really* is just a subjective and imprecise way of saying that certain C-fibers in particular nerves of my somatic sensory system have been activated by a physical injury of a given type.[9] Pain, in this account, is nothing over and above the firing of C-fibers. The problem, of course, is that talk of pain and talk of C-fiber activation—though certainly related—are not at all interchangeable ways of referring to the same phenomenon but rather distinct aspects (the subjective experience and the neurobiological description) of that phenomenon. The Churchlands are, in a sense, making the same mistake that Harris does, treating neurobiology as a fundamental and self-contained explanation of the mental, entirely sidestepping the fact that our subjective experiences have a qualitative richness that is simply not captured by a (technically correct) scientific account.

Leonard makes a similar mistake in "The Grasshopper Experiment," when Penny is practicing to be a bartender. Quite proud of herself, Penny announces, "Okay, here we go, Leonard, one tequila sunrise." Pleased, Leonard replies, "Thank you! You know, this drink is a wonderful example of how liquids with different specific gravities interact in a cylindrical container." True, a tequila sunrise (a drink made of three parts tequila, six parts orange juice, and one part grenadine syrup) is a wonderfully colorful way to demonstrate the layering of liquids characterized by different specific gravities, but that is decidedly *not* the reason people ask for tequila sunrises in bars, nor does that bit of information have anything interesting to tell us about the experience of drinking a tequila sunrise (try it and find out for yourself). Something like this also happens in "The Friendship Algorithm," when Sheldon realizes that climbing a rock wall has a distinctive qualitative feel to it that reading and learning about climbing a rock wall does not. Indeed, the former made Sheldon pass out, while the latter didn't.

## The Ramifications

The term *scientism* is almost never used in a positive sense; rather, it is ordinarily meant as an insult, usually hurled by (some) philosophers and humanists at scientists who seem to trespass on territory that does not belong to them. True, Howard's attempt to mathematically quantify the delicate art of human dating is amusing, as is Leslie and Leonard's experiment. And Sheldon's attempt at friendship is simply comical. Yet what accounts for the animosity associated with scientism?

Consider that staunchly valuing a scientific approach to things may hamper our ability to see the "bigger picture." These days, for instance, our society seems to be in the thrall of a quantification frenzy: we wish to measure (and compare) people's intelligence or learning or happiness by using simple, linear scales that afford us a feeling of precision and scientific accuracy. The risk, of course, is that we may miss the structure (and beauty?) of the forest because we are focused on counting the individual trees, discounting the importance of anything that is not amenable to a scientific-quantifying approach (think again of Sheldon's friendship algorithm) or straitjacketing complex phenomena (such as intelligence, learning, or happiness) into easily digestible numbers that make our decisions and our entire worldview much simpler than they would otherwise be.

Even Sheldon seems to get close to understanding this point during a conversation with his sister Missy in "The Pork Chop Indeterminacy." Introducing her to the rest of the gang, he says, "She is my twin sister, she thinks she is funny, but frankly I've never been able to see it." Missy knowingly replies, "That's because you have no measurable sense of humor, Shelly." Without skipping a beat, Sheldon rhetorically asks, "How exactly would one measure a sense of humor? A humor-mometer?" The delightful play on the term *measurable* shows that Missy, and not Sheldon, has a sense of humor exactly because humor resists quantifiable analysis.

Too much emphasis on science also risks becoming a sterile end, in and of itself, as in this exchange from "The Cooper-Hofstadter Polarization," where the boys proudly show Penny a new piece of software that Howard developed, which allows people from all over the world to take control of Leonard and Sheldon's apartment's fixtures:

Leonard: See?

Penny: No.

Sheldon: [impatiently] Someone in Szechuan province, China, is using his computer to turn our lights on and off.

Penny: Oh, that's . . . handy. Ahem, here is a question: why?

When the four scientists answer, in unison, "Because we can," Penny shakes her head in exasperation. The exercise is fascinating to the boys because it shows that it can be done, even though there are much better (but less "scientific") ways of accomplishing the same goal. Penny would simply have them use the light switch (or, at most, buy a universal remote from Radio Shack.)

Philosophers who criticize scientistic approaches to human problems seek to highlight the ethical issues raised by a science-based view of everything. When we attempt to reduce, or reinterpret, the humanities and our everyday experience in scientific terms, we not only are bound to miss something important, we also risk dehumanizing our own and other people's existence, possibly even becoming callous about the dangers of doing certain types of science on the ground that the latter represents in itself the highest conceivable goal. For instance, since the Large Hadron Collider (LHC), the world's highest energy particle accelerator, has gone into service near Geneva (Switzerland), there has been discussion of the possible dangers posed by some of the experiments planned for the facility. The controversy is briefly featured in "The Pork

Chop Indeterminacy." Leonard informs Raj, "Some physicists are concerned that if the Supercollider actually works, it will create a black hole and swallow up the earth, ending life as we know it." Raj unsympathetically answers, "What a bunch of crybabies."

True, there doesn't seem to actually be any measurable (!) risk of a black hole suddenly materializing inside the LHC and destroying the Earth, but science does have a long history of questionable effects on human life, from the tragedy of the eugenic movement (which from 1909 through the 1960s was responsible for the forced sterilization of sixty thousand individuals deemed to be genetically "unfit" in the United States) to the invention of nuclear weapons and the development of biological warfare. So an argument can be made that we shouldn't necessarily carry out certain types of scientific research just "because we can," as the boys explained to Penny. Science needs the guidance of external disciplines—such as ethics—as well as a serious engagement with public discourse to avoid eugenics-type Frankenstein scenarios. Yet this assumes the very thing that a scientistic approach denies: that meaningful rational discourse is possible or relevant outside of science itself.

Even if scientists know best, should science be used to improve the human condition without the explicit consent of the people whose lives are affected, in order to achieve the alleged improvement? And what constitutes an "improvement" in our existence, anyway? This question is implicitly posed in "The Gothowitz Deviation," when Leonard discovers that Sheldon is using positive reinforcement (a behavioral control technique devised by B. F. Skinner) with Penny—giving her chocolate every time she does something he likes:

Leonard: You can't train my girlfriend like a lab rat.
Sheldon: Actually, it turns out I can.
Leonard: Well, you shouldn't.

Sheldon: There is just no pleasing you, is there, Leonard? You weren't happy with my previous approach in dealing with her, so I decided to employ operant conditioning techniques. . . . I'm just tweaking her personality, sanding off the rough edges, if you will.

Leonard: No, you are not sanding Penny!

Sheldon: Oh c'mon, you can't tell me that you are not intrigued by the possibility of building a better girlfriend.

The exchange is hilarious, but the underlying issue—the interplay between science at all costs and a consideration of extrascientific ethical values—has led to some horrifying outcomes, even in recent history. One of the most notorious cases is the Tuskegee syphilis experiment, conducted in Tuskegee, Alabama, between 1932 and 1972. Doctors working with the U.S. Government began a study of 399 black men affected by syphilis, as well as an additional 201 used as controls, without telling the men in question that they had the disease. More crucially, once an effective cure became available—with the development of penicillin in the mid-1940s—the researchers knowingly withdrew treatment from the subjects. The study continued for decades and was terminated only because of a leak to the press, with the resulting controversy eventually leading to federal legislation to regulate scientific research that affected human subjects, as well as to the establishment of the Office for Human Research Protections.[10]

## The Analysis

So, what exactly is the problem with scientism, and what solutions are available to us? The answers to these two questions are actually among the several comedic premises that make *The Big Bang Theory* work so well as a show: respectively, the tendency of scientists to overreach, and the push back we can generate by applying some common sense (along with, perhaps, good philosophical reflection). Again, there should be no question that science is by far the best toolbox that humanity has come up with to discover how the world works. Science also needs much defending, as it has been under increasing attack recently, with large portions of Americans denying the theory of evolution, rejecting the notion of anthropogenic climate change, or believing that somehow vaccines cause autism.[11] As Carl Sagan aptly put it in his *The Demon-Haunted World*, a classic collection of essays about pseudoscience and assorted nonsense, science is like a very precious candle in the dark, which deserves our respect and requires our protection.

Yet it should be equally clear that science has a proper domain of application (however large). This implies that there are areas where science doesn't belong or it is not particularly informative or has nothing to do with what we really want. One of the benefits of *The Big Bang Theory* is its effectiveness in demonstrating this point, especially through many of the lighthearted exchanges between Penny and Sheldon.

One such exchange is particularly relevant to the debate about scientism. In "The Work Song Nanocluster," Sheldon volunteers to help Penny make her new "Penny Blossom" business enterprise become as profitable as possible. A bit surprised, Penny asks, "And you know about that stuff?" Sheldon, slightly scoffing, answers, "Penny, I'm a physicist. I have a working knowledge of the entire universe and everything it contains." Rather annoyed, Penny asks a question to test Sheldon's hypothesis: "Who's Radiohead?" This time skipping many beats, Sheldon musters, "I have a working knowledge of the *important* things in the universe." This is a near perfect example of the fallacy of scientism: physicists may one day be successful in arriving at a theory of everything, but "everything" has a very specific and limited meaning here, referring to the basic building blocks of the universe. It does not follow, either epistemologically or ontologically, that one can then simply apply the Cartesian method to work one's way up from superstrings to the cultural significance of Radiohead.[12] Moreover, Sheldon is offering a not-so-implicit value judgment here. Yet one could reasonably ask, why is theoretical physics the only important mode of discourse? Or, more to the point, how could Sheldon prove or justify this position within science alone? Value judgments, again following David Hume, seem distinct from scientific discourse exactly because what is or can be done is no sure guide to what ought to be done.

Moreover, it is downright pernicious for science, as well as for society at large, when prominent scientists such as Stephen Hawking declare an entire field of inquiry (philosophy) dead. Hawking does so, while at the same time engaging in some (bad) philosophical reasoning throughout his book, particularly when he comments on the very nature of science—a classic domain of study for philosophy. Or consider again Sam Harris, who wrote an entire tome about how science can provide us with values, rejecting without argument one of the most fundamental distinctions made by philosophers, the one between empirical facts and values.[13] Harris does this while at the same time making a very particular (and entirely unacknowledged) set of philosophical choices right at the beginning of his book, such as taking onboard a consequentialist ethical philosophy as the basis for his ideas about human happiness.

A much more reasonable view, I think, is that natural science, social science, philosophy, literature, and art each must have a respected place at the high table of societal discourse, because they are all necessary—and none sufficient—for human flourishing. Or, as it was so beautifully put in "The Panty Piñata Polarization,"

> Sheldon: Woman, you are playing with forces beyond your ken.
> Penny: Yeah, well, your ken can kiss my Barbie.

Philosophically, I can see no better way to articulate the message: sometimes, science is just not the point, and it certainly isn't the only point.

## NOTES

1. The actual equation looks like this: $N = R * fp * ne * fl * fi * fc * L$. Where $N$ is the number of civilizations in our galaxy with whom communication is possible; $R$ is the average galactic rate of star formation per year; $fp$ is the fraction of stars with planets; $ne$ is the average number of potentially life-sustaining planets per star; $fl$ is the fraction of planets actually developing life; $fi$ is the further fraction developing intelligent life; $fc$ is the fraction of civilizations developing communication technology; and $L$ is the length of time these civilizations produce detectable signals. You can play with the equation yourself here: <www.activemind.com/Mysterious/Topics/SETI/drake_equation.html>.

2. In case you are really curious, here are the first and the fourth: "The first was never to accept anything for true which I did not clearly know to be such; that is to say, carefully to avoid precipitancy and prejudice, and to comprise nothing more in my judgment than what was presented to my mind so clearly and distinctly as to exclude all ground of doubt." And: "The last, in every case to make enumerations so complete, and reviews so general, that I might be assured that nothing was omitted."

3. See *Dreams of a Final Theory* (New York: Vintage Books, 1992), chap. 7.

4. Right at the beginning of *The Grand Design*, written with Leonard Mlodinow (New York: Random House, 2010).

5. See *Consilience: The Unity of Knowledge* (New York: Vintage Books, 1999).

6. The irony of the title comes from the fact that *consilience* is a word also invented by the above mentioned philosopher William Whewell, to indicate a type of reasoning by which one uses convergent lines of evidence to arrive at a particularly strong conclusion, as Sherlock Holmes does in his famous adventures in logic and crime detecting, and very much unlike what Wilson achieves in his book.

7. See *The Moral Landscape: How Science Can Determine Human Values* (New York: Simon and Schuster, 2010).

8. Ibid., chap. 3, "Belief."

9. C-fibers are neural structures found in the peripheral nerves of our system, and their primary function is to convey information from there to the central nervous system; they are one of two types of fibers responsible for the sensation of pain.

10. Disturbingly, however, some federal agencies can still engage in human research without consent, via a presidential executive order, presumably under the increasingly all-encompassing excuse of "national security."

11. For a fuller discussion of the relationship between science and pseudoscience, see my own *Nonsense on Stilts: How to Tell Science from Bunk* (Chicago: University of Chicago Press, 2010).

12.  Epistemology is the branch of philosophy that deals with what we can know, while ontology is the branch that attends to the existence of things. In this context, reductionism may be ontologically insufficient to explain reality, if it turns out that there are truly novel ("emergent") phenomena at higher levels of complexity that cannot be directly reduced to lower levels. Even if ontologically feasible, reductionism surely does not work epistemologically, because it would make for an unwieldy account of reality above the quantum level. For instance, while engineers certainly agree that a bridge is, ultimately, made of quarks (ontology), attempting to describe its macroscopic physical properties by developing a detailed quantum mechanical model of it (epistemology) would be sheer folly.

13.  To be fair, even some philosophers, such as W. V. O. Quine, have questioned the existence of a sharp distinction between facts and values, but they have done so within strict limits and based on careful arguments. Harris, instead, simply thinks that philosophical arguments are capable only of increasing the degree of boredom in the universe and accordingly dismisses them out of hand—an exceedingly anti-intellectual attitude exhibited by a self-styled public intellectual.

# COOPER CONSIDERATIONS: SCIENCE, RELIGION, AND FAMILY

*Adam Barkman and Dean A. Kowalski*

Sometimes family members don't see eye to eye. Yet through our differences, there is almost always something to be learned. The Coopers from *The Big Bang Theory* provide rich ground for a "learning through family differences" thesis. True, precious few of us have fathers who once wrestled a bobcat for licorice. Yet many of us must navigate relationships with our siblings, even though most of us aren't as different as Sheldon and Melissa, and all of us have had to negotiate some differences with our parents. As we'll see, Sheldon and Mary Cooper can learn from their differences, and we in turn can learn from them.

## Magic Maharaja Macs?

Mary Cooper obviously has loved Sheldon dearly ever since he fell out of her at the Kmart. She comforted him in the aftermath of his "ass-kickings" at the hands of the neighbor kids—before and after his failed sonic death ray solution. She didn't stand in his way as he left for college at the tender age of eleven, and she accepted his decision to study science, which resulted in a physics Ph.D. at age sixteen. Yet aside from an occasional trip to California—land of the heathen—to mollify Shelly's meltdowns, Mary doesn't leave Texas. She has led most of her life surrounded by those who tend to look, think, and act more or less as she does—that is to say conservative, biblically based Christians.

It's not that Mary is completely ignorant of other cultures or faiths. In "The Luminous Fish Effect," she tells the gang about an Indian gentleman from her church, Dr. Patel. She elaborates, "It's a beautiful story. The Lord spoke to him and moved him to give us all 20 percent off on LASEK—you know, those that needed it." Yet neither Raj nor Howard is Christian. Mary acknowledges this fact by interrupting one of her prayers, turning to Raj and Howard, and saying, "Now, after a moment of silent mediation, I'm gonna end with 'in Jesus' name,' but you two don't feel any obligation to join in. [beat] Unless, of course, the Holy Spirit moves you." Mary bows her head and takes Howard's hand; Howard uncomfortably takes Raj's, and then everyone eats the meal Mary prepared for them.

The awkwardness continues in Mary's more direct inter-actions with Raj. In "The Electric Can Opener Fluctuation," Sheldon learns that Leonard, Howard, and Raj had falsified some of his magnetic monopole data. (In their defense, he was being a giant North Pole "dic-tator.") Sheldon thought that he finally had confirmed string theory, but his reputation is now ruined. He goes home, looking for his mother's comfort. The guilty trio travel to Texas to apologize and bring Sheldon back to California. Mary cordially greets them. Approaching

Raj, she inquires, "What about you? Radge, isn't it?" Raj looks at his feet and shakes his head affirmatively. Mary continues, "Oh, you still having trouble talking to the ladies?" She (knowingly) chuckles to herself but continues, "Because you know, at our church, we have a woman who is an amazing healer. Mostly she does crutch and wheelchair people, but I bet she'd be willing to take a shot at whatever Third-World demon is running around inside of you."

Given the progress of neurobiology and psychology, it's difficult to believe that some sort of supernatural demon causes Raj's selective mutism. In "The Maternal Capacitance," Dr. Beverly Hofstadter is "fascinated" by Raj's condition. She admits it "is quite rare" but attributes it to "a pathological fear of women." Mary's diagnosis of Raj probably relies on Scripture, not science. In the Gospel of Mark, Jesus speaks to "demons"; these "unclean spirits" possess people, causing great suffering. Jesus heals their suffering by casting out the demons.[1] Furthermore, the Gospel of Mark affirms that "signs accompany those who believe: in my name they will cast out demons; . . . they will lay their hands on the sick and they will recover."[2]

If Mary believes, as a number of conservative Christians do, that the Bible is the inerrant Word of God, then her introducing Raj to her friend at church is much more credible. Yet biblical inerrancy is a hotly contested topic among scholars. Nevertheless, is the devout believer required to interpret Scripture in this way? Genesis 41:57 states, "All the countries (all the earth) came to Egypt to buy grain from Joseph." Reading "all" literally, would that include Scotland or those native to North America? Similarly, 2 Chronicles 9:23 asserts, "All the kings of the earth . . . sought Solomon to hear his wisdom." Did Celtic or Korean kings seek Solomon's presence? And did the Genesis patriarch Seth live to be exactly 912 years old?

Contemporary philosopher Peter van Inwagen argues that God might have good reason not to inspire biblical authors to always convey literal truths. He notes, "A scientifically accurate rewriting of Genesis would turn it into something all but useless, for the result would be inaccessible," having "little pedagogical value for most people at most times."[3] This may also apply to references to "demons" in the New Testament. Biblical authors simply may not have been in the proper historical position to share scientifically based insights about psychological maladies. Moreover, by invoking popular beliefs of the time, even if not literally true, Mark's basic message about Jesus seems emboldened: Jesus is a great healer of various maladies—physical, psychological, spiritual—apart from the literal existence of demons.[4]

Perhaps the most awkward interaction between Mary and Raj is found in "The Luminous Fish Effect." As Mary cooks the gang dinner, she approaches Raj and says, "I made chicken, I hope that isn't one of the animals that you people think is magic?" Mary probably intends to be considerate of Hinduism's traditional beliefs in karma and reincarnation, but her question drips with condescension. Mary may contend that Hindu belief and practice contain elements of "magic," but it is incredibly unlikely that Hindus see it that way. In fact, a devout Hindu might instead see the biblical Jesus as something of a magician.

Because religious belief and practice seem central to the human experience, the issue of religious diversity is of paramount importance. The haughty derision associated with dubbing the beliefs of others "magical" seems inappropriate. Tolerance and dialogue seem the better course.[5] After all, if Mary had been raised in India, it is very likely that she would practice some form of Hinduism. Perhaps this means that all religious beliefs are in some sense true or equally valid. The problem with this approach is that different religions believe contradictory things. They can't all be right. Christians believe that the One God is personal, but Hindus deny this. Christians believe Jesus is divine, but Jews deny it. So, how can we tell which beliefs are true? Is anyone in a justified position to claim that another's religious beliefs are simply false? Furthermore, if not all religious beliefs can be true, how should adherents of one religion conceptualize the beliefs of other religious adherents?

Anyone serious about his or her religion ought to take these questions seriously. Philosophers tend to conceptualize religious diversity into three competing camps: exclusivism, inclusivism, and pluralism. The exclusivist says that not all religious beliefs are true and that religious adherents professing false doctrines cannot achieve salvation or enlightenment. The inclusivist, similar to the exclusivist, believes that not all religious beliefs are true; however, she also believes that there are multiple paths to salvation or enlightenment. The pluralist believes that all religious beliefs, in some sense, are true or equally valid (at least, among the major religious traditions), and that there are multiple paths to salvation or enlightenment.[6]

## Scientist Sons Scolded

Mary is not above being stern or practicing tough love. In "The Luminous Fish Effect," growing weary of waiting for Sheldon to come to his senses, she strides to his bedroom closet, retrieves a pair of pants, and declares, "Put those on." A pajama-clad Sheldon asks, "What for?" Mary replies, "Because you're going to go down to your office, you're going to apologize to your boss, and get your job back." As Sheldon is about to start a fit, Mary rhetorically asks, "I'm sorry, did I start that sentence with the words 'if it pleases your highness'?"

Yet five minutes before she tells her son to "get cracking" so they can "shove off" to Dr. Gablehauser's office, Mary spies Sheldon by the edge of his bed, working on something "that looks awful fancy." We can only wonder how many times she has started conversations in this way. Nevertheless, Sheldon informs his mother that it's his "idea of what DNA would look like in a silicon-based life form." Mary's demeanor immediately changes. He has ceased being her little "snicker-doodle" and has (again?) assumed the role of scientist in need of reminder: "But intelligently designed by a creator, right?" It's far from clear that, at least in her mind, there is any question here. She is blunt: DNA of any kind can result only from intelligent design (and not even her genius son is intelligent enough to be the designer she has in mind).

Mary's rhetorical question reminds us of the tumultuous relationship between science and religion in the United States. The conflict was recently revived, in part, by biochemist Michael Behe with his idea of "irreducible complexity." In his words: "By irreducibly complex I mean a single system composed of several well-matched, interacting parts that contribute to the basic function, wherein the removal of any one of the parts causes the system to effectively cease functioning."[7]

Although Behe prefers the molecular machine examples of cilium or blood clotting, the eye is a classic example of a system that seems irreducibly complex. An eye missing half of its parts doesn't see half as well; it doesn't see at all. According to Behe, this is supposed to be evidence that some systems cannot form gradually, piece by piece, via Darwinian processes. The problem is that given Darwinian theory, functions can be selected for only if they provide some evolutionary advantage. Nonfunctional systems ("half-eyes") cannot be advantageous; thus, some biological systems—those that require all of their parts to have a beneficial function—must have been created all at once by some intelligent designer.

This may be a case where Mary could benefit by further discussion with her son and his scientist colleagues. (Does anyone have Professor Crawley's new phone number?) Darwin himself anticipated this sort of criticism. Rather than envisioning half an eye, he had us consider an organism that possesses light-sensitive cells of some sort. This would pose an evolutionary advantage over animals that lacked them. Thus, this trait would be selected for and, presumably, would be refined and made more complex over time.[8]

Contemporary microbiologists apply Darwin's basic insight to Behe's position on molecular machines—including the bacterial flagellum, his favorite example of an irreducibly complex system. The flagellum works like an outboard motor. Its rotation makes the bacterium's filament tail whip around in a corkscrew fashion. This motion works like a propeller, allowing the bacterium to "swim." The motor is a complex structure of forty proteins. Take any one away, and the motor doesn't work, which is why Behe believes that it is irreducibly complex. Recent studies, however, have found a structure very similar to the flagellum that performs a different task. Bubonic plague–carrying bacteria use the filament as if it were a syringe. The "plunger" contains a subset of the proteins that compose the flagellum "motor." It doesn't spin, but it transports the poison through the "syringe" and into another cell. This apparatus doesn't help the bacterium swim, but it functions perfectly for transmitting disease. Therefore, there is a sense in which natural selection could favor structures similar to those Behe deems irreducibly complex, which leads microbiologist Kenneth Miller to conclude, "That's why the irreducible complexity argument falls apart."[9]

The deeper philosophical worry here is that people such as Mary Cooper must be wary of a "god-of-the-gaps" approach to their religious beliefs. This approach is sometimes invoked when scientists have difficulty, under the current paradigm, immediately explaining some newly found natural phenomenon. Some believers are quick to conclude that "it must be the product of design," only to have scientists later offer a plausible naturalistic explanation. This process, if repeated a sufficient number of times, has an erosive and corrosive effect on religious belief.

The context of Darwinian evolution reminds us of Mary chastising her son for his (short-lived) professional goal of teaching in Texas. Recall in "The Electric Can Opener Fluctuation" that Sheldon initially refuses to travel back to California with Leonard, Raj, and Howard, announcing, "No, this is my home now. Thanks to you [motioning to the guilty trio], my career is over and I will spend the rest of my life here in Texas trying to teach evolution to creationists." Mary will have none of this talk: "You watch your mouth, Shelly. Everyone's entitled to their opinion." Sheldon retorts, "Evolution isn't an opinion, it's fact." Mary quickly adds, "And that is your opinion." Sheldon, looking toward his friends again, states, "I forgive you. Let's go home."

Mary's point about everyone being entitled to their opinion is true, but probably not in the way she intends. Yes, everyone should have the right to speak on a topic; it would be dismissively rude to silence anyone simply because you don't wish to hear what he or she has to say. Yet it doesn't follow from this that everyone's opinion is equally weighty or plausible. Sheldon and Howard are both entitled to their opinion about whether "Toby" is a snowy field cricket, but Professor Crawley's opinion rules the day because he is the resident expert on insects. Sometimes an opinion is more trustworthy exactly because the person offering it is an expert in the field. A scientist, for example, would be in a better position than a nonscientist to gauge the legitimacy of Darwinian evolution.

There is a great deal more that needs to be explored. It is commonplace to distinguish between microevolution and macroevolution. The former deals with small changes in biological systems that result from various environmental pressures. The latter deals with larger changes that are more difficult to observe. It's quite plausible for Leonard's dog Mitzie to have given birth to an albino puppy—well, before she died—but it is implausible for her to have given birth to a rabbit. Some scientists counter that, ideally, given enough small "micro" changes and enough time, you might observe "macro" changes. Still, some wonder, even assuming the Earth is very old, whether enough time has elapsed to account for the great diversity we observe in the animal kingdom. What of the fossil record? Does it contain unexpected gaps or not? For that matter, we must get clearer about what a "scientific fact" is, when a theory is "true," and what role observation plays in scientific research.

With all of this work still to do, perhaps Mary is better advised to first make friends with Bernadette, rather than being so quick to scold Sheldon. This harkens back to English philosopher John Locke's (1632–1704) sage advice: "He that believes without having any reason for believing may be in love with his own fancies, but neither seeks truth as he ought nor pays the obedience due his maker, who would have him use those discerning faculties he has given him, to keep him out of mistake and error."[10] If educated opinions are weightier than noneducated, even believers seem well-advised to explore science.

## Monumental Math Mysteries

In "The Luminous Fish Effect," Mary provides some context for Sheldon's egg-scrambling, fish-glowing, poncho-weaving meltdown: "He gets his temper from his daddy. . . . He's got my eyes. . . . All that science stuff, that comes from Jesus." It's not uncommon for parents to describe their children in this way. Furthermore, given Mary's religious moorings, it's not surprising that she believes Sheldon's most spectacular gift— his keen mind—comes from God. In fact, there might be more than meets the eye in her contention that "all that science stuff comes from Jesus."

The first issue implicit in Mary's claim is whether we would expect the existence of theoretical physicists simply given Darwinian processes. Contemporary philosopher Alvin Plantinga argues that we would not expect this if naturalism were true.[11] In fact, he contends that the probability of unaided Darwinian processes resulting in the existence of a Sheldon Cooper is extremely low (to say nothing of Albert Einstein or Stephen Hawking). Moreover, he says that the probability of our cognitive faculties effectively tracking truth at all is very slight in a thoroughgoing Darwinian approach. In a strict Darwinian approach, the advanced human brain guarantees propagating the species, not truth. Beyond that, Plantinga states that if thoroughgoing Darwinians accept his contentions about cognitive reliability, this actually serves to undercut their approach. If Darwinians are correct that the probability of human cognitive reliability is low, then they have no reason to believe their theory is true! Thus, the fact that Sheldon exists is reason for Mary to believe that he ultimately has supernatural origins.

The second issue implicit in Mary's claim is the fact that Sheldon—and the rest of us, of course—is alive in the first place. Plantinga's complex argument aside, it's well-known that Darwinian processes only explain how biological systems behave. Darwinian theory doesn't explain the existence of biological systems. What are the odds that life would develop on Earth from "primordial soup" all by itself? Scholar Stuart Pullen uses recent laboratory attempts to show that the odds of just one protein molecule emerging unaided from prebiotic materials are incredibly small, specifically, "1 time is $2^{350}$ tries or 1 time in $2.2 \times 10^{105}$ tries."[12] Such numbers are difficult to fully comprehend, but that's the whole point. The odds of life emerging from nonlife are so astronomically remote that its happening is a virtual impossibility.

Some scholars apply this kind of reasoning to make cosmological conclusions. What are the odds that the universe would possess conditions suitable for life in the first place? Given what is currently known about the laws of physics and corresponding mathematical constants, that the "big bang" would produce a universe such as ours seems incredibly unlikely. According to theoretical physicist Paul Davies, if the initial explosion of the big bang had differed in strength by as little as one part in $10^{60}$, the universe would have either quickly collapsed back on itself or expanded too rapidly for stars to form. In either case, life would be impossible. Philosopher

John Jefferson Davis likens the accuracy of one part in $10^{60}$ to firing a bullet at a one-inch target on the other side of the observable universe, twenty billion light-years away, and hitting the target.[13] These sorts of considerations lead various scholars to conclude that between the hypotheses that we are here by blind chance or we are here as the result of intelligent design, it must be the latter because the odds of the former are so astronomically remote.

Of course, we haven't yet tackled the issues of why we have the fundamental laws of physics we do or the corresponding mathematical constants we do, when others seem logically possible. Why only these laws? Why only these constants? Furthermore, we haven't explained why the big bang happened in the first place. At best, thoroughgoing naturalists must take these facts as brute, with no further explanation possible, but is this conclusion intellectually satisfying? Might there be some sort of ultimate explanation? If so, it will certainly take us beyond the realm of physics. No wonder Sheldon once claimed that his work delving into theoretical physics will help him "tear the mask off nature and stare at the face of God."[14]

Math is hard. Even fictional physicists such as Sheldon know this. Recall his quip to Penny in "The Luminous Fish Effect." She stops by to ask whether he needs anything from the market; he smirks, "Oh, well, this would be one of those circumstances that people unfamiliar with the law of large numbers would call a coincidence." Can the same be said about finding apparent evidence of design in the cosmos? It's difficult to say, but perhaps we should follow Beverly and Sheldon. In "The Maternal Capacitance," when they acknowledge that they feel very comfortable around each other, Sheldon remarks, "It's surprising because I generally don't feel comfortable around—well, anyone." Beverly concurs, "Nor I." Intrigued, Sheldon asks, "What are the odds that two unique individuals as unique as ourselves would be connected by someone as comparatively workaday as your son?" More intrigued, Beverly inquires, "Is that a rhetorical point, or would you like to do the math?" Sheldon: "I'd like to do the math." Thus, whether the intuitions of those who see design in the universe hold up depends on our doing the math (or at least on someone ensuring the math is done correctly).

Sheldon and scientists such as him (Leonard, Bernadette) are uniquely suited to determine whether the statistical improbabilities of getting life from nonlife or cosmological fine-tuning hold up. As philosopher Philip Kitcher points out, the kind of probability-based arguments often employed by proponents of design depend on background knowledge. Whether something is statistically unlikely depends on many related factors. The more we know about these factors, the more likely our probability judgments are to be trustworthy. Yet do we know enough about the primordial soup or the initial conditions of the big bang to justify probability statements about them? Kitcher wrote,

> The origin of life is a very hard problem precisely because we have so little idea about the constraints on a solution. . . . The challenge is to go further, to specify how it might have been done. To respond to that challenge, you have to guess, to make assumptions about the initial conditions—and some inspired guess-work, followed by ingenious experimental research, has revealed that some aspects of original life can be simulated. What the decades of research also reveal is that our ignorance of those initial conditions is so extensive, and the range of possible assumptions so vast, that probability estimates are likely to be deceptive.[15]

Increasing scientific knowledge can and will help us make more informed judgments about some of the most important questions there are. By being careful about the science, Sheldon is more assured about the math. In being more confident of his math, he will (perhaps) be in a better position to conclude that it's God's face he's staring at when he makes his Nobel Prize–winning breakthrough.

## Lifelong Lessons

Clearly, Mary can learn quite a bit from her son. Given his vast knowledge of physics, she could better grasp van Inwagen's point about why the author(s) of Genesis might not convey literal scientific truths about creation. Becoming more familiar with his colleagues, she may develop a deeper appreciation for other faiths or at least the fact of religious diversity. Sheldon could explain to her all of the paradigm-shifting advancements, making a god-of-the-gaps approach to religious belief tenuous, yet with his continued advancements into theoretical physics, he might actually bolster her belief that all of this "science stuff comes from Jesus." (Of course, he thought that teaching *Penny* "a little physics" was difficult—what must it be like to have one's mother as a student?)

Sheldon could benefit from his mother's religious inclinations, especially as they pertain to his research. His religious leanings are clouded anyway. In "The Zarnecki Incursion," he exclaims, "Why hast thou forsaken me, O deity whose existence I doubt," but in "The Panty Piñata Polarization" he admits, "No, I don't know what Jesus thinks about." Most scientists do perfectly well with their pragmatic assumption of not including God in their research, yet by reminding Sheldon of the possibility of more ultimate explanations for what he discovers, Mary may inch him toward more intellectually satisfying conclusions.

Of course, Sheldon and Mary Cooper are very different people with vastly different perspectives. The one thing they have in common is their stubbornness. If they could only communicate, they might find that Sheldon can help broaden Mary's perspectives and Mary can, in a way, deepen Sheldon's perspectives. These effects certainly seem beneficial, and if the

*Coopers* can benefit by communicating with one another, what does that say about us and our family relationships?

## NOTES

1. See, for example, Mark 5:6–14 and 7:24–30. It's interesting that not all instances of Jesus laying hands on his followers involved casting out a demon. At 7:32–37, Jesus cures a deaf and mute man by putting his fingers in the man's ears and by touching the man's tongue.

2. Mark 16:17–18. Yet the vast majority of biblical scholars hold that verses 9–20 of chapter 16 are not original to Mark. See, for example, Bart D. Ehrman, *Misquoting Jesus* (San Francisco: HarperCollins, 2005), 65–68.

3. Peter van Inwagen, "Genesis and Evolution," in David Shatz, ed., *Philosophy and Faith* (New York: McGraw-Hill, 2002), 365.

4. Fundamentalist biblical Christians are surprisingly diverse. Some believe the Earth is quite young, others hold that it is quite old. This diversity also leads to different interpretations of specific biblical passages. Professor Barkman reminds us that some biblical Christians uphold the literal existence of demons, and doing so leads to intriguing philosophical implications for the problem of evil. See, for example, Alvin Plantinga, *God, Freedom, and Evil* (Grand Rapids, MI: Eerdman's, 1977).

5. Sheldon arguably overcompensates for his mother's apparent unfamiliarity with Hinduism. In "The Pirate Solution," he is quick to qualify Raj's claim that in Hinduism, "cows are gods." Because it is conceivable that a religion "from the inside" may appear differently from more "outside" academic perspectives, perhaps Sheldon's blunt critique is a bit harsh. Dialogue and friendly inquiry seem preferable to Sheldon simply telling Raj what Hindus actually believe. (Yet then again, we are talking about Sheldon here.)

6. For a notable exclusivist voice, see Alvin Plantinga, "Pluralism: A Defense of Religious Exclusivism," in Thomas Senor, ed., *The Rationality of Belief and the Plurality of Faith* (Ithaca: Cornell University Press, 1995), 191–215. For an influential inclusivist voice, see Karl Rahner, "Religious Inclusivism," reprinted in Michael Peterson, ed., *Philosophy of Religion: Selected Readings* (New York: Oxford University Press, 1996), 502–513. The leading advocate for religious pluralism is John Hick. See his *An Interpretation of Religion* (New Haven, CT: Yale University Press, 1989).

7. Michael Behe, *Darwin's Black Box* (New York: Simon & Schuster, 1996), 39.

8. Charles Darwin, *The Origin of Species* (New York: New York University Press, 1998), 187.

9. The discussion of the bacterium flagellum is indebted to NOVA's *Judgment Day: Intelligent Design on Trial* (Boston: WGBH Educational Foundation, 2007), scene 7. Miller's quote is also taken from this source. For additional examples of Darwinian processes selecting for novel functions from systems that perform other functions, see Kenneth R. Miller, *Finding Darwin's God* (New York: Harper Perennial, 2007), 140–161. To be fair, Behe, in his latest book, has offered responses to the sorts of concerns Miller raises; see Michael Behe, *The Edge of Evolution* (New York: Simon & Schuster, 2008).

10. John Locke, *Essay Concerning Human Understanding* (1690), IV.xvii. 24.

11. Alvin Plantinga, *Science and Religion: Are They Compatible?* (Oxford: Oxford University Press, 2011), 17. For a sort of precursor to Plantinga's argument, see Locke, *Essay Concerning Human Understanding*, IV.x.10.

12. Stuart Pullen, *Intelligent Design or Evolution?: Why the Origin of Life and the Evolution of Molecular Knowledge Imply Design* (Raleigh, NC: Intelligent Design Books, 2005), 102.

13. The claims by Davies and Davis are quoted in Robin Collins, "A Scientific Argument for the Existence of God," in Michael Murray, ed., *Reason for the Hope Within* (Grand Rapids, MI: Eerdmans, 1999), 49.

14. For an accessible and highly influential attempt to rationally justify God's existence via similar considerations, see Richard Swinburne, *Is There a God?* (New York: Oxford University Press, 1996).

15. Philip Kitcher, *Living with Darwin* (New York: Oxford University Press, 2007), 98–99. Elliot Sober is another philosopher who doubts that we have a sufficient grasp of background assumptions to determine whether the universe is the product of design. See his "The Design Argument," in William E. Mann, ed., *The Blackwell Guide to the Philosophy of Religion* (Malden, MA: Blackwell, 2005), 117–147.

# PART FOUR

# "I NEED YOUR OPINION ON A MATTER OF SEMIOTICS": LANGUAGE AND MEANING

# WITTGENSTEIN AND LANGUAGE GAMES IN *THE BIG BANG THEORY*

*Janelle Pötzsch*

Leonard: I am just saying, you can catch more flies with honey than with vinegar.

Sheldon: You catch even more flies with manure, what's your point? ["The Gothowitz Deviation"]

It's a bit surprising that Sheldon Cooper, with his 187 IQ, struggles so mightily with irony, sarcasm, and figures of speech. We can understand poor Sheldon a bit better, though, if we see him through the lens of the Austrian philosopher Ludwig Wittgenstein (1889–1951), who ultimately characterized language use as a kind of game. Language users need to master not only proper grammar and vocabulary, but also the implicit rules of language, including how words function in context. As we shall see, Sheldon's constant bewilderment highlights the "conventional" roots of everyday language, giving us a glimpse of how Wittgenstein came to his view of language in *Philosophical Investigations* (*PI*).

## "The Philosophy Is Theoretical, but the Fun Is Real"

Wittgenstein came to prominence in 1918 with his *Tractatus Logico-Philosophicus* (*TLP*), in which he tried to formulate an ideal, unambiguous language based purely on logic.[1] In the *TLP*, he claimed that a sentence is a logical picture of a fact and that every sentence has only one precise meaning, corresponding to the fact it represents. This view implies that sentences are logically independent of one another. Yet sadly, for overly analytical people such as Sheldon Cooper, who prefer to deal with literal meanings, this project turned into a dead end. Wittgenstein gradually realized that language and the use of it require more than logic. No sentence can be understood in complete isolation; instead, sentences are dependent on one another. Therefore, one cannot assign meaning without getting entangled with ambiguities or contradictions because a word's meaning depends on its context and not (merely) on the thing it might represent. Wittgenstein would muse later, "The question 'What is a word really?' is analogous to 'What is a piece in chess?' "[2] To understand what the chess piece represents requires understanding the rules of chess. To understand what a word represents requires understanding the rules of language.

Consequently, to employ and understand language adequately, one has to consider the social context in which it is used. Because social features cannot be conveyed in logical terms or characters, Wittgenstein realized that his so-called picture theory of language, according to which language represents or even copies our world and its logical structure, was mistaken. Therefore, he gradually developed a "use-theory of meaning," implying that the actual use of language is decisive for the constitution of meaning.

Because Wittgenstein's books are considered to represent two distinct theories in the philosophy of language, scholars usually distinguish between the early Wittgenstein of the *TLP* and the later Wittgenstein of the *PI*. Sheldon remains invariably trapped in his logic-centered worldview when it comes to dealing with language. In this way, Sheldon often resembles the early Wittgenstein of the *TLP*, still trying to find a purely logical structure in language. Yet Sheldon (alias early Wittgenstein) encounters a world in which language is employed as described in the *PI* of the later Wittgenstein, who realized that we have to focus on the way language is actually used in order to make sense of it. This is sometimes called the philosophy of ordinary language. One cannot *assign* meaning, one has to *learn* it because "the meaning of a word is its use in the language."[3]

Consequently, application is crucial for both correct use and understanding of language. Due to his narrow, logic-centred understanding of language, however, Sheldon misses what people actually are expressing. Sometimes Sheldon's cluelessness is so obvious, it seems that Sheldon is speaking a different language, albeit with familiar words. Recall from "The Spaghetti Catalyst":

> Penny: So, how've you been?
> Sheldon: Well, my existence is a continuum, so I've been what I am at each point in the implied time period.

Instead of taking Penny's question as a common way to inquire about one's recent physical and mental health, or whether he or she has any interesting news to share, Sheldon interprets the verb "to be" in its abstract sense of "existence." He simply ignores the common usage of a language pattern and applies his own logic instead. The logic, in some sense, is correct, but it is inappropriately applied, given the context.

We encounter a similar case in "The Jiminy Conjecture." As Sheldon slowly makes his way down the elevator shaft in search of "Toby," Wolowitz advises, "Be careful!" Sheldon curtly responds, "If I weren't careful, your telling me to be careful would not make me careful." Sheldon does not interpret Howard's exclamation as a way to express concern for another person's well-being but takes it as an ascription of characteristics. Again, he fails to recognize the context of Howard's admonition. And in "The Gothowitz Deviation," an exasperated Penny exclaims to Leonard, "You know what, I give up. He's impossible." Sheldon quizzically responds, "I can't be impossible, I exist. I believe what you meant is 'I give up. He's improbable.'" Again, Sheldon misses the point of Penny's message. Obviously, he still has to learn that this is not how language works.

## "So, What Does That Mean?"

The later Wittgenstein aimed at analyzing how the meaning of language is actually constituted. In the very first paragraph of the *PI*, he quoted from the *Confessions* of Augustine, in which the latter recounts how he was (allegedly) taught his language as a child:

> When they (my elders) named some object, and accordingly moved towards something, I saw this and I grasped that the thing was called by the sound they uttered when they meant to point it out. . . . Thus, as I heard words repeatedly used in their proper places in various sentences, I gradually learnt to understand what objects they signified.[4]

Wittgenstein objected that this exemplifies only one particular "picture of the essence of human language" because Augustine did not mention any "difference between kinds of word" but merely depicted "a system of communication."[5]

This, however, is a very limited view because we do much more than exchange information when we talk to people.

Sheldon often assumes this sort of limited view of language, which causes him to overlook the social, as well as informative, functions of language. Consider again "The Jiminy Conjecture":

> Penny: If it makes you feel any better, I am not feeling so hot either.
> Sheldon: Why would that make me feel better?
> Penny: I don't know, empathy?

Here Sheldon infers a causal connection between sharing one's sorrows and a lifting of one's spirits. He misses that such a connection does not exist on a logical level but on an emotional one. A person can feel better precisely because she had the ability to share her thoughts or anxieties with a sympathetic friend.

This social function of language is much more fundamental than the exchange of information it makes possible. A traveler in a foreign country may well be able to learn the meaning of words by pointing and explanations of the natives, but this works only because this traveler already *knows* a language. Wittgenstein remarked, "And now, I think, we can say: Augustine describes the learning of human language as if the child came into a strange country and did not understand the language of the country; that is, as if it already had a language, only not this one."[6] Imagine that you are trying to explain to someone who does not speak your language the meaning of the word "table" by pointing at one and saying the term "table." Why should this person assume you are referring to the *construct* of the table as such and not to its material or color? As Wittgenstein noted, "Only someone who already knows how to do something with it can significantly ask a name."[7] The very fact that a person asks for an explanation of something implies that she already possesses some knowledge of the subject matter. For example, recall the following exchange from "The Desperation Emanation":

> Sheldon: Amy has asked me to meet her mother.
> Leonard: Yeah. So?
> Sheldon: What does that mean?
> Leonard: Well, you know how you're always saying that Amy is a girl who's your friend, and not your girlfriend?
> Sheldon: Sure.
> Leonard: You can't say that anymore.

If Sheldon didn't attach any importance to Amy's request, he wouldn't have consulted Leonard.

There are some episodes in which Sheldon exhibits at least some awareness of social context. Again, in "The Jiminy Conjecture," Leonard admits that his first sexual encounter with Penny was not as he had imagined. Later the guys mock Leonard in front of Penny. Penny asks what's going on. As a result of Sheldon's very clear and forthright explanation, Penny becomes uncomfortable and abruptly leaves. Leonard follows her out, hoping to explain (or otherwise defuse) the situation. Sheldon consequently remarks, "I sense I may have crossed some line here." Before Raj can explain it to him, Howard interjects, "Don't tell. Let's see if he can figure it out." It takes Sheldon an embarrassingly long time before the answer dawns on him, but he does eventually get it—sort of.

That Sheldon must learn social appropriateness, and sometimes painfully so, makes him appear childlike. This occasions many laughs, but it also serves as a vivid example of Wittgenstein's objection to Augustine's view of language acquisition. It seems children cannot acquire an understanding of their mother tongue the way Augustine claims, because the mind of a child is a *tabula rasa*, a blank slate.[8] This slate will be written on by the experiences a person has during her lifetime. We can also say that Sheldon's mind is a tabula rasa when it comes to grasping social cues. It was much more blank before he met Leonard and was introduced to Raj, Howard, and eventually Penny. The early Wittgenstein wrote, "The limits of my language are the limits of my world."[9] This aptly describes Sheldon. Due to his sole focus on logic, he has developed too narrow a view of language and the world.

## "Be Serious, We're Playing a Game Here"

The later Wittgenstein called any way of employing language a *game*. Such games can be "Giving orders, and obeying them—Describing the appearance of an object. Reporting an event. . . . Making up a story; and reading it—Play-acting. . . . Asking, thanking, cursing, greeting, praying."[10] Yet the term *game* is not meant to imply that language use is unimportant or comical. Rather, it serves to illustrate the multiple aspects of language. One cannot say precisely what games such as *Mystical Warlords of Ka'a*, *Halo 3*, *Dungeons and Dragons*, or *Jenga* have in common. Nevertheless, they are all grouped into the same category of "game" because they intuitively share at least some characteristics. In Wittgenstein's own words: "I can think of no better expression to characterize these similarities than 'family resemblances'; for the various resemblances between members of a family: build, features, . . . temperament etc. etc. overlap and criss-cross in the same way. And I shall say: 'games' form a family."[11]

Even though such distinctions may seem blurry, Wittgenstein considered them to be sufficient: "Is an indistinct photograph a picture of a person at all? Is it even always an advantage to replace an indistinct picture by a sharp one? Isn't the indistinct one often exactly what we need?"[12] This analogy might not be that convincing when it comes to pictures, but as for language, keeping its meanings unfixed implies keeping language alive and diverse and thus also multifunctional. Trying to be too precise can cause more harm than good, making you miss the essential point, which happens often to

Sheldon. Recall the following exchange from "The Luminous Fish Effect":

> Penny: You know, I always say "when one door closes, another one opens."
> Sheldon: No, it doesn't. Not unless the two doors are connected by relays or there are motion sensors involved. Or if the first door closing creates a change of air pressure that acts upon the second door.

Sheldon tries to establish a causal connection between opening doors, interpreting ordinary language by the same standards he applies to his theoretical work. Thus, he completely misses the fact that Penny's saying is offered in empathy.

To help remedy Sheldon's wooden approach to language, Wittgenstein suggested that we imagine language as an old, winding city where one has to find one's way in "a maze of little streets and squares, of old and new houses, and of houses with additions from various periods."[13] Notice how Sheldon tries to navigate through different situations and their respective social protocols, which he sometimes meets with suspicion, as if he were still finding his way. Recall from "The Dead Hooker Juxtaposition":

> Sheldon: Hold on. You honestly expect me to believe that social protocol dictates we break our backs helping Wolowitz move, and then he only need buy us a pizza?
> Leonard: I'm sorry, that really is how it works.
> Sheldon: You're tricking me. You tell me the truth, what do we get?

Interestingly, Wittgenstein also claimed that lying is a language game to be learned and properly navigated. Dogs and babies are unable to lie because they cannot participate in the game.[14] Sheldon participates in this game but not very well. His navigational skills with respect to lying are poor because it does not fit into his science-centric worldview.[15] Again, he seems to share the view of the early Wittgenstein that language can be logically mapped onto reality. A lie is a distortion of reality because its speaker claims something that does not exist. How eager Sheldon is in his pursuit of mapping language onto reality becomes apparent when he tries to lie. In such situations, he becomes obsessed with details to make things seem as real as possible. For instance, in "The Loobenfeld Decay," he creates a Facebook page and a blog to make Penny believe his story of a drug-addicted cousin due to whose drug-intervention he and Leonard cannot make it to her gig. And in "The Irish Pub Formulation," he steals hair from an orangutan to "prove" that Leonard spent the night with a red-haired bartender and not with Raj's sister.

## "Figured Out the Magic Trick Yet?"

Another characteristic well illustrated by the term *game* is the importance of the *context* of an utterance: every game contains more or less specific rules regulating its practice that should be known by anyone who wants to participate in it. The same goes for language, because the full meaning of an utterance becomes clear only in its social context. It is helpful to consider the social framework in which a remark takes place to ensure that one interprets it adequately. Think, for example, of the language of advertising, as illustrated in "The Robotic Manipulation." When Penny suggests that Sheldon meet Amy in person in the hopes of knowing her better, Sheldon responds, "And you don't think I can achieve the required intimacy via text messaging?" To Penny's response that this is unlikely, Sheldon adds, "Hmm. It appears that the phone companies have been lying to me." Clearly, reaching out and touching someone via the phone is a poor substitute for getting to truly know a girl-who-is-a-friend.

This example again highlights Sheldon's childlike language qualities. Like many children, Sheldon is unfamiliar with the language game of advertising, whose sole aim consists of enticing people to buy the advertised objects. Children (and Sheldon) tend to take things at face value and are not yet able to distinguish between reliable and unreliable information. This, again, harkens back to Wittgenstein's different "kinds" of words.

The tendency to take persons at their word and thus interpret their sayings literally is indeed very typical of Sheldon. In "The Gorilla Experiment," Leonard playfully asserts, "The more the merrier." Sheldon, not amused, replies, "No, that's a false equivalency, more does not equal merry. If there were two thousand people in this apartment right now, would we be celebrating? No, we'd be suffocating." Another telling example of this occurs in the episode "The Big Bran Hypothesis." In this season 1 episode, Sheldon sneaks into Penny's apartment during the night to clean it up. An infuriated Penny asks him in the morning, "What kind of doctor removes shoes from asses?" An ordinary person might take this as a thinly veiled threat of bodily harm (as is Penny's intention). Given the context, Penny is clearly expressing anger and disappointment; she is not inquiring about a surgical procedure. Sheldon, however, replies, "Well, depending on the depth, either a proctologist or general surgeon." Sheldon gives no indication that he grasps Penny's intended meaning. In this way, his answer is embarrassingly childlike.

This season 1 episode—as opposed to the example in the season 4 episode, in which Sheldon asks Leonard about the meaning of asking to see another person's mother—illustrates very well Sheldon's lack of social skills. The prospect of meeting Amy's mother occurs at a time when he can begin to employ some previously acquired knowledge. Still, he has a great deal of time to ponder the situation. He is often at a loss when it comes to immediate social contact, where we sometimes have to rely on our intuition to deal with people because we don't have time to think things over again and again. Sheldon's outlandish reply to Penny's rhetorical question has its cause in his inability to set utterances and their context in a relation—in this situation, to consider a person's anger and the influence it might have on her remarks. Even if Sheldon is learning, he still has a long way to go.

He continues to display an inability to quickly take social circumstances and conventions into account in the later episodes. In "The Irish Pub Formulation," from season 4, Raj's sister Priya comments, "Oh, Sheldon. You haven't changed a bit, have you?" He quizzically answers, "Why would I change?" Leonard's retort, "The hope has been that you'd eventually bend to public opinion," suggests that Sheldon is perhaps unwilling to take conventions into account, even if he could. He is convinced that his approach to the world is correct—so why bend to the public opinion of ordinary folk? This attitude seems to be another major obstacle for his language acquisition. As Wittgenstein remarked, "[A] philosophical problem has the form: 'I don't know my way about.'"[16] The first step to handle problems is to acknowledge them. We know especially from "The Pirate Solution" that Sheldon is quite unwilling to do that:

Sheldon: I looked over the board and it turns out you were right.
Raj: So you were wrong?
Sheldon: I didn't say that.

## "It's a Nonoptional Social Convention," Stupid!

To employ a language game correctly requires awareness of both language patterns *and* corresponding activities. Which action is considered appropriate for which language game is laid down by social convention. Consequently, the meaning of a language is based on an agreement among members of a language community. This community shares not only a language but also specific behavioral manners, which manifest themselves in its language games. Therefore, children are taught more than their mother tongue; they are taught the corresponding lifestyle of their community as well. In Wittgenstein's words, "Hence the term 'language-*game*' is meant to bring into prominence the fact that the *speaking* of language is part of an activity, or of a form of life."[17]

Our view of the world is influenced by our language. Such a reciprocal dependence of language and forms of life can harbor negative consequences because our view of the world can be limited by our language. Recall, for example, the following dialogue from "The Maternal Congruence":

> Sheldon: I've made tea.
> Leonard: I don't want tea.
> Sheldon: I didn't make tea for you. [beat] This is my tea.
> Leonard: Then why are you telling me?
> Sheldon: It's a conversation starter.
> Leonard: It's a lousy conversation starter.
> Sheldon: Oh, is it? We're conversing, check-mate.

This exchange exemplifies the connection between Wittgenstein's language games and Sheldon. Wittgenstein stressed the high conventionalism of ordinary language, which implies that many of our remarks have a fixed meaning. Usually, if a person mentions she has made tea, it is taken as an invitation to share a cup, just as Leonard assumes. The humor of Sheldon's reply derives from its clash with this convention. Yet if you give it a second thought, Sheldon's response is far from out of place. Rather, it exposes the logical flaw in Leonard's assumption that the tea mentioned was for him. As Wittgenstein might say, Leonard is a victim of the confining aspect of language. We become so dependent on it that it eventually influences our way of thinking: "A *picture* held us captive. And we could not get outside it, for it lay in our language and language seemed to repeat it to us inexorably."[18] Sheldon is never held captive in this particular way because he relies not on conventions but on logic when dealing with language.

With his slowly emerging knowledge of "social conventions," and his occasionally correct application of them, Sheldon begins to fulfill Wittgenstein's demand "don't think, but look!"[19] His successes are inconsistent, but he is getting better. We thus get the somewhat paradoxical picture of Sheldon as representing either a child still lacking "conventional wisdom" when it comes to language use, or, which fits well with his status as a scientist and his know-it-all character, an admittedly unwitting Wittgensteinian philosopher who encounters logical flaws and questionable implications in our language. Arguably, Sheldon's social naiveté mirrors Wittgenstein's youthful bravado in proffering a purely logical account of language. Just as Wittgenstein eventually came to a more mature understanding of language, so will Sheldon (perhaps).

## "Believe in Magic, You Muggle!"

The view of language that Sheldon Cooper represents is at best naïve and at worst unfounded and inapplicable. Similar to the early Wittgenstein, Sheldon adheres to a theory of language according to which language represents or even copies our world such that both share a logical structure. This is the so-called picture theory of language. The later Wittgenstein moved to a theory in which the actual use of language was decisive. This is the "use theory of meaning," an understanding of language that Sheldon Cooper is only beginning to grasp.

In the end, the social conventions governing our language are decisive in helping us navigate our world. It is precisely Sheldon's rejection of language conventions and his adherence to logic that cause him trouble when it comes to social interactions. Strangely enough, he knows of the importance of social conventions in general, which is why he succumbed to buying Leonard a birthday gift in "The Peanut Reaction." Yet unlike the later Wittgenstein, Sheldon does not (yet?) understand, at least fully, that conventions are equally important for language. Whether he will ever realize this is one of the mysteries to be solved by future episodes. Just as it took Wittgenstein some time to arrive at his more mature views, perhaps the same is true of Dr. Cooper who apparently has yet to find his "way out of the [logical] fly-bottle."[20]

## NOTES

1. Ludwig Wittgenstein, *Tractatus Logico-Philosophicus*, trans. D.F. Pears and B.F. McGuinness (London: Routledge, 1961).

2. Ludwig Wittgenstein, *Philosophical Investigations*, trans. G.E.M. Anscombe (Oxford: Blackwell, 1967), §108. Hereafter *PI*.

3. *PI*, §43.

4. Ibid., §1.

5. Ibid., §1 and §3.

6. Ibid., §32.

7. Ibid., §31.

8. The English philosopher John Locke (1632–1704) is typically associated with this term. See his *An Essay Concerning Human Understanding*. Oxford: Oxford University Press 2008.

9. *Tractatus Logico-Philosophicus*, sentence 5.6.

10. *PI*, §23.

11. Ibid., §67.

12. Ibid., §71.

13. Ibid., §18.

14. Ibid., §249, 250.

15. Compare this to Sheldon's most adored fictional character, Mr Spock from *Star Trek*, who stems from a whole society that has eschewed emotion for an existence dictated by logic. In this society, it is postulated that lying would neither be necessary nor desirable because it would be illogical. Besides, as Sheldon points out in "The Loobenfeld Decay," a "lack of physiological response while lying is characteristic of a violent sociopath"; he might be pondering not only the logical, but also the moral implications of lying. This again ties in with his evangelical upbringing (so much on the language-lifestyle-thing).

16. *PI*, §123.

17. Ibid., §23. Emphasis in the original.

18. Ibid., §115. Emphasis in the original.

19. Ibid., §66.

20. Ibid., §309.

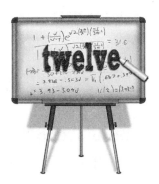

# "I'M AFRAID YOU COULDN'T BE MORE WRONG!": SHELDON AND BEING RIGHT ABOUT BEING WRONG

*Adolfas Mackonis*

Leonard, Sheldon, and Raj are brilliant physicists, and Howard ("*Mr.* Wolowitz") is a gifted engineer, but even the smartest guy, Sheldon Cooper, with his impressive list of degrees—B.S., M.S., M.A., Ph.D., Sc.D.—sometimes errs. For instance, he misidentifies "Toby" in "The Jiminy Conjecture" as a snowy field cricket. And in "The Bozeman Reaction," his belief that he would be safer living in Montana is almost immediately disconfirmed. Sheldon's errant beliefs are not simply about factual matters, though. Sometimes they're about concepts, including what it means to be wrong. In this chapter, we'll see how Sheldon is sometimes wrong about the nature of being wrong, and we'll highlight some philosophical issues associated with that interesting error, all in the hope of shedding some light on the character of Sheldon Cooper.

## "More Wrong?"

Recall this exchange from "The Hofstadter Isotope" between Sheldon and comic book store owner Stuart:

> Stuart: Ooh, Sheldon, I'm afraid you couldn't be more wrong.
> Sheldon: *More* wrong? Wrong is an absolute state and not subject to gradation.
> Stuart: Of course it is. It's a little wrong to say a tomato is a vegetable. It's very wrong to say it's a suspension bridge.

Here the debate is whether there are degrees of falsehood. Sheldon claims that there cannot be degrees of falsehood, but he does not give an argument in support of his claim. He does say that it is "an absolute state" but that merely rephrases his point without really supporting it. This is so typical of Sheldon. Recall in "The Cooper-Hofstadter Polarization," when a perturbed Leonard asks, "So the entire scientific community is supposed to just take your word?" Sheldon replies, "They're not supposed to, but they should." Stuart, on the other hand, holds that there are indeed degrees of falsehood and even gives a description of a situation that seems intuitively powerful enough to refute Sheldon's claim.

Stuart's view suggests an analogy with scientific exploration. It certainly seems that science gets closer and closer to the truth. In Ancient Greece, the philosophers Leucippus (5th century BCE) and Democritus (c. 460–370 BCE) claimed that all physical matter is composed of tiny indivisible particles called atoms. Around the year 1800, John Dalton proposed a modern atomic model based on experimentation. Later, scientists discovered various subatomic particles. Gradually, scientific knowledge became more and more detailed. Now scientists dispute whether loop quantum gravity or string theory best explains the physical world, occasioning the "conversation" between Leslie and Leonard in "The Codpiece Topology" about which should be taught to their imaginary future children. Just as science confirmed the views of Leucippus and Democritus, it is widely believed that it will also resolve the debate between loop quantum gravity and string theory. Once it does, we will be closer to understanding the truth about the universe. There are truths about the universe yet to be learned, but with each scientific discovery, we get closer and closer to the truth. So, the idea of "closeness to truth" seems intelligible.

## "In None of Them Am I Dancing"

Apart from the connection to scientific advancement, Stuart's implicit position seems intuitive on its own merits. There certainly seems to be such a thing as closeness to truth. People often say, "There is some truth in that," or, "That is fairly close to the truth." So, if truth comes in degrees, why can't falsity? After all, it would be absurd to claim that "A tomato is a suspension bridge" is no more wrong than to claim that "A tomato is a vegetable," even if both are false. The second seems closer to the truth. The trick is articulating how and why.

Some philosophers rely on "possible worlds" to specify closeness to the truth. A possible world is a complete description of how things could have been, even if things are not actually that way. For any statement or state of affairs, either it or its denial (but not both) is included in a possible world's description. For example, there are no possible worlds in which Sheldon both is and is not originally from Texas. In some possible worlds, though, Sheldon does not have a twin sister. A bit paradoxically, in some possible worlds, Sheldon Cooper *is* a physicist attempting to win a Nobel Prize, but in others—the actual world—he is a (fictional) television character played by Jim Parsons. In this way, the actual world—the real world—is one possible world among others, but it stands out exactly because it represents actuality and not fiction.

*The Big Bang Theory* conveys the idea of "possible worlds," at least as it is sometimes employed by theoretical physicists. In "The Gothowitz Deviation," Sheldon provides Penny, now Leonard's girlfriend, with a glimpse of his understanding of possible worlds:

> Penny: Morning, Sheldon. Come dance with me.
> Sheldon: No.
> Penny: Why not?
> Sheldon: Penny, while I subscribe to the many worlds theory, which posits the existence of an infinite number of Sheldons in an infinite number of universes, I assure you that in none of them am I dancing.
> Penny: Are you fun in any of them?
> Sheldon: The math would suggest that in a few I'm a clown made of candy. But I don't dance.

It's unclear from this exchange, though, whether Sheldon subscribes to the actual existence of these possible worlds, existing in various parallel dimensions or some such. (Imagine an infinite number of actual Sheldons—oy vey.) The vast majority of philosophers subscribe to a weaker notion of possible worlds by focusing on merely logically possible descriptions or, simply, the ability to consistently imagine the state of affairs in question. This interpretation of "possible worlds" is sufficient for our purposes of exploring the debate between Sheldon and Stuart.

Conveniently enough, Sheldon also expresses this weaker form of possible worlds. Recall the spat between Sheldon and Raj in "The Hot Troll Deviation":

Raj: I'm telling you, if xenon emits ultraviolet light, then those dark matter discoveries must be wrong.

Sheldon: Yes, well, if we lived in a world where slow-moving xenon produced light, then you'd be correct. Also, pigs would fly, my derriere would produce cotton candy, and *The Phantom Menace* would be a timeless classic.

The interesting feature of this exchange is that Sheldon and Raj disagree about the actual properties of (slow-moving) xenon, namely, whether it emits light. Sheldon sarcastically retorts that Raj is correct about xenon in a different—or fictional—world. Xenon doesn't actually emit light, at least according to Sheldon. Assume for the sake of argument that Sheldon is correct about xenon and Raj is mistaken. The larger point, at least implicitly, is that Sheldon suggests Raj's claim is *wildly* false. Its being true doesn't require only one thing about the actual world to be different, but a host of things, including flying pigs.

Accordingly, one strategy for determining whether a statement is more wrong than another is how far removed it is from the actual world. Take any two false theories. For example, take the theory that a tomato is a vegetable; for simplicity's sake, let's call it "vegetable theory." Take a second theory that a tomato is a suspension bridge; let's call it "suspension bridge theory." Vegetable theory is wrong (or false), because, strictly speaking, a tomato is a fruit, rather than a vegetable. This is probably what Stuart had in mind. The actual world contains the following states of affairs regarding tomatoes: is a fruit, is edible, comes from a plant, isn't a human-designed thing, isn't a building. Vegetable theory is different from the actual state of affairs in one feature (isn't a fruit) but similar in the other stipulated features. Thus, the truth of vegetable theory requires only one rather small alteration from the actual world. Suspension bridge theory is different in multiple facets regarding actual tomatoes. Hence, the vegetable theory is different from the actual world in only one aspect, and the suspension bridge theory is different from the actual world in at least six aspects. It seems that Stuart had in mind exactly this understanding of truth-likeness or false-likeness, when he said that it's a little wrong to say a tomato is a vegetable, but it's very wrong to say it's a suspension bridge.

Even so, our discussion of possible worlds probably shouldn't be interpreted as solving all aspects of the problem of truth-likeness. The vegetable example is fairly simple, and the measure of similarity by counting matching features to the actual world might not be the best measure. Perhaps one very large alteration (Sheldon is a robot) somehow outweighs one smaller change (Wolowitz has a Ph.D.). So, there is more work to do. Nevertheless, you can't deny that Stuart's example about tomatoes, vegetables, and suspension bridges makes a very good point about different things being wrong in different degrees.

Stuart's move is clever on another level. If someone such as Sheldon says that being wrong isn't subject to gradation, then, logically speaking, just one (true) example to the contrary suffices to refute him. This is exactly what Stuart gives Sheldon; the comic book store owner shows the theoretical physicist that he is wrong about being wrong. Sheldon may be the smarter guy, but Stuart, at least this time, has logic on his side. This would (or should) make any lifelong fan of Mr. Spock take notice.

## "I Think You Mean I'm Improbable"

Perhaps Sheldon might resort to logic in a different way to defend himself about being wrong. Recall "The Pirate Solution," where Sheldon (apologetically) admits that Raj is correct about a calculation but denies that this means he is wrong:

Sheldon: I looked over the board and it turns out you
   were right.
Raj: So you were wrong.
Sheldon: I didn't say that.
Raj: That's the only logical inference.
Sheldon: Nevertheless, I didn't say it.

Given that Sheldon and Raj argued about the very same thing, and given that Raj is indeed right, is Sheldon's wrongness the only logical inference? The answer is both yes and no. More particularly, it depends on the logic one adheres to in this situation.

Raj's position that Sheldon's being wrong "is the only logical inference" assumes what philosophers call classical logic. One of the fundamental principles of this logic is the law of excluded middle: every (meaningful) statement has to be either true or false. There's no other possibility. It's called the law of excluded middle because it excludes the possibility of any middle ground between true and false. This sheds light on another law of classical logic—the law of noncontradiction, which holds that a statement can't be both true and false. In other words, a statement can't contradict itself. Hence, if Raj is right and Sheldon contradicts him, then Sheldon must be wrong.

People often like to say, though, that the world isn't only black and white; there are shades of gray. Many-valued logics have been developed exactly for this reason. For example, if one wants to capture three states of affairs—true, false, and indeterminate—one can use for that a corresponding three-valued logic. In many-valued logics, one can have as many truth-values as one wants to. There's only one basic principle for calculating truth-values (where 1 means completely true, 0 means completely false, and all of the other possible truth-values are between 0 and 1): the degree of false = 1 − the degree of truth; and the degree of truth = 1 − the degree of false. For example, if the truth-value of "*A*" is 0.8, then the truth-value of "not *A*" is 0.2, or if "*B*" is true to the degree of 0.4, then "not *B*" is true to the degree of 0.6.

Therefore, given many-valued, nonclassical logic, there's a way for Raj to be right and for Sheldon not to be wrong. We can say, for example, that Raj is right but not completely, and, because of that, Sheldon isn't completely wrong but rather very slightly, yet still somewhat, right. So the only way for Sheldon not to be wrong and for Raj to be right is if there are degrees of truth and falsity. Yet this comes with a price. Recall the debate between Sheldon and Stuart in "The Hofstadter Isotope." There, Sheldon was emphatic that being wrong was not subject to gradation. So, his new implicit position with Raj, if correct, seemingly makes him wrong about his previous position with Stuart! (And no, Sheldon, that's not sarcasm, just logic.)

## The Cooper-Wrongness Paradox

*The Big Bang Theory* is replete with examples of Sheldon professing his incredibly large and accurate knowledge base (thanks in part to his eidetic memory, no doubt). He goes so far as to smugly tell Penny in "The Prestidigitation Approximation" that "Oh, oh, please, if I don't know, you don't know. That's axiomatic." In "The Bat Jar Conjecture," she humorously reveals his hubris by asking him questions such as "Which Ridgemont High alumnus was married to Madonna?" and "Who replaced David Lee Roth as the lead singer of Van Halen?" He is ignorant of both answers. She possesses knowledge he lacks, thus falsifying his claim.

In "The Jiminy Conjecture," Sheldon puts forward a similar claim to Wolowitz: "Howard, you know me to be a very smart man. Don't you think if I were wrong, I'd know it?" There is more than a sliver of arrogance here, too, but note that it differs from the claim made to Penny in the following way. There may be topics about which Sheldon is ignorant, but he would not assert something as true that wasn't. He would never (knowingly) make that sort of error. As we'll see, this position harbors some interesting implications about truth and knowledge.

Given Sheldon's implicit position expressed to Howard, it seems to follow that if Sheldon correctly asserts something, then he knows what he's right about, so he knows what's true. It also seems to follow that if Sheldon incorrectly asserts something, then he knows what he's wrong about, so he knows that the contrary thing is true. For any assertion Sheldon makes, it is either correct or incorrect, but either way he knows what is true. Hence, if Sheldon's statement to Howard is true, then Sheldon never holds a false belief! If someone would object and reply that Sheldon might know when he's wrong, but this doesn't mean that he knows when he's right, then consider this. If Sheldon knows he's wrong every time he's wrong, then the only time he wouldn't know he's wrong would be the time when he's right.

True, this argument contains a false premise because it's not the case that Sheldon (always) knows when he is asserting something false. His mistaken attribution of Toby as a snowy field cricket is an obvious example, but so is (it seems) the claim he makes to Stuart about truth and falsity not admitting of degrees. Yet even ignoring those examples, interesting philosophical insights follow. Seemingly, it can be proved that when Sheldon is wrong, he *can't* know that he's wrong at all.

Let's assume for the sake of the argument that Sheldon knew that he asserted something false, say, Toby's being a snowy field cricket. For this to happen, two things have to be true. First, it has to be true that Sheldon knows that Toby is actually a common field cricket. In other words, in order to know that you're wrong, you have to know what's right. Second, it has to be true that Sheldon knows that he doesn't know that Toby is a common field cricket. In other words, in order to know that you're wrong, you have to know what you're wrong about.

Now, if you know something, then this thing you know has to be true. Truth is a necessary condition of knowledge. You may believe that *The Big Bang Theory* moved from Tuesday to Thursday nights on CBS, but you cannot know this. This is grounded in the intuition that knowledge is opposed to ignorance. Your belief about the change in the CBS schedule demonstrates your ignorance of the facts, not the knowledge of them. Hence, if Sheldon knows that he doesn't know that Toby is a common field cricket, then it's also true that Sheldon doesn't know that Toby is a common field cricket. Yet this contradicts our beginning assumption, namely, that Sheldon knows that Toby is a common field cricket. If we made a supposition and inferred a contradiction from it, then our supposition has to be false. (Philosophers sometimes call this an indirect proof.) We made a supposition that Sheldon knows that he's wrong and derived a contradiction. Therefore, this supposition is wrong: Sheldon can't know that he's wrong!

Where's the paradox? A paradox is something that has contradictory qualities. On one hand, Sheldon claims that if he were wrong, he'd know it. On the other hand, we just saw that Sheldon can't possibly know that he's wrong about something. The paradox may be further strengthened: that he's wrong about his claim to Wolowitz is the only (relevant) thing Sheldon can know for sure.

## "Of Course I'm Right—What Are the Odds I'd Be Wrong Twice in One Week?"

Even though, conceptually speaking, Sheldon can't know that he's wrong, there's a sense in which Sheldon can be wrong and know about it, thanks to inductive inference.

Inductive inferences note similarities or regularities among a group of data and then make generalized conclusions about them. These conclusions are often predictive. Given what we have observed in the past, conclusions about future events are made. For example, suppose that for the last fifty consecutive Saturdays, you observed that Sheldon awakens at 6:15, pours a bowl of cereal, adds a quarter cup of milk, sits on his end of the couch, turns on BBC America, and watches *Doctor Who*. Given these prior experiences and knowing what a creature of habit Sheldon tends to be, someone such as Leonard can confidently predict Sheldon's behavior next Saturday morning at 6:15 A.M.

The connection to Toby the field cricket is fairly obvious. Yes, Sheldon mistakenly identifies him as a snowy field cricket, but the chances that he will utter another falsehood in the next seven days are incredibly low. This belief is strengthened by all of Sheldon's past experiences, especially noting how rare it is that he utters a falsehood. So, in a way, his being proved wrong about Toby has interesting ramifications for his other beliefs (all things being equal). Yet there's a hitch. The worry has to do with Sheldon's affirmation that "Of course, he's right" about his other knowledge claims in light of misidentifying Toby. If he means that he must be right about all of his other beliefs in the current seven-day window, he again runs the risk of being wrong about being right.

The potential error is rather straightforward: any generalization based on past experiences could, no matter how unlikely, turn out to be false. Recall "The Dumpling Paradox," in which Sheldon finds Penny sleeping on his couch one Saturday morning; as he ponders the situation, his cereal quickly loses all of its molecular integrity, and he misses the beginning of *Doctor Who*. Or consider Leonard's season 1 lamentation that girls like Penny never end up with guys who own time machines. In his experience—perhaps in anyone's experience—girls like Penny simply don't become involved with guys who are preoccupied (obsessed?) with classic science fiction and fantasy memorabilia. Yet no matter how many unfortunate time machines owners you may have observed, this doesn't guarantee that the next time machine owner can't have a girlfriend like Penny. The Scottish philosopher David Hume (1711–1776) is often credited for his succinct formulation of the relevant worry: "That the sun will not rise tomorrow is no less intelligible a proposition, and implies no more contradiction, than the affirmation, that it will rise."[1] Thus, Sheldon cannot know, at least not with any certainty, that his false belief about Toby guarantees that his other recent knowledge claims are true.[2]

Although we can't ever be sure that our inductive inferences are true, at least we can sometimes be sure when our inductive inferences are false. The statement "Girls like Penny never end up with guys who own time machines" isn't guaranteed simply because we can't possibly observe each and every future time machine owner's private life. If, however, we observe at least one time machine owner who has a pretty girlfriend like Penny, for example, Leonard during the third season, then we're more than definitely justified to believe that the generalization "Girls like Penny never end up with guys who own time machines" is false. This result may finally comfort Sheldon. He can't ever be sure that his inductive generalizations are true, but, at least, he can sometimes know when his generalizations are false. He may, at last and in some sense, be wrong and know about it.

## "Throw All the French around You Want, It Doesn't Make You Right."

Sheldon shows us how nonrational factors often impinge on one's rationality. He has grown so accustomed to being right that it is difficult for him to accept that he is wrong or even doesn't know something. The final question of the Physics Bowl competition in "The Bat Jar Conjecture" is excellent evidence of this. Sheldon would rather lose to Leslie and the guys than allow another member of his team to answer correctly. He would rather lose the competition than not answer all of the questions himself.

This sort of psychological idiosyncrasy also sometimes leads Sheldon to argue irrationally. Recall another part of Sheldon's discussion with Stuart in "The Hofstadter Isotope" about who is the logical successor to the Bat Cowl if Batman's death proves permanent:

> Sheldon: Removing Joe Chill as the killer of Batman's parents effectively deprived him of *his* raison d'être [reason for existence].
> Stuart: You can throw all the French around you want, it doesn't make you right.
> Sheldon: Au contraire [on the contrary].

The implication is that by simply infusing his argument with words from the French language, Sheldon's position is somehow established. Yet this is a faulty inference, and Stuart is wise to call him on it.

As their argument wears on into the wee hours of the morning, and after Penny falls asleep—which reminds us of why we're inclined to say guys like Leonard don't wind up with girls like Penny—Stuart finally relents.

> Stuart: Okay. Look, Sheldon, it's late. I've gotta get some sleep.
> Sheldon: So I win.
> Stuart: No, I'm tired.
> Sheldon: So I win.
> Stuart: Fine, you win.
> Sheldon: Darn tooting, I win.

Here again, Sheldon appeals to something other than the subject matter of the argument. Now Sheldon plays on Stuart's tiredness in order to "prove" his point. Stuart won't be allowed to leave until he accepts that Sheldon is right. The implication is that if Stuart gives up and goes home, Sheldon's conclusion is thereby established. Yet again, this is faulty reasoning. Stuart knows this, but he simply needs a break from Sheldon. Again, Stuart has logic on his side.

Philosophers have a name for the type of "argument" Sheldon is employing here: logical fallacy. Logical fallacies, of which there are many kinds, are faulty pieces of reasoning because they do not and cannot establish a rational link between premises and a conclusion of an argument. Nevertheless, they are often rhetorically persuasive. Instead of logically proving something, they psychologically or emotionally persuade the listener to accept a position.[3]

That Sheldon sometimes resorts to logical fallacies to persuade his dialogue partner is telling. Very much unlike his favorite *Star Trek* character, he is so overcome with the emotional need to be right that he is willing to sacrifice logic. Perhaps, in the end, this as much as anything else explains why Sheldon cannot accept that Stuart is correct about truth admitting of degrees; why, if Raj's competing calculation was correct, his was not mistaken; and why he takes his ill-advised "axiomatic" position about Penny's knowledge base. And so, we see a pattern develop. Rather than admit he was wrong or simply doesn't know, he invariably resorts to nonrational behavior, including rhetorical ploys. In this, perhaps Sheldon is again wrong about being wrong—at least, that's what Spock might say.

## NOTES

1. David Hume, *An Enquiry Concerning Human Understanding* (New York: Oxford University Press, 2007), p. 18.

2. Actually, Hume is invariably credited with formulating an even deeper problem about induction. He famously argued that the very process of induction as a way to extend our knowledge is flawed. Inductive inferences, especially those that make predictions from past observations, ultimately assume what they are trying to prove: that some natural occurrence (the sunrise) will continue to happen as it has repeatedly in the past.

3. Of course, employing logical fallacies may have pragmatic or perhaps even evolutionary benefits.

# THE COOPER CONUNDRUM: GOOD LORD, WHO'S TOLERATING WHOM?

*Ruth E. Lowe*

The characters of *The Big Bang Theory* are an eclectic bunch. Penny and her scientific neighbors have different tastes, social habits, cultural backgrounds, and interests, yet they are drawn together, and somehow, they make it work. When we live in a free society, we are expected to accept that people are different and that everyone should be free to live his or her life according to those differences (so long as we're not harming one another). It's a simple, perhaps heavy-handed, message of tolerance, and in some cases it's easier said than done. What if my way of life deems yours so objectionable that we can't get along?

Look at the Coopers. Conventional wisdom suggests that it's easier for a scientist to be tolerant than it is for a religious fundamentalist. Mrs. Cooper believes that by faith one comes to know truth. Not the kind of truth that merely applies today or in this place, religious truth tends to be the capital "T" variety that holds for all times and in all places. In contrast, Dr. Cooper holds fast to the scientific tradition, which is tied to observable fact and as such must recognize its own limits and fallibility. Scientists once told us the Earth was flat; now we know it is round—well, actually not "round," but you get the idea; even gravity is up for grabs these days. Scientists are aware that their findings are probably not the last word on a subject, whereas religious evangelists preach the Truth.

Does that mean, though, that scientists are better equipped to tolerate religious persons than vice versa? Is Sheldon more tolerant than his mother? Does that make Sheldon a better citizen in a free society? The answers are not simple and straightforward. In fact, *The Big Bang Theory* shows just how complicated the relationship is between a person's worldview and tolerance. To observe this, let's put Sheldon (the scientist), Mrs. Cooper (the religious fundamentalist), a couple of antirealist philosophers, and their concomitant worldviews in competition with one another. Remember the Physics Bowl in "The Bat Jar Conjecture?" Well, this is the Tolerance Bowl.

## Who's Tolerating Whom?

The connection between how we see the world and how we choose to organize ourselves politically is probably as old as politics, but we don't have to look back that far to see what it might mean in contemporary political arrangements. In the late 1950s, Isaiah Berlin famously argued that liberalism, the view that individuals should be free from restraints placed on them by the state, is simply the best response to pluralism, a view that emphasizes the diversity of values that one might reasonably pursue.

Berlin argued that reasonable, rational people will develop very different ways of going about their lives. Given that people reasonably choose different goals and come up with different ways of achieving them, it is absurd to think that one person can make the right choice for everyone. As a result, individuals should be equally free from (illegitimate) coercion by the state or other citizens.[1] Of course, in any society, some coercion is necessary. In a liberal democracy, for example, coercion that protects individual freedoms and equality can be legitimate.

The upshot is a free society, where Sheldon and his mother can have different beliefs, values, and ideas about what makes a good life. They both benefit by keeping their controversial values more or less private, because in doing so, they support the public value—namely, freedom—which allows them the opportunity to live their lives according to their own ideas. Even though it seems like a chore, they both have a good reason to exercise tolerance. Politically speaking, they agree that it is better to be free and live with deep disagreement than to live under the kind of tyranny that is necessary for agreement on multiple levels of association.

The idea that tolerance and tyranny stand on opposite sides of the freedom question is appealing but not without its problems, as this memorable moment from "The Electric Can Opener Fluctuation" shows:

> Sheldon: I will spend the rest of my life here in Texas trying to teach evolution to creationists.
> Mrs. Cooper: You watch your mouth, Shelly. Everyone's entitled to their opinion.
> Sheldon: Evolution isn't an opinion, it's fact.
> Mrs. Cooper: And that is your opinion.

At first blush, Mary gets a lot of tolerance points here because she *says* she won't tolerate intolerance. In doing so, however, she is imposing a kind of tyranny on Sheldon, a tyranny that is meant to force him to move out of her house and back to California. Let's call the relationship here, between tyranny and tolerance, the "Cooper conundrum." It is an expression of tolerance that is functionally intolerant.

Mrs. Cooper believes that the world was created by God over seven days; Dr. Cooper believes the universe is the product of evolution over billions of years. Neither will be convinced that the other is correct. Indeed, Sheldon is seldom convinced that anyone else is right about anything, as he reminds us in "The Boyfriend Complexity": "As usual, you're all *wrong*." Obviously, this approach costs Sheldon a few tolerance points, but Mary also loses some when she bulldozes through Raj's ethnicity in "The Electric Can Opener Fluctuation" with comments such as "You know, at our church we have a woman who's an amazing healer. . . . I bet she'd be willing to take a shot at whatever Third World demon is running around inside of you."

Sheldon's commitment to being right and his mother's commitment to the truth of her own beliefs are not conducive to accepting the fact of reasonable disagreement—the idea that different people can have very different, perfectly reasonable, ways of looking at the world. As a result, the Coopers don't seem to embrace what is fundamental to the liberal tradition, the pluralist approach to right and wrong. Why is that? Why do they find it so difficult to tolerate each other?

## Worlds Apart or Words Apart?

The scientist and the fundamentalist seem to be worlds apart, or, at the very least, they look at the world in completely different ways. For Dr. Cooper, scientific method reveals facts about the world; for Mrs. Cooper, God is a fact in the world. They live in the same world, observing the same physical reality, but they see the world in very different ways. Sheldon's mother brings those differences into stark comic relief, for example, in "The Electric Can Opener Fluctuation," when she says things such as, "Hold your horses, young man. Here in Texas, we pray before we eat. . . . This is not California, land of the heathen."

Despite appearances, however, the worldviews of Sheldon and his mother may not be that far apart. According to the philosopher Donald Davidson (1917–2003), a conceptual scheme, like a worldview, is a package of beliefs, values, and concepts that are in some way linked to the way we talk about the world (our language practices) and the way we organize ourselves socially (our political practices). Davidson argued that the notion of radically different conceptual schemes (worldviews) is itself a paradox. The argument goes something like this: Different conceptual schemes make sense only in relation to an overarching conceptual scheme shared in common; however, the existence of a common conceptual scheme disproves radical difference between conceptual schemes. As a result, we cannot make sense of the idea that there is radical difference between conceptual schemes.[2]

Here's one way to understand the paradox: Penny and Leonard come from different social worlds—waitress and wannabe actress v. physicist. Yet if they were radically different, they wouldn't even be able to communicate. They understand how different they are only because they can appeal to what they have in common, an overarching scheme. They're both Americans, they speak the same language, and so on. These similarities mean that their worlds aren't so different, after all.

Davidson developed an integrated approach to problems of knowledge, action, language, and mind. So it's not surprising that he argued that the way we talk about the world is closely linked with how we view the world. As a result, the language practices of a given group express, or reflect, the conceptual scheme of the group.

We recognize a language as a language on the basis of our own. So, if we came across a radically different language, it would not look, to us, like a language. If it is possible to employ the concepts of one language to make sense of another, the difference between them is not radical. In other words, if Klingon was radically different from English, it is doubtful that the speakers of English would recognize Klingon as a language. And what kind of a world would it be without Klingon Boggle?

What holds for the translatability of languages holds for the intelligibility of reasoning as well. If we encountered reasoning radically different from our own, we wouldn't recognize it as reasoning. If we are able to make sense of it as reasoning, it doesn't embody radical difference. The very idea that others might have a completely different way of explaining, organizing, and categorizing their experience of the world is internally inconsistent with how we explain, organize, and categorize experience. If we share the same world, then we share, for the most part, the same apparatus for making sense of it. Hence, if we can make sense of difference, it is because the contrast is not significant; understandable difference is only moderately different.

Davidson's ideas are not without controversy, but at least they help show how much Sheldon and his mother have in common. Recall the following exchange from "The Luminous Fish Effect":

> Mrs. Cooper: Oh, well, that looks awful fancy, what is that?
> Sheldon: It's my idea of what DNA would look like in a silicon-based life form.
> Mrs. Cooper: But intelligently designed by a creator, right?

Despite their disagreement, Mary and Sheldon share and deploy a plethora of concepts to voice that disagreement—DNA, life form, intelligent design. They understand each other because underneath the disagreement about which is the right way to view the world, they share a world in which different groups have different opinions about the world.

In a world with different opinions, we don't have to look far to see that like attracts like. Mrs. Cooper says her normal kids are much easier to deal with. It's easy for Sheldon to get along with Beverly Hofstadter and Amy Farrah Fowler, yet he finds the company of his own mother and Penny exceedingly taxing.

So, they're still neck and neck in the Tolerance Bowl. They find it equally difficult to tolerate each other and people who think differently. That's not to say that they're not capable of being tolerant. In fact, Sheldon feels that his forbearance capacity is constantly tested, as he reminds us in "The Desperation Emanation": "Leonard, you are my best friend. I've known you for seven years, and I can barely tolerate sitting on the couch with you." So, why is tolerance such a burden for Sheldon? Does it have something to do with his way of looking at the world?

## The Mutual Exclusion Dogma

Surprisingly, Sheldon and Mrs. Cooper share more than just the same world and a bunch of concepts; they also share a particular way of looking at the world. They are both so committed to the truth of their beliefs that they often talk *past* each other, rather than *to* each other, as in the following phone conversation from "The Electric Can Opener Fluctuation": "No, mother, I could not feel your church group praying for my safety. The fact that I'm home safe is not proof that it worked, that logic is Post Hoc Ergo Propter Hoc. No, I'm not sassing you in Eskimo talk."

Mrs. Cooper is committed to a fundamentalist notion of truth, and although Dr. Cooper does not subscribe to the same set of beliefs, he does appeal to the truth of logic. In other words, the way Mary believes and orients her life around God parallels the way Sheldon believes and orients his life around science. This sort of orientation falls under the umbrella of metaphysical realism. Roughly speaking, it's the idea that there is an objective reality that exists independent of how we talk or think about it.

In contrast, Davidson argued that a worldview with that type of orientation is misguided. The idea that we cannot make sense of radically different worldviews, plural, he cautioned, does not mean that we can make sense of a worldview, a singular grand master scheme, either. The idea that there is one scheme out there somewhere is problematic. We cannot appeal to God or some sort of unified theory to justify the idea that one way of looking at the world is better than the rest. The mistake, according to Davidson, is to think that there is some sort of independent ground out there at all.

If there is no giant meter stick out there that we can use to adjudicate disagreement, then we are left with provisional understandings in a socially conditioned reality—the truth is, there is no truth. This antirealist paradigm is a worldview in which, simply, *what we have is what we have*, nothing more, and nothing less.

This issue is often couched as a *created* or *discovered* problem in philosophy. Do we create truth, social reality, human nature? Or are those things out there waiting to be discovered? Is it just our understanding of those things that's incomplete? In the antirealist picture, there is nothing out there to be discovered; social reality is created.

Historically, Western civilization has been particularly guilty of justifying oppression on the basis of a natural order. The world, it was thought, simply dictated that some races were meant to serve others, and this discovery made it possible to enslave or otherwise take advantage of some races on moral grounds. Sheldon, of course, is quite comfortable with the idea of natural orders, lest we forget his quip from "The Financial Permeability": "I think I'd be willing to be a house pet to a race of super intelligent aliens." (No doubt, Sheldon would like to live in a world where his inferiors would similarly defer to his superiority.)

Most of us think differently; our social reality has changed. It is a fact that there are people of different races in the world, but the world does not tell us that one race is better than the rest, that one race deserves a better life than the others. Racism is not somehow "in" the world; it is created through social relations. In "The Boyfriend Complexity," Raj asks, "Is that racist? It feels racist." He's asking, "What do we have here?" and Howard's answer is his socially conditioned understanding: "Don't be oversensitive. He's calling you illiterate, not your race." Through dialogue, they sort out what kind of comments are ethically contentious. In that, they're building a shared concept of racism.

Giving up on the idea that the world can somehow ground or justify our opinions, it seems, makes it easier to accept that other people (perfectly reasonable people) can have very different (yet equally legitimate) worldviews. Yet Sheldon believes he knows more about what's out there than anyone else. Recall an exchange from "The Work Song Nanocluster." Sheldon mockingly asserts, "Penny, I'm a physicist. I have a working knowledge of the entire universe and everything it contains." When Penny asks, "Who's Radiohead?" he doesn't know, so he must, in order to be consistent with his premise, reject the question (or, at least, its importance).

Both the Coopers would disagree with the antirealist paradigm. Whether they believe they have access to God or the unified theory of everything doesn't matter; what does matter is that they both believe that there is something out there. In contrast, Davidson rejects the idea that there is any sort of independent ground out there, and as a result, the most we can say about the truth of a statement is that it is relative to the language in which it was spoken.[3]

Given Sheldon's Spock-like commitment to logic, you might think Sheldon could happily agree with Davidson on this point, but that requires accepting the fallibility of his own beliefs. Sheldon's scientism doesn't seem to allow for that degree of fallibility. For Sheldon, the truth of string theory, although not proven, is not merely one truth among many, it is the capital "T," Truth, which everyone, including Leslie Winkle, will come to accept—eventually. Dr. Cooper, it seems, is religiously scientific in "The Benefactor Factor" when he proclaims his purpose is "to tear the mask off nature and stare at the face of God."

This sort of commitment to first, the truth of one's beliefs, and second, the belief that an independent reality will ultimately prove those beliefs "true" doesn't make sense in the Davidsonian worldview. Realists—be they religious, scientific, or metaphysical—are operating in a paradigm in which reality is revealed to them as truth. Truth is not relative to the language of the community. Truth is relative to an independent ground that can be discovered, and it is the standard against which evaluations of true and false, right and wrong, and good and evil are made.

In contrast, Davidson's paradigm is less concerned with absolute right or wrong, and as a result, the fallibility of what is known or believed today is a given. I can still believe what I believe, but the idea that what I believe might change over time makes it easier to accept the idea that people can reasonably disagree. Acknowledging the ultimate fallibility of one's beliefs encourages tolerance by getting around some of the obstacles thrown up by the Coopers' realism. So, the antirealist outlook makes it much easier to accept pluralism. Different people, if they are free to do so, will have different views of the world, and that's really all we can say. The differences alone are not enough to prove one worldview better than another. At this point you might think that antirealists, such as Davidson, are going to clean up in the Tolerance Bowl. Yet there is a kind of dogma lurking in the what-we-have paradigm, a dogma that functionally excludes the metaphysical realism of Sheldon and Mrs. Cooper.

## World Speak or Person Speak

If Davidson is right, realist reasoning (scientific or religious) about truth is not reasoning at all; it is so radically different from the what-we-have paradigm, it fails to meet the only features of reasonableness that can be known, those that represent reasoning in the what-we-have worldview. If Davidson is right, both Coopers are excluded from the realm of reasonable people.

Building on Davidsonian ideas, Richard Rorty (1931–2007) famously quipped: "The world does not speak. Only we do."[4] This suggests that the line between appearance and reality, what is made and what is created, is itself a creation—not a discovery. If all we have is what we have, then objectivity is a myth. We simply can't step outside our point of view, our worldview.

If we cannot achieve any sort of critical distance from where we are, then we cannot see our worldview in relation to another worldview. We can only see alternative points of view from our own; we can only deploy the concepts from our own point of view to interpret the actions of others.[5] This isn't to say that we cannot, over time, learn new concepts and different ways of looking at things. We can expand the number of shared concepts between different worldviews. Penny comes to understand what the guys are up to in "The Bat Jar Conjecture" by translating their actions into her own terms. "Wow, so in your world, you're like, the *cool guys.*" Howard: "Recognize."

The process of recognition comes about, according to Rorty, because there is no objective criterion of "cool guyness" out there. Instead, what a cool guy is, is contingent on social conditions. To say that Dr. Cooper's claims about evolution are made relative to a scientific worldview or that Mrs. Cooper's comments about creationism are made relative to a religious worldview really isn't saying anything *about* the difference between them, except to say they are different.

The implications of this idea present a significant challenge in modern political and moral arrangements because if Rorty was right, then no one can be shown to be wrong. Or more succinctly, to say "you're wrong" is really only stating an opinion. Once again, both Coopers would be quite uncomfortable with such a loosey-goosey approach to facts or truth. So, once again, they are equally disadvantaged on the tolerance scale. Yet the antirealists, it turns out, don't fare much better.

If, as Rorty suggested, we lose access to what makes evaluations of difference and disagreement meaningful, then we really are stuck with what-we-have—stuck with it in such a way that we cannot even account for the idea of genuine pluralism. If we can't see the significant contrast between our own worldview and the worldviews of others, we have no good reason to acknowledge that different worldviews exist out there. We tend, in that case, to see our worldview as the only worldview and, in doing so, lose sight of the reason we need tolerance in the first place.

So, antirealism seems to offer a worldview that encourages tolerance through the recognition of fallibility but then loses any tolerance points gained because it cannot account for the level of diversity that makes disagreement meaningful in pluralist associations. Whether your way of looking at the world falls under the antirealist or the realist umbrella, believing that you're more right, more reasonable, more in touch with reality than others makes it difficult to tolerate people who think differently.

## The Tolerance Tally

So, who wins the Tolerance Bowl? Who's more tolerant: Sheldon, his mother, or the antirealist philosopher? If we base the decision on worldviews, they all come out about even. We've seen how giving up on the idea that all of the answers we need to run a society come from correctly interpreting God or discovering a theory of everything makes it easier to be tolerant of others. Rejecting the idea that the world "out there" exists to justify some beliefs but not others makes it easier to accept that all of the worldviews in *The Big Bang Theory*—Jewish, East Indian, Texan, and Nebraskan—are equally reasonable and worthy of public recognition. Yet adhering to the what-we-have idea, as if it were the only right way to think, can make it just as difficult to acknowledge and tolerate different points of view.

So, if we can't judge who's more tolerant than whom on the basis of their worldviews, can we answer the question another way? As a scientist, Sheldon works in a tradition that is inherently fallibilist, yet his unyielding commitment to his own hypotheses makes tolerating others an annoying chore. Recall his crass admission from "The Cooper Nowitzke Theorem": "The truth can indeed be a finger down the throat of those unprepared to hear it. But why should I cater to second-rate minds?" Similarly, Mrs. Cooper's religious beliefs clearly color her view of the world—including who is ultimately responsible for her son's acumen—as she states in "The Luminous Fish Effect": "All that science stuff, that comes from Jesus."

Despite the fact that they appeal to different meters, neither would be comfortable with the idea that what we have is what we have. Both Coopers, however, understand the difference between fact and opinion, and they both allow, perhaps more grudgingly in Sheldon's case, that everyone is entitled to his or her opinion. In "The Hot Troll Deviation," Sheldon is pretty clear that everyone is free to be wrong, "Yes, well, if we lived in a world where [insert statement he disagrees with here], then you'd be correct. Also, pigs would fly, my derrière would produce cotton candy, and *The Phantom Menace* would be a timeless classic."

Ultimately, though, the Coopers must make room for the worldviews of others in order to have the space for their own. So, we're left with the Cooper conundrum. Neither Shelly nor his mom can tolerate intolerance, and, as we've seen, that can be a complicated, even contradictory, idea. Maybe tolerance is a puzzle, the type that is never really solved; it's just the type that makes us stop and think about who's tolerating whom and why.[6]

## NOTES

1. Isaiah Berlin, "Two Concepts of Liberty," in his *Four Essays on Liberty* (Oxford: Oxford University Press: 1969), 122.

2. I owe the "worlds" versus "words" comparison to Donald Davidson, "On the Very Idea of a Conceptual Scheme," in *Inquiries into Truth and Interpretation* (Oxford: Oxford University Press, 2001), 184-89.

3. Ibid., 195.

4. Richard Rorty, *Contingency, Irony, and Solidarity* (Cambridge University Press: New York, 2005), 6.

5. Ibid., 48.

6. My thanks to the webmaster at <http://bigbangtrans.wordpress.com> for episode dialogue.

# THE MENDACITY
# BIFURCATION

*Don Fallis*

Boy, you have a lot to learn about lying!
—Sheldon Cooper, Ph.D., to Leonard Hofstadter, Ph.D.

Sheldon Cooper is a lousy liar. Just think of his unconvincing claim that "Leonard is going to *the office*" (complete with stilted delivery and awkward hand gesture) in "The Lizard-Spock Expansion."[1] Or recall that horrible fake smile in "The Griffin Equivalency" that is supposed to suggest that Sheldon is happy for Koothrappali for being named one of *People* magazine's "thirty under-30 to watch." As he admits to Penny in "The Bad Fish Paradigm," "when I try to deceive, I myself have more nervous tics than a Lyme disease research facility."

Although Sheldon claims in "The Boyfriend Complexity" that he'll "have no truck with plots" and in "The Irish Pub

Formulation" that he's "deeply uncomfortable with impromptu dishonesty," feeling guilty is not what makes Sheldon a lousy liar. If it serves his interests, Sheldon has no compunction about lying or about asking other people to lie for him, as when he gets Leonard to tell Amy Farrah Fowler that he is not at home in "The Desperation Emanation." Sheldon is a lousy liar simply because he does not know how to do it well; it's just one more social skill that he does not have.[2]

Unsurprisingly, Sheldon is also pretty bad at detecting lies. For instance, in "The Creepy Candy Coating Corollary," Sheldon is fooled by Wil Wheaton's (aka Ensign Crusher's) lie about why he did not show up for the 1995 Dixie-Trek. Wheaton convinces Sheldon that he missed the Star Trek convention only because his "Nana" died, and, as a result, Sheldon lets him win the *Mystic Warlords of Ka'a* tournament. Also, in "The Electric Can Opener Fluctuation," Sheldon's friends trick him into thinking that he has detected "evidence of paradigm-shifting monopoles" because "it was the only way to keep you from being such a huge 'Dick-ensian.'" Even when he does detect that people are trying to deceive him, Sheldon is bad at figuring out *what* they are trying to deceive him about. For instance, in "The Boyfriend Complexity," when Raj and Howard are trying to hide the fact that they accidentally kissed, Sheldon can tell that something is up, but his theory about what's up is way off:

> Sheldon: I'm going to propose a hypothesis. Last night, Raj accidentally made contact with an alien civilization and has been ordered by the United States government to keep it a secret.
> Raj: Nothing happened. Can we please just change the subject?
> Sheldon: That sounds rehearsed. We are not alone.

With his inability to tell and detect lies, Sheldon can give us more than just laughs. As we shall see, he can actually teach us quite a lot about how to lie well, and he can teach us something interesting about exactly what lying is.

## Should We Be Learning How to Lie Better?

Before we look at what Sheldon can teach us about how to lie well, we should first ask ourselves a question: is lying something that we should be trying to learn how to do well in the first place? The German philosopher Immanuel Kant (1724–1804) famously argued in *The Metaphysics of Morals* that it is always wrong to lie. Kant's idea was that it would be wrong for *me* do something if it would be self-defeating for *everyone* to do it. For instance, if everyone lied whenever they liked, no one would believe what anyone else said. In that case, there would clearly be no point in lying to anyone. Although very few philosophers agree with Kant that lying is *always* wrong, most philosophers hold that it is *usually* wrong to lie. For instance, in *Lying: Moral Choice in Public and Private Life*, Harvard philosopher Sissela Bok argues that it is wrong to lie more often than we tend to think because we often underestimate the personal and social costs of lying.[3]

Given all of that, it might seem that it is just as well that Sheldon is not a good liar. His lack of skill deters him from doing what would be a bad thing. For instance, he is clearly reticent to lie about Leonard going to the office because, given that he knows that Leonard is *not* going to the office, "How can I say it convincingly?"

There are, however, at least some circumstances where it is morally permissible to lie. For instance, it is probably acceptable to tell a lie to avoid needlessly hurting someone's feelings, as when Leonard and Sheldon lie to Penny in "The Loobenfeld Decay" about not being able to go hear her sing. In fact, we are probably morally *required* to lie if it will save a life or save the universe. Penny seems to agree. In "The

Electric Can Opener Fluctuation," she tells Sheldon about the time "Kirk has to take over the ship, so he tells Spock all that stuff he knew wasn't true." She relies on this dire *Star Trek* circumstance to presumably provide Sheldon with an example of how sometimes lying can be justified, thereby softening his feelings of betrayal.

Indeed, some philosophers claim that lying is quite often a good thing. For instance, Plato (429–347 BCE) claimed in *The Republic* that the "philosopher kings" should tell "noble lies" to the hoi polloi (that is, to the masses or the riffraff) for the good of society. Also, Friedrich Nietzsche (1844–1900) asserted in *The Will to Power* that the *Übermenschen* (that is, the "overmen" who are engaged in transcending human values and creating new ones) should lie. Lying is actually part of their greatness; they choose to be whomever they wish to be.[4]

For both Plato and Nietzsche, though, there are constraints on *who* is allowed to lie. For Plato, only philosopher kings were allowed to lie, and Nietzsche was not keen on hearing lies from timid, inferior people with their "slave morality." Yet clearly these constraints do not rule out Sheldon.[5] He is quite a special and superior individual (or, at least, he thinks he is). In "The Codpiece Topology," Sheldon explains that he is "a published theoretical physicist with two doctorates and an IQ which can't be accurately measured by normal tests." Moreover, in "The Worksong Nanocluster," he tells Penny that he has "a working knowledge of the entire universe and everything it contains." He plans to win the Nobel Prize, describing himself as a "visionary." And—as if that weren't enough—he proudly reminds us in "The Wheaton Recurrence" that he was "the co-captain of the East Texas Christian Youth Holy Roller Bowling League Championship team seven- to twelve-year-old division."

Because it is sometimes necessary to lie, it can be important to do it well. Fortuitously, Sheldon has quite a lot to say on the topic, but why should we listen to what he has to say, given that he is such a lousy liar?

## Should We Listen to What Sheldon Has to Say about Lying?

Sheldon is a bad liar, but that doesn't mean that he doesn't know about lying. After all, he *is* a genius who, as we find out in "The Pancake Batter Anomaly," has an IQ of 187. In other words, although he lacks what Aristotle (384–322 BCE) called practical wisdom (or *phronesis*), Sheldon does have theoretical wisdom (or *sophia*). Or, as Oxford philosopher Gilbert Ryle (1900–1976) might express the distinction, he does not have much *know how*, but he has a lot of *know that*.[6]

For instance, Sheldon recommends in "The Loobenfeld Decay" that a lie be delivered "casually, no rapid breathing, no increase in perspiration." In other words, a liar should try to avoid any outward signs of deceit that a person (or a polygraph) might detect. Of course, it's worth remembering that, as Sheldon tells Leonard, "lack of a physiological response while lying is characteristic of a violent sociopath."

When people are caught lying, though, it is not typically because they look nervous. We usually catch people lying because what they say does not fit with what we already know or later find out. As Sherlock Holmes advised would-be human lie detectors, "we must look for consistency; where there is a want of it we must suspect deception."[7] So, there are other rules for lying well that also need to be followed.

Most notably, Sheldon insists on the importance of making your lie "plausible" and "weaving an un-unravelable web" of supporting evidence. If Penny "googles Leopold Houston [the imaginary drug-addicted cousin who figures in Sheldon's lie to her] she'll find a Facebook page, an online blog depicting his descent into drug use, and a desperate yet hopeful listing on eHarmony.com." Basically, as Sheldon puts it in "The Desperation Emanation," "the key to a good lie lies in the details."

Furthermore, it is vitally important for the liar to keep all of these details straight. Otherwise, it's easy to get tripped up.

As Nietzsche warned us in *Human, All Too Human*, "he who tells a lie seldom realizes what a heavy burden he has assumed; for, in order to maintain a lie, he has to invent twenty more."[8] In a similar vein, the English thinker Thomas Fuller noted that "it is easy to tell a lie, but hard to tell only one lie." Sheldon finds this out firsthand when he tries to hide the fact that he had dinner with Penny in "The Spaghetti Catalyst" (right after Penny and Leonard broke up):

> Leonard: Hey, where you been?
> Sheldon: I told you, walking.
> Leonard: For an hour and a half?
> Sheldon: I got lost.
> Leonard: How could you get lost? Your phone has GPS.
> Sheldon: Satellites are down. Solar flares.
> Raj: There are no solar flares right now.
> Sheldon: Yes, there are.
> Raj: Dude, I'm an astrophysicist. If there were solar flares, I'd be all up in it.
> Sheldon: I'm sorry. I misspoke. What I meant to say was my battery died.

As Sir Walter Scott poetically pointed out, it is very easy for the web to get tangled, which is why it is so crucial to make sure that it is "un-unravelable."

Finally, there is another important suggestion implicit in Sheldon's worry that he will not be able to say something convincingly if he knows that it is false. Namely, you will be more successful at deceiving people if you believe that what you are saying is true. Thus, if you want to deceive others, you should begin by deceiving yourself. As Nietzsche pointed out, "With all great deceivers there is a noteworthy occurrence to which they owe their power. In the actual act of deception . . . they are overcome by belief in themselves. . . . Self-deception has to exist if a grand effect is to be produced. For men believe in the truth of that which is plainly strongly believed."[9]

## Is Sheldon Really a Bad Liar?

In suggesting that he has only *theoretical* knowledge of how to lie well, maybe we have not been giving Sheldon enough credit. There are actually several occasions on which Sheldon seems to lie quite effectively. For instance, Penny never realizes that Sheldon does not have a drug-addicted cousin. Also, in "The Desperation Emanation," Amy Farrah Fowler's mother seems pretty convinced that Sheldon is "having regular intercourse with her daughter."

Yet most notably, in "The Monopolar Expedition" and several other episodes, Sheldon's friends find that "Once again, you've fallen for one of my classic pranks. *Bazinga!*" For instance, in "The Lunar Excitation," the gang goes up on the roof to shoot a laser at one of the reflectors that the *Apollo 11* astronauts put on the moon. Sheldon says that he "should've brought an umbrella" because "with skin as fair as mine, moon burn is a real possibility." Of course, with the possible exception of Penny's date Zack (who is happy to hear that the moon will not blow up because "we set our laser to stun"), nobody is going to believe that moon burn is a real possibility. Yet it's a lie even if you merely intend people to believe that *you believe* what you are saying. And in these *Bazinga!* cases, Sheldon's cluelessness actually works in his favor. Although it is clear that what Sheldon is saying is crazy, his friends have to countenance the possibility that he nevertheless really believes what he is saying.

Now, someone might claim that such practical jokes are not really lies. According to the traditional philosophical definition, however, you *lie* if you say something false with the intent to deceive.[10] So, Sheldon is lying. In fact, according to Kant, even lies told "out of frivolity" are always morally objectionable.[11] Of course, if a group of friends enjoys playing practical jokes on one another, Kant seems to be a bit of a killjoy in claiming that their doing so is immoral.

Sheldon also has success in "The Bus Pants Utilization" when he makes a convincing but insincere apology for his bad behavior in order to be reinstated as a member of Leonard's "Smartphone App" project. At first, he is unwilling to do this because "Mrs. Mary Cooper didn't raise her no liars." Yet Penny suggests that "all you have to do here is say you're sorry to Leonard, but say it sarcastically." Sheldon finally agrees to do so because Leonard "will hear it as an attempt to mend fences, as opposed to the withering condemnation you and I will know it to be." When he says how "deeply sorry I am for my earlier behavior," however, he *is* lying because he says something that he believes to be false with the intent to deceive. In this case, Sheldon succeeds in convincing Leonard that he is sincere. Of course, it could be that Sheldon is successful only when he *thinks* that he is not *really* lying but merely being sarcastic or joking around.

## Does Lying Require Intending to Deceive?

The traditional philosophical definition of lying goes all the way back to the early Christian philosopher Saint Augustine's (354–430) *De Mendacio*, but this definition is too narrow. Although you lie if you say something that you believe to be false with the intent to deceive, it is not the only way to lie. Or, as philosophers would put it, intending to deceive may be a *sufficient* condition for lying, but it is not a *necessary* condition.

For one thing, lying does not require that you intend to be believed outright. For instance, in "The Lunar Excitation," Raj tells a lie that he does not expect Sheldon to simply believe. He just intends to create doubt in Sheldon's mind.

> Raj: Sheldon, I've hidden the dirty sock from the roof somewhere in your apartment. Unless you are willing to come with us to meet this girl, it will remain there forever.
> Sheldon: You're bluffing.
> Raj: Are you willing to risk it?
> Sheldon: Curse you.

Even though they are not intended to be believed outright, such bluffs still count as intentional deception of a sort. Yet it turns out that you can lie even if you do not intend to deceive anyone at all. For instance, Sheldon tells a *bald-faced lie* in "The Excelsior Acquisition."[12] This is a lie that everyone, the liar and the person lied to, knows is a lie.

Sheldon is found guilty of running a red light while taking Penny to the hospital with a dislocated shoulder. He is so upset about the verdict that he insults the judge by saying, "I would like to point out that I am at the top of my profession while you preside over the kiddy table of yours!" The judge finds him in contempt of court and throws him in jail until he apologizes, which Sheldon finally agrees to do. Because he is not really sorry, though, he is lying. He tells Penny later, "I was forced to issue an undeserved apology, simply because I refuse to urinate in a stainless steel bowl in front of criminals."

The judge is well aware that the apology is insincere, but he doesn't care. There is still a point to requiring someone to apologize, even if he or she does not really mean it. It's humiliating to have someone else force you to say something that you do not want to say. In this case, it serves as a deterrent to Sheldon's talking back to the judge. (In fact, because Sheldon's humiliation takes place in open court, it serves as a deterrent to everyone else as well.) Also, there is still a point to apologizing even if the person to whom you are apologizing knows that you do not really mean it. Sometimes it can even get you out of jail!

## Does Lying Require Intending to Violate a Social Convention?

Given the existence of such bald-faced lies, we need to come up with an alternative definition of lying. Even if liars do not always break the rule against deceiving others, they seem to break some rule when they "go on the record" with something that they believe to be false. So, a few philosophers, including myself at one point in time, have claimed that lying is about intending to violate a certain *social convention*, rather than about intending to deceive.[13]

Social conventions are informal rules that we typically obey in our interactions with other people. Moreover, these are rules that we think we *ought* to obey. For instance, there are many rules of politeness. You don't blow your nose and then show the handkerchief to the people at the next table in the restaurant. (In "The Pancake Batter Anomaly," Sheldon does just this and then asks them, "Would you call that moss green or forest green?") In addition, there are rules with respect to how we communicate with one another using language. In his *Studies in the Way of Words*, Berkeley philosopher Paul Grice (1913–1988) identified several *norms of conversation*, such as, "Do not make your contribution to the conversation more informative than is required," "Avoid obscurity of expression," and "Do not say what you believe to be false."[14] According to my alternative definition of lying, you lie if you intend to violate this last norm of conversation. Thus, even though Sheldon does not intend to deceive the judge, he is lying if he intends to violate the norm of conversation against saying what he believes to be false.

Unfortunately, my alternative definition of lying is also too narrow. In fact, someone such as Sheldon is potentially a counterexample. It is pretty clear by now that even though he is not always very good at it, Sheldon can lie. Yet as Leonard points out in "The Luminous Fish Effect," Sheldon does not understand social conventions.

Leonard: What happened?
Sheldon: I'm not quite sure. It involves a part of the human experience that has always eluded me.
Leonard: [sarcastically] That narrows it down.

Now, even if you are not aware that there is a particular social convention, you can certainly violate that social convention.

The incident with the handkerchief clearly establishes this. Yet you cannot *intend* to violate that social convention if you do not know that it exists.

Among the social conventions that Sheldon does not understand are the norms of conversation.[15] For instance, he famously does not get sarcasm. In "The Big Bran Hypothesis," when Leonard asks, "For God's sake, Sheldon, do I have to hold up a sarcasm sign every time I open my mouth?" Sheldon credulously replies, "You have a sarcasm *sign*?" Likewise, in "The Financial Permeability," he has to keep asking, "Was *that* sarcasm?"

This particular bit of cluelessness is especially important here. According to Grice, we have to understand the norm of conversation against saying what we believe to be false in order to understand sarcasm.[16] When someone says something that she clearly believes to be false, such as, "I hope I'm a waitress at the *Cheesecake Factory* for my whole life," and there is no apparent reason for her to be lying, we conclude that she means to communicate something other than what she literally says, usually the exact opposite of what she literally says. In other words, when someone "blatantly fails to fulfill" the norm of conversation against saying what she believes to be false, we suspect sarcasm. By contrast, Sheldon simply takes people at their word, no matter how surprising that word is in any given instance.

In addition, Sheldon does not understand that it is not always socially appropriate to say whatever happens to be true. For instance, in "The Luminous Fish Effect," Sheldon tells the new department head that he is "a glorified high school science teacher whose last successful experiment was lighting his own farts." When he gets home, Sheldon says to Leonard, "I can't believe he fired me." As he explains, "I didn't say anything that wasn't true."[17] Also, Sheldon does not understand why Leonard lies to Penny in "The Loobenfeld Decay."

> Sheldon: I'm uncomfortable having been included in your lie to Penny.
> Leonard: What was I supposed to say?

Sheldon: You could have told her the truth.
Leonard: I could not have said that, it would have hurt
    her feelings.
Sheldon: Is that a relevant factor?

To be fair, however, there is some evidence that Sheldon is learning some of these social conventions. For instance, in "The Bad Fish Paradigm," he tells a joke "subverting the conversational expectations." Also, when Leonard tries to tell him that "The Electric Can Opener Fluctuation" ruse was no big deal, Sheldon replies, "You're right, Leonard, it's not a big deal. All you did was lie to me, destroy my dream, and humiliate me in front of the whole university. That, FYI, was sarcasm. I, in fact, believe it is a big deal."

In addition, even before he started to learn about how sarcasm works, Sheldon was well aware that there was a norm of conversation against saying what he believes to be false. It is very clear that his mother succeeded in teaching him that. He still does not completely understand exactly how this norm of conversation works in actual practice, but he certainly knows that there is such a norm of conversation. So, he can (and frequently does) intend to violate it.[18] Thus, Sheldon can lie according to my alternative definition of lying.

Yet we can imagine someone who is even more socially clueless than Sheldon, and who is not aware that there is a norm of conversation against saying what he believes to be false. In fact, Barry (no relation to Saul?) Kripke might be such a person. After all, even Sheldon could accurately say of him in "The Friendship Algorithm," "Kripke lacks the basic social skills that we take for granted." If such a person were to say something that he believed to be false with the intent to deceive, it seems pretty clear that he would be lying. He would not be lying, however, according to my alternative definition of lying because he could not intend to violate a norm of conversation that he did not even know about.

So, it looks as if someone can lie without intending to violate the norm of conversation against saying what he believes to be false. In other words, there appears to be a counterexample (even if only a hypothetical one) to my alternative definition of lying—but that's alright. Unlike Sheldon, I can admit that I was wrong.[19]

## NOTES

1. To be geeky for just a moment, the name of the game should actually be "rock-paper-scissors-Spock-lizard," rather than "rock-paper-scissors-lizard-Spock." That way, as with the original game "rock-paper-scissors," the items are listed in order of increasing power. See <www.samkass.com/theories/RPSSL.html>.

2. Interestingly, Amy Farrah Fowler, Sheldon's "girl-slash-friend," is apparently very good at telling lies. Recall in "The Wildebeest Implementation" when Bernadette says that she is "not a very good liar," Amy responds, "I'll teach you. I did two years of Cub Scouts before they found out that I was a girl." Also, she is pretty good at detecting lies. For instance, in "The Toast Derivation," Amy can tell that Penny is lying about not being upset about Leonard dating Priya because "your flaring nostrils indicate otherwise."

3. See Immanuel Kant, *The Metaphsics of Morals*, ed. Mary J. Gregor (Cambridge: Cambridge University Press, 1996), and Sissela Bok, *Lying: Moral Choice in Public and Private Life*, (New York: Random House, 1978).

4. See Plato, *Republic*, trans. Francis MacDonald Cornford (Oxford: Oxford University Press, 1945), and Friedrich Nietzsche, *The Will to Power*, trans. Walter Kaufmann and R.J. Hollingdale (New York: Vintage Books, 1967).

5. Of course, Mary Cooper has apparently instilled some degree of slave morality into him. Recall Sheldon's admission from "The Classified Materials Turbulence": "For what it's worth, my mother says that when we deceive for personal gain, we make Jesus cry."

6. Gilbert Ryle, "Knowing How and Knowing That," *Proceedings of the Aristotelian Society* 46 (1946): 1–16.

7. Sir Arthur Conan Doyle, *The Complete Sherlock Holmes* (New York: Doubleday, 1930), 1065. Speaking of Sherlock Holmes, here is a quiz for you: Which of these lines was said by Sherlock and which was said by Sheldon? "I don't guess. As a scientist, I reach conclusions based on observation and experimentation." and "I never guess. It is a shocking habit—destructive to the logical faculty."

8. Friedrich Nietzsche, *Human, All Too Human*, trans. R.J. Hollingdale (Cambridge, UK: Cambridge University Press, 1986), 40.

9. Ibid., 40.

10. See Bok, *Lying*, 15; see also Don Fallis, "What Is Lying?," *Journal of Philosophy* 106 (2009): 29 56.

11. Kant, *The Metaphysics of Morals*, 183.

12. See Fallis, "What Is Lying?" 41–43. For other fun examples of bald-faced lies, see Roy Sorensen, "Bald-Faced Lies! Lying without the Intent to Deceive," *Pacific Philosophical Quarterly* 88 (2007): 251–264.

13. See Fallis, "What Is Lying?" 34–37; Eve E. Sweetser, "The Definition of *Lie*: An Examination of the Folk Models Underlying a Semantic Prototype," in Dorothy Holland and Naomi Quinn, eds., *Cultural Models in Language and Thought* (Cambridge: Cambridge University Press, 1987).

14. Paul Grice, *Studies in the Way of Words* (Cambridge, MA: Harvard University Press, 1989).

15. For more on this point, see chapter 11, "Wittgenstein and Language Games in *The Big Bang Theory*," by Janelle Pötzsch in this volume.

16. Paul Grice, *Studies in the Way of Words* (Cambridge, MA: Harvard University Press, 1989), 34.

17. Later, in the same episode, Sheldon has to make another openly insincere apology here in order to get his job back: "Um, as you know, several weeks ago in our first encounter we may have gotten off on the wrong foot, when I called you an idiot. And I just wanted to say that I was wrong . . . to point it out."

18. There are numerous occasions on which Sheldon violates the norms of conversation against contributing more than is required and against avoiding obscurity. For instance, in "The Hamburger Postulate," Penny says to him, "Okay, sweetie, I know you think you're explaining yourself, but you're really not." Yet he may not be totally aware that these norms of conversation exist.

19. I would like to thank Andrew Cohen, Tony Doyle, Sydney Johnson, Dean Kowalski, Kay Mathiesen, Bill Taylor, and Dan Zelinski for helpful suggestions on this chapter.

# PART FIVE

# "THE HUMAN EXPERIENCE THAT HAS ALWAYS ELUDED ME": THE HUMAN CONDITION

# MOTHERS AND SONS OF *THE BIG BANG THEORY*

*Ashley Barkman*

Let's face it, Mrs. Koothrappali, Mary Cooper, Mrs. Wolowitz, and Beverly Hofstadter have made their sons "mama's boys"—men who are essentially controlled or unhealthily influenced by their mothers. Consequently, the men of *The Big Bang Theory* linger near the bottom of Maslow's hierarchy of needs, shrinking away from personal growth and fulfillment. They are clueless about true masculinity, which, according to author and physician Leonard Sax, calls for men to use their strength in the service of others.[1] This all makes for good comedy, and it also provides us with the opportunity to explore the psychological and philosophical implications of imbalanced and unreflective relationships between mothers and sons.

## Raj: The "Selective Mutism" Mutant

Raj's parents are traditional, yet worldly. Living in India, they judge and meddle in Raj's life through the webcam lens of their computer. They are concerned about his limited earning potential as an academic and wait impatiently for grandchildren (so, he should not wear the "tighty-whiteys!"). Not bothering to conceal their disappointment in Raj for not being married, they arrange a blind date for him with Lalita Gupta, unaware that he is unable to speak to women (outside of his family) without the help of alcohol (or other meds). Poor Raj is prone to social anxiety and suffers from a "nervous bladder." I wonder why?

Raj simply can't assert himself authoritatively. His sister Priya rekindles her relationship with Leonard in "The Cohabitation Formulation," and Raj "forbids" it. When Leonard goes directly to Raj's apartment to see Priya, Raj does his best to uphold the traditional Hindu Code of Manu, declaring (insofar as he declares anything), "It's completely inappropriate for a single woman to entertain a man in private. If you insist on talking, you must do it on the couch!" They, of course, ignore Raj, who tries again: "All right, you may talk in the bedroom, but I want this door to remain open!" The door slams. Raj keeps up appearances: "All right, just this once you may close the door. But keep in mind I'll be right out here monitoring the situation!" From the couch, he dials his phone and says, "Oh, damn it. Leonard, when you get this message, call me." Perturbed, he again dials his phone and says, "Priya, this is your brother. When you get this, tell Leonard to check his voicemail."

Raj's weak will is reflected in his propensity for addiction—to gaming and to Internet pornography—and his need for alcohol in order to talk to women. His selective mutism, which Beverly Hofstadter says in "The Maternal Capacitance" may "stem from a pathological fear of women," restricts him from growing as a man. Because Raj presumably suffered its symptoms in India, his parents' ignorance of his selective mutism reflects negligence on their part. Indeed, aside from scholarly accomplishments, they have not helped him develop confidence as an adult.

Raj seems to suffer his parents' judgmental meddling in the karmic hope of being "reborn as a well-hung billionaire with wings." Yet perhaps he should first work on being able to talk to women.

## Sheldon: Roots in Fundamental(ist) Particles

Mary Cooper is obviously concerned about Sheldon's welfare. In "The Luminous Fish Effect," she declares, "I love the boy to death," yet she goes on to admit, "but he has been difficult since he fell out of me at the Kmart." She seems to keep tabs on Sheldon, as vividly demonstrated by her premature phone call in "The Electric Can Opener Fluctuation" and Sheldon's response: "Oh, hi, Mom. No, I told you I'd call you when I got home, I'm not home yet. (*Walks through door.*) Alright, I'm home." When she swiftly reminds Sheldon of her concern that he return home safely from the North Pole, he reports, "No, mother, I could not feel your church group praying for my safety. The fact that I'm home safe is not proof that it worked, that logic is Post Hoc Ergo Propter Hoc." He pauses, slightly exasperated. "No, I'm not sassing you in Eskimo talk."

That Mary Cooper deftly manages Sheldon's idiosyncrasies is evidence that he was deeply cherished as a child. When he was sick, she sang "Soft Kitty" to him and applied VapoRub (counterclockwise) on his chest. By way of an improvisation session with Penny, we learn that "Shelly-bean" grew up with a lot of affection and that he loves his "mommy" and looks to her for security and comfort, even as a grown man.

For her part, Mary is grateful that Leonard called her in "The Luminous Fish Effect," alerting her to "Shelly's" latest meltdown. After arriving in California, she is kind to Sheldon—making him his favorite dinner—but also tough, admonishing him to get with it so that he can get his job back. Mary subsequently works her magic on Dr. Gablehauser, sealing the deal (and it remains to be seen whether he will become Sheldon's "new daddy"). The fact that she is able to so quickly repair Sheldon's "nonrelationship" with Amy is testament to how much she loves—and knows—her adult son.

Still, Mary Cooper's relationship difficulties with her husband might have negatively affected Sheldon's upbringing. The parental arguments that he overheard seem to have resulted in trauma, such that even as an adult, Sheldon is deeply uncomfortable witnessing arguments. In "The Guitarist Amplification," for example, we see his extreme discomfort when Penny and Leonard argue, then Howard and Raj, then Raj and his parents, and then Howard and his mother. Sheldon is so sensitive to such arguments that he removes himself from the situation as a frightened child would. Ultimately, Penny and Leonard find him sitting on the floor at Stuart's comic book store, hiding from the source of his discomfort. Poor Sheldon comes home only after Penny and Leonard buy him comics and a toy.

Another source of tension between Sheldon and Mrs. Cooper is her Christian fundamentalist beliefs. Mary always kept the Bible near—including when Sheldon wouldn't eat his brussels sprouts as a child. She sees everything through a religious lens, including Sheldon's intellectual gifts. In "The Luminous Fish Effect," she shares with the gang, "[Sheldon] gets his temper from his daddy. He's got my eyes. All that science stuff, that comes from Jesus." After Sheldon's blow-up with Dr. Gablehauser, Mary visits Sheldon in his room and asks what he's been up to. Sheldon reports that he's been working on what silicon-based DNA would be like. Without skipping a beat, Mary adds, "But if it were created by an intelligent designer, right!"

Sheldon has another breakdown when he discovers the gang falsified his magnetic monopole data in "The Electric Can Opener Fluctuation." His friends have betrayed him, but his mother hasn't, so he travels back to Texas. After making him grilled cheese (complete with a smiley face carved in the bread), Mary requires that they say grace before eating. Sheldon protests, but Mary persists, declaring, "This is not California, land of the heathen. Gimme. By His hand we are all . . ." "Fed," Sheldon mutters. Eyes closed, Mary continues, "Give us, Lord, our daily . . ." "Bread," Sheldon adds. The Coopers are grateful for every cup and every plateful. Mrs. Cooper concludes, "Amen. Now, that wasn't so hard, was it?" Sheldon retorts, "My objection was based on considerations other than difficulty." When Leonard, Raj, and Howard finally arrive to apologize and take Sheldon back to California, Dr. Cooper obstinately reports, "No, I shall stay here and teach evolution to creationists." Mary reminds her son that everyone has their opinion. Sheldon protests, "But evolution is not opinion, it's a fact!" "And that is your opinion!" Mrs. Cooper quickly interjects. Sheldon thus boards the next flight with his friends.

## Howard: A Sociological Cliché

Oblivious to Howard's accomplishments as a successful engineer with a master's from MIT, Mrs. Wolowitz treats her son like a thirty-year-old boy, cooking him dinner every night, doing his laundry, and taking him to the dentist (sometimes going for ice cream afterward.) By treating Howard like a child, Mrs. Wolowitz has made him overly dependent on her, instilling "learned helplessness" in him. Howard may *try* to convince himself and others that his mother doesn't live with him, but Beverly Hofstadter's assessment from "The Maternal Capacitance" rings true: he perpetuates the "sociological cliché" of "a Jewish male living with his mother." Whereas Mary Cooper calls Sheldon on occasion, Howard's mother calls him every day at work to see whether he's had a healthy bowel movement—even though they share a bathroom.

The Wolowitzes have a codependent relationship that Howard can no longer easily escape. In "The Cohabitation Formulation," after making love to Bernadette, Howard announces that he should get going home. When Bernadette suggests he stay the night, Howard is skeptical, saying, "Well, I'd love to, but you know my mother needs me in the morning." Annoyed, Bernadette responds, "Please, I think the woman can manage to put a wig on by herself." Howard presses, "It's not just the wig. It's pinning her hair up, drawing on her eyebrows. It's a two-person job." Ultimately, he "compromises" and agrees to stay another five or ten minutes.

Howard really has no idea how to balance his relationships with his mother and Bernadette. How Bernadette puts up with Howard at all is one of the show's great mysteries. Returning to "The Cohabitation Formulation," he announces to Bernadette,

> Listen, my mom's going to Palm Springs to visit her sister. That's two whole nights in a row I can sleep over with you all the way to morning. Unless the desert air dries out her sinuses, in which case I'll have to schlep out there with the big humidifier.

Flabbergasted, Bernadette replies, "That's it? That's your big solution to all of our problems? If your mom's nose holds up, we get two nights together?" Bernadette finally makes him choose between her and his mother. He hesitates. She leaves. When he (impulsively) reconsiders and they move in together, Howard perfunctorily believes that Bernadette will simply assume the role of his mother, which includes taking him to the dentist. Bernadette throws him out, and Howard schleps home, explaining to his mother that he's not a sex criminal.

One expects a thirty-year-old, gainfully employed man to at least have his own place. There are rumblings of this at "Casa Wolowitz," but they seem to be veiled threats more than anything else—the proverbial (but unspoken): You don't know how good you've got it! Howard should be forging his own path, becoming independent of his mother by finding ways to define himself as a man. Yet instead of encouraging Howard to grow, helping him mature as an individual, Mrs. Wolowitz has encouraged Howard to remain an overgrown child. Even his delusion that he is a ladies' man and his "disgusting" (according to Penny) antics toward women reveal that he has yet to mature.

By the end of season 4, Howard and Bernadette have worked through some of his problems and gotten engaged, but we are left wondering what will happen when Bernadette becomes the breadwinner with the Ph.D. Will Howard become an assertive man, realizing his potential while continually seeking personal growth, or will his mother simply be replaced by Bernadette, whose angry voice now eerily echoes Mrs. Wolowitz's? Whatever the case, Mrs. Wolowitz has failed her son in her inability to see him as a man, to acknowledge his accomplishments, and to encourage his growth toward self-actualization.

## Leonard: Hofstadter's Monkey

Dr. Beverly Hofstadter provides a stark contrast with the other three mothers of *The Big Bang Theory*. She is a successful academic, an accomplished psychiatrist and neuroscientist. Cold and distant, Beverly is extremely frank and has difficulty appreciating or conveying any sort of emotion, including pride in her children's accomplishments. When she informs Leonard's friends in "The Maternal Capacitance" that her son Michael is a tenured law professor at Harvard and her daughter has grown a pancreas in a gibbon, Howard aptly comments, "You must be very proud." Yet she abruptly replies, "Why? They're not my accomplishments." She reacts similarly in "The Maternal Congruence" regarding Michael's upcoming nuptials. Beverly admits that her son's fiancée is "a remarkable girl": the youngest appeals court judge in New Jersey and a two-time Olympic bronze medalist. When Leonard notes, "You must be very happy," she dryly responds, "Why? I'm not marrying her." When glimmers of emotion do surface, she tends to explain them away. When Penny asks about her recent divorce in "The Maternal Congruence," she shares, "I did feel something akin to grief and perhaps anger, but that's the natural reaction of the limbic system by being betrayed by a loathsome son of a bitch."

Beverly Hofstadter likes to perform lab experiments and is quick to do brain scans on those she meets. In fact, research seemingly consumes her. Leonard suffered the brunt of his mother's textbook approach to life, being raised more like a test subject than a son. For example, when Leonard was potty training, Beverly hooked electrodes to Leonard's head to measure his brain waves. Instead of exchanging Christmas presents, his family exchanged research presentations. As Leonard grew older, Beverly started to treat Leonard as if he were something of a colleague. For example, when, as an adolescent, Leonard attempted a science experiment to determine the positive effects of classical music on plant growth, Beverly disparaged him. His experiment was too derivative on his brother's earlier experiment charting the negative effects of rock music on plant growth. Echoing that experience, Beverly chides an adult Leonard for not doing original research, saying that if she wanted to know what the Italians had accomplished, she could just read *their* paper.

To say that Leonard's upbringing lacks maternal warmth is an understatement. When Beverly visits in "The Maternal Capacitance," Leonard asks what's new. Beverly matter-of-factly tells Leonard that his favorite uncle died. Looking back,

Leonard shares, "The only warm memories I have of my child-hood are of my Uncle Floyd." Leonard subsequently confides in Penny that he'd once built a "hugging machine." He found a manikin, wrapped it in an electric blanket, and fashioned it with two mechanical arms, all in the hope of providing himself with simulated warmth. The truly sad and funny thing was that his dad borrowed it. Leonard's invention is reminiscent of a famous psychology experiment in which young monkeys preferred a cloth-wrapped wireframe mother to a sterile and bare wireframe mother. Some semblance of warmth and comfort is better than none, and Leonard (as well as his  father) would agree.

Aside from giving birth to children, Beverly has no other maternal inclination. She remains emotionally detached from the world and from her children. Leonard, as a product of an affectionless childhood, remains socially underdeveloped, especially toward women. He is often manipulated by the women in his life, from Joyce Kim (the North Korean Spy) to Leslie Winkle to Dr. Stephanie Barnett to Mrs. Latham (the wealthy donor) to Penny and Priya. As a result of his mother's overly critical and analytical approach, he is often fearful of expressing his opinion, especially if he disagrees with what others say. He seeks affirmation but can find it only in the praise he receives from his experimental physics work.

## Aristotle, Justice, and Special Obligations

Plato (428–348 BCE) and Aristotle (384–322 BCE) tended to see injustice as a kind of inequality that occurred when someone didn't receive what he or she deserved, given that person's social role or station. In this account, a son (or a daughter) is owed certain treatment from a parent exactly because he (or she) is that person's child, and an adult son (or daughter) is owed treatment distinct from that due him/her as a child. Clearly, the mothers of *The Big Bang Theory* have failed in treating their sons properly. Raj, Sheldon, Howard, and Leonard have thus been treated unjustly.

Aristotle held that the wrongs against those close to us are worse than wrongs against strangers. He said that our moral obligations, at least in part, are shaped by our personal relationships:

> The duties of parents to children and those of brothers to each other are not the same nor those of comrades and those of fellow-citizens, and so, too, with other kinds of friendship . . . and the injustice increases by being exhibited toward those who are friends in a fuller sense; e.g., it is a more terrible thing to defraud a comrade than a fellow-citizen, more terrible not to help a brother than a stranger, and more terrible to wound a father than anyone else.[2]

Consequently, the wounds suffered at the hands of one's parents are "more terrible" than similar wounds inflicted by strangers. On this score, the harm Sheldon suffers at the hands of Todd Zarnecki is less significant than, say, the harm Leonard suffered as a result of Beverly's maternal neglect.

Some contemporary philosophers press Aristotle's point to argue that our obligations and the severity of breaking them are completely defined by the closeness of our personal relationships.[3] This view becomes problematic, however, given the common-sense intuition that we have at least minimal moral obligations to complete strangers. Zarnecki does something wrong in liberating Sheldon from his *World of Warcraft* (virtual) belongings. Even so, this doesn't negate the other common-sense intuition that the wrongs a parent does to his or her child are somehow "more terrible" than they otherwise might be.

Even if our moral obligations are not completely defined by the closeness of our relationships, parents nevertheless do seem to have special obligations to their children. A parent is obligated to care for his or her child in ways that other adults are not. When Sheldon has one of his meltdowns, we wouldn't fault Mrs. Koothrappali for not making the trip from India to attend to him. She's not his mother, after all. If a parent's moral obligations in caring for his or her child include taking steps to ensure that the child matures in healthy ways, then clearly the mothers of *The Big Bang Theory* may be (to some degree) morally blameworthy for their respective sons' social and psychological shortcomings.

## Cognitive Dissonance and Psychological Courage

Assuming that something has gone morally astray between *The Big Bang Theory* mothers and their sons, how did it occur and what, if anything, might be done about it *now*? Any definitive analysis would require carefully exploring family histories. Short of that, and given only what we know of the characters through season 4, it seems that "cognitive dissonance" is partly to blame, calling for "psychological courage" on part of the mothers and their respective sons.

According to cognitive dissonance theory, there are occasions when we feel the tension of two clashing beliefs or mental cognitions that thereby call for resolution. The negative effects of cognitive dissonance are felt when a person is emotionally invested in a belief, but new evidence arises that creates conflict with it. It's easy to imagine how each of *The Big Bang Theory* mothers might have experienced this. It must have been difficult for Mrs. Koothrappali to realize that her son's best professional interests are served by working at a research university in America. How will she impress on him her traditional values? Likewise, Mary Cooper is clearly invested in her Christian fundamentalist worldview. What should she do once she realizes that her genius son may one day win a Nobel Prize in science? What if Sheldon's studies clash with the faith-based beliefs she's impressed on him? After Mr. Wolowitz departed, Mrs. Wolowitz became very invested in her son's well-being. It's easy to see how she wouldn't want any harm to come to him. Yet he is slowly becoming an adult, the new (or next) Mr. Wolowitz. Beverly is most comfortable in the laboratory and prizes a scientific and analytical approach to the world. Yet she has children at home who require her care.

How should a parent deal with cognitive dissonance regarding his or her children? According to contemporary philosopher Daniel Putman, the quick answer is: honestly.[4] The parent should not ignore the evidence, hide behind some social role, or implement some sort of ad hoc additional belief to deflect the tension. This kind of honesty requires "psychological courage," though.

Aristotle advised that courage should become part of our overall character so that we can properly address threatening situations that involve physical harm or moral integrity. Yet psychological courage is unique, in that the fear we must face properly concerns the loss of psychological stability; in some ways, one's psyche itself is threatened. As Putman explains, "This is the courage it takes to face our irrational fears and anxieties, those emotions that hold us in bondage. These can range from habits and compulsions to phobias."[5]

Accordingly, a lack of honesty, falling prey to self-deception, can result in a lack of personal autonomy, but practicing psychological courage can ensure that each of us is the owner of his or her own life. Mary Cooper might attempt discussions about the rationality of religious belief—including, perhaps, reasons behind the "Big Bang"—rather than reverting to her methods of indoctrination. Mrs. Wolowitz must be honest with herself that Howard is not "her little boy" anymore. In fact, he is about (it seems) to get married. Being honest with herself about her son's new role will (potentially) allow her new and exciting ways to care for him and his family. Beverly should stop hiding behind her professional role and realize that expressing emotion (while sober) will not make her any less of an academic. It will not hamper her abilities to impartially process data, and doing so can only aid Leonard's emotional stability.

Of course, the benefits of psychological courage also apply to *The Big Bang Theory* sons. Consider Sheldon's propensity to delve into the world of comic books when those around him bicker and fight. This avoidance defense mechanism was put into place long ago, due to the dissonance he experienced about his parents' constant arguments. Mom and Dad seem to love one another, but why do they fight all of the time? Furthermore, perhaps he could work harder to find ways to enter into give-and-take *discussions* with his mother about religious belief. Jesus will still love him, if Mary is right. Raj should seek counseling for his selective mutism and come clean to his parents about his communication difficulties with attractive women (or even effeminate men). Howard can no longer hide behind the role of son any longer. He must begin to act more like man. Of course, he is comforted by his mother buying him popsicles and making him mouth-watering brisket, but he is about to become a husband and, potentially, a parent himself. He may soon begin to buy popsicles for the next Mr. Wolowitz—*his* son! (Yikes!).

Despite the fact that he received the least amount of motherly attention and concern, Leonard has come the furthest in terms of practicing psychological courage. Recall in "The Maternal Congruence" his candid questions of Beverly, "How come you didn't tell me that you and Father were getting a divorce? How come you didn't tell me you had surgery? How come you didn't tell me my dog died?" Despite his fear of facing rejection—again—he confronts Beverly in the hope of a more intimate mother-son relationship. Beverly begins to reciprocate by giving him an uncomfortable hug but then states, "There. It's late. Now, go to bed. I'm getting a warm feeling spreading through my heart." Leonard dutifully does as she asks, but Sheldon enters the scene shortly afterward to ask, "Why is Leonard softly banging his head against his bedroom door?"

The courage Leonard expresses can only benefit his future relationship with his mother. Leonard's courage has helped him in the past when he successfully wooed Penny (at least for a while—despite Sheldon's "haughty derision"). Remarkably, he maintains a healthy sense of humor, gets annoyed at Sheldon but doesn't hold grudges, and is still empathetic. If Leonard continues to deal honestly with his relationships issues, perhaps his friends will follow his lead. Let's face it, he's pretty much their only hope.

## NOTES

1. Leonard Sax, *Boys Adrift: The Five Factors Driving the Growing Epidemic of Unmotivated Boys and Underachieving Young Men* (New York: Basic Books, 2009), 181.

2. Aristotle, *Nicomachean Ethics*, trans. W. D. Ross (Oxford: Oxford University Press, 1925), 1160a1–1160a6.

3. See, for example, Nel Noddings, *Caring: A Feminine Approach to Ethics and Moral Education* (Berkeley: University of California Press, 1984).

4. See Daniel Putman, *Psychological Courage* (Lanham, MD: University Press of America, 2004).

5. Ibid., 2.

# PENNY, SHELDON, AND PERSONAL GROWTH THROUGH DIFFERENCE

*Nicholas G. Evans*

The most interesting friendship in *The Big Bang Theory* is also the most surprising: Penny and Sheldon. Penny is carefree and lax, whereas Sheldon is neurotic and rigid. Strained and turbulent, the friendship struggles amid their differences, often to comic effect. Consider "The Panty Piñata Polarization," in which Penny earns her second "Sheldon-strike" by purposely handling some of Sheldon's takeout food. Not to be deterred, Penny immediately plops herself down in Sheldon's "0–0–0–0" spot on the couch, earning her third strike, at which point Sheldon banishes her from the apartment. Penny retaliates by simultaneously using all of the washing machines on Sheldon's laundry night, and Sheldon counters by displaying her "female undergarments" on a nearby phone line, chortling, "Mua-ha-ha." The conflict spirals out of control, as an unstoppable force—Penny's stubbornness—meets an immovable object: Sheldon's idiosyncrasies. To "shorten the war by five years and save millions of lives," Leonard covertly provides Penny with Sheldon's kryptonite: his mother's phone number. Penny calls Mrs. Cooper, who, in turn, calls her son. Sheldon is powerless to resist (and he still is unsure of what Jesus thinks). He slowly walks across the hall and warily congratulates Penny, saying, "Well played." She slowly nods in acknowledgment, whispering, "Thank you." Mutual respect and friendship thus take shape.

Difference is an important but sometimes underappreciated feature of friendship. Difference pushes us to discover more about ourselves by exposing us to alternate ways of valuing life. Throughout the series, the friendship between Penny and Sheldon has been rocky, but it has always maintained an authenticity that has caused the characters to grow. Moreover, the other friendships don't provide the same types of opportunities for discovering more about the characters and, more important, ourselves.

## Are Penny and Sheldon Really Friends?

Even though Sheldon sometimes acts for the sake of, or due to the conventions he believes exist around, friendship, it's not clear that Sheldon has any friends. In the "Middle Earth Paradigm," Sheldon surmises that friendship entails having "one's back" during confrontation and providing tea to the upset, and platitudes to the upset, such as "There, there," although he admits that beyond this point, his abilities to conform to convention lapse. In "The Jerusalem Duality," he goes so far as to declare, "While Mr. Kim . . . has fallen prey to the inexplicable need for human contact . . . social relationships will continue to baffle and repulse me." This calls into question whether Sheldon possesses the capacity for friendship. Even if a glimmer of the relevant capacities subsists, Sheldon also has well-established interpersonal problems. Recall Sheldon's claim in "The Desperation Emanation" about his roommate: "Leonard, you are my best friend. I've known you for seven years, and I can barely tolerate sitting on the couch with you." If Sheldon's friendship with Leonard—undoubtedly the most enduring in the show—is still fraught with problems such as a strong aversion to physical proximity (much less physical contact!), we might think that genuine friendship with Penny is almost impossible.

Friendship has interested philosophers ever since that "warm summer evening" in ancient Greece—that is, at least as far back as Aristotle (384–322 BCE).[1] Philosophical approaches deal with friendship as a relationship that involves intimacy and particular attitudes toward people. In ancient times, this was commonly characterized by the Greek concept of *philia*, the affection between two individuals (contrasted with *eros*, which is typically sexual in nature, or *agape*, which is a different type of love, such as the type of love Christians might think God has for humanity).[2] Much debate about friendship, then and now, is about what makes friendship different from, say, our relationships with acquaintances or romantic partners.

Three aspects of friendship seem universal. The first is mutual care; what defines friendship is the shared affection between two friends. Romantic affection might be one-sided, with bedfellows Howard Wolowitz and Leslie Winkle coming to mind, but you can't be friends with someone if you do not both care about each other in some respect.

The second aspect is intimacy. Friendships are intimate, in the sense that they are a deeper kind of relationship than mere acquaintances. Precisely what constitutes this intimacy is debatable. It may be that friends are intimate in the sense that they function as "mirrors" for each other, providing a perspective on their character and self-concept. Alternately, it could be through the sharing of secrets or sensitive personal information. For example in "The Bad Fish Paradigm," Penny rather abruptly asks Sheldon "as a friend" to conceal from Leonard the fact that she did not complete community college. Sheldon quizzically replies, "So, you're saying that friendship contains within it an inherent obligation to maintain confidences?" When Penny quickly responds, "Well, yeah," Sheldon redirects, "When did we become friends?" (He seemingly wishes to verify that he has incurred an obligation.) Or, and perhaps most intuitively, it seems that friends are intimate in the sense that they direct and interpret each other's conduct. One participates in activities with friends that one might not otherwise because this is part of what it is to be friends with someone.

On a related note, the third aspect constitutive of friendship is shared activity. Two people are considered friends, in part, when they are mutually involved with projects or parts of each other's lives. Even in remote or nonparadigm cases of friendship, such as "pen-pals," the action of becoming friends involves setting aside time for mutual or coordinated activity (for example, writing letters or even sharing Facebook time).

This isn't the place to engage in questions of (a) which of these properties of friendship are central or most important to an account of friendship, or (b) how much of each property (say, what strength of intimacy) serves to mark the line between friends and "more than friends".[3] Rather, we need to consider in which of the three ways Sheldon and Penny are friends.

It seems clear that as far as Sheldon displays affection to people at all, he does so with Penny. His affections toward her are obviously disproportionate with his other relationships (including Amy). He even expresses sincere gratitude: Sheldon hugs Penny, not once but twice! The rarity of this is confirmed by Leonard's affirmation: "It's a Saturnalia miracle!"[4] Moreover, Sheldon's interactions with Penny often display a sense of care we don't see with others. In "The Adhesive Duck Deficiency," he helps Penny when she slips in the bathtub, which includes driving her to the hospital, despite his insistence that "I don't drive" and his horror at Penny's check engine light ablaze. In "The Gorilla Experiment," he agrees to teach her "a little physics" (as if there were such a thing)—even though his time is "both limited and valuable"—simply because she wishes to impress Leonard.

Perhaps the strongest indication of Penny and Sheldon's friendship is the directive and interpretive aspects of their relationship—what makes their friendship intimate. Penny and Sheldon do not act as static characters—rather, episodes often center on the changes that each undergoes in the course of their relationship. Penny, for example, becomes more sensitive to Sheldon's supposed idiosyncrasies. When Bernadette, Howard's girlfriend, is introduced to the central group of friends in "The Gorilla Experiment," Penny—independently of Sheldon's guidance or intervention—perfunctorily explains the significance of Sheldon's "0–0–0–0" spot to her. And of course, we cannot forget her haunting rendition of "Soft Kitty," complete with applying menthol vapor rub (counterclockwise, lest Sheldon's chest hairs mat), when Sheldon becomes ill in "The Pancake Batter Anomaly."

Sheldon, for his part, is drawn into situations in which Penny's actions test him. For example, in "The Adhesive Duck Deficiency," Sheldon only briefly points out that her dislocated shoulder was caused (in part) by the lack of friction on her shower floor. Rather than belabor that point, he moves to navigate (and not reorganize) Penny's room, handle her wardrobe (even though her panties are not organized per days of the week), and, of course, somehow manage her nudity (even though he seems to have difficulty discerning arms from other nearby body parts). Sheldon's trials and tribulations continue, as he must next (somehow) quash his mysophobia (fear of germs) while waiting with Penny in the hospital, and (albeit awkwardly) comfort her as they wait for the doctor to examine her shoulder. Yet there's more. When they return to Penny's apartment, he sings "Soft Kitty" to her (even though she's not technically sick). If that weren't enough, they sing it together, in the round! Their relationship is now cemented; insofar as Sheldon has any friends, Penny is certainly among them.

## Penny's and Sheldon's Friendship and the Importance of Difference

The friendship Penny and Sheldon enjoy, though genuine, is marked by deep personal differences. Sheldon is meticulous, hyperintellectual, clean, and obsessive. Penny is messy, emotive, at times willfully ignorant, and tends to wing things more than she plans them. Nevertheless, Penny and Sheldon grow, not despite their differences and conflicting characters, but *because* of these differences.[5] Consider Sheldon from season 1 (or, to Leonard's recollection, seven years previous when Leonard first met Sheldon), and the difficulties he had with Penny and his other friends. These difficulties persist, of that there is no question. Yet how far he has come! His jokes are more numerous and more self-aware. His claim to "having more tics than a Lyme disease facility" in "The Bad Fish Paradigm" is actually quite clever (and a Sheldon Cooper original). He is far less prone to tantrums and even has a modicum of social awareness. In "The Agreement Dissection," he agrees to go dancing with Penny, Bernadette, and Amy. Sheldon's conduct with female characters develops—he copes with being kissed by Beverly Hofstader and later by Amy Farrah Fowler.[6] If there lay a continuum of character, Penny and Sheldon's progression on this continuum would be toward each other. This is not to say they become the same; rather, they develop parts of their character through their interaction that they would not otherwise develop.

There are things Sheldon simply could not learn from, say, his friendship with Amy that he can through Penny, precisely because of the conflict it produces. Sheldon, for example, is unlikely to learn about valuing people for their own sake from Amy, who is just as willing to instrumentalize others for her own curiosity as Sheldon is. Just think of "The Herb Garden Germination," when they spread lies in order to track the memetic origins of gossip. With Penny, Sheldon is forced to accept that sometimes we do things *out of* or *for the sake of* friendship, not simply in the process of going through the motions of being friends. This produces a change in Sheldon during the course of the series that simply wouldn't happen if Penny wasn't in Sheldon's life.

Someone might object, though, that this isn't distinctive about friends. All sorts of people offer us reflections or differences. If it is only our reflection in others that causes change, presumably everyone, at least in theory, would change us. What makes friends special in this regard?

Here the idea of direction and interpretation comes into play. It is not enough that I am enlightened as to my own character through my friends by virtue of our differences. Conflict between friends is transformative because the reasons we come into conflict with our friends *are reasons that matter to those friends*. If I upset my friend and do not care that I have upset my friend, then most of us would say I'm not much of a friend at all! (Sheldon at least suffered from digestive distress—"he couldn't poop"—when he and Leonard were feuding in the season 1 episode "The Cooper-Hofstadter Polarization.") Part of being friends is being directed and interpreted by them— valuing what happens to them because it happens to *them*. This direction and interpretation is not the goal of friendship or what we do out of friendship, but rather what we do because we are friends.

Our families change us, but often we are not given the same opportunities for growth through our families—we and our family members are more alike than we might like to admit. Our romantic partners also give us opportunity for growth, but serious differences can jeopardize romantic relationships. We are just that much more vulnerable to our partners or spouses than to our friends, and, as such, differences that might aggravate us about friends can end romantic relationships. Sheldon's obvious intellectual prowess is a challenge for his and Penny's friendship, but Leonard's intellectual prowess plays off Penny's insecurities to the point that she ends their romantic relationship.

## Modern and Classical Friendship

By stressing the differences between friends, this view departs significantly from more classical views. Aristotle, in particular, believed that each of his three forms of friendship is grounded in similarity. Perhaps you are friends with someone because each of you finds the other witty or pleasant in some way. Perhaps you are friends with someone because each of you shares a common goal, for example, splitting the cost of rent or gas by carpooling—much as Sheldon and Leonard do. Aristotle provided a similar analysis for his highest form of friendship. True or complete friends, he claimed, are similar, in that they share a project of approaching *eudaimonia*, which today we generally understand as flourishing or the best way to live.

Yet my view is not a complete departure from more classical views such as Aristotle's. The coming together of viewpoints and values is still part of my account of what friends accomplish together and value in each other. With Penny and Sheldon, both begin (and remain) flawed people—people just like you and me, which may indeed be what makes them such compelling characters! Sheldon, insofar as he could pursue Aristotle's eudaimonia at all, would be much more comfortable doing so with Leonard Nimoy (or at least Spock!) than with Penny. Penny couldn't be further from his ideal. Moreover, there are too many differences between Penny and Sheldon for them to enjoy true friendship—at least according to Aristotle.

During the course of the show, however, Sheldon's and Penny's commitment to shared values grows through disagreement and resolution. More important, though, is the dynamic tension they continue to exhibit—Sheldon still wants to win his Nobel Prize and can't understand someone wanting to be an actor; Penny has no desire to become a string theorist and pursues her dream of acting. Yet in attempting to reach their various pinnacles of existence, they come to value each other's motivations as plausible (if not personally attractive) ways of flourishing as the distinct individuals they are.

Sheldon and Penny understandably have distinct interests, but without the growth they display—growth achieved through their friendship—we (the veiwers) would probably disparage their initial attempts at leading the good life. With the benefit of hindsight, Sheldon and Penny would probably agree that their initial ways of living were (respectively) deficient. Moreover, it is not obvious that Sheldon's initial unemotional, near-sociopathic rationality is any better than Penny's antiscientific, emotional, and impulsive nature. Without their friendship, they are unable to grow out of what they come to recognize—begrudgingly!—as unacceptable ways of living.

So, understanding friendship primarily in terms of our differences is distinct from more classic views in three ways. First, it allows for a wider appreciation of the various ways people can suitably live. Second, it places value on ways to flourish that aren't—and never will be—our own. Third, it allows for more vivid insights into and self-reflection about the rightness or wrongness of our own ways of living. This departure, then, is primarily a consequence of a more modern and pluralistic interpretation of what it is to live a morally good life. A central tenet of classical thought remains—that friends are so valuable because their and our own flourishing are valued by us, and they can help us flourish. What has changed is how varied that flourishing might be, and how our friends help us realize what corrections we might make in our own beliefs about the good life.

## Good Friendship and Good Friends

Close or strong friendships are conducive to moral development. This is, in part, what makes the relationship between Penny and Sheldon so important. They aren't merely good at being friends—they are friends who make each other (morally) better people. In our modern world, especially with the ascendance of online culture, friendships can—literally—begin and end with the click of a button. Though they could move away from each other when things get rough, as Sheldon attempts to do in "The Bozeman Reaction," or forcibly ignore or avoid each other, as when Sheldon banishes Penny from the apartment in "The Panty Piñata Polarization," they don't end their friendship. Despite their differences, Penny and Sheldon's friendship doesn't merely survive, it thrives.

Our capacity for growth leaves us vulnerable to our friends; the opportunity to change invites the opportunity to be hurt along the way. Yet this is surely something important about friendships. Unless we are so narcissistic as to presume our own perfection or so averse to risk that we couldn't stand even the chance of being hurt, the way we grow with and through our friends is to our benefit. And without diversity and difference between friends, as Penny and Sheldon have shown us, our growth will be limited.

This is not to say that any old difference will do. Much as there are conditions under which friendships are formed, there are deal breakers as well. A person might not be able to be friends with those who discriminate against her. Likewise, a person might not be able to be friends with someone whose sense of justice is absent or radically different. There are differences that preclude friendship, but these differences are surely extreme cases.

In contrast, personal interests, natural abilities, political affiliations (except the most extreme kinds), religious orientations, and other differences surely serve as the basis for growth.

Of course, this requires an attitude of acceptance, of the kind we see developing in the friendship between Penny and Sheldon. If we can learn to emulate them, our lives will certainly grow in the richness that the contrast of beliefs within a genuinely caring friendship can produce.

## NOTES

1. For more on Aristotle's classic views of friendship, cast largely as they are in similarities between those who are friends, please see chapter 2 in this volume, "You're a Sucky, Sucky Friend," by Dean A. Kowalski.

2. A quality summary of these and other philosophical approaches to friendship (and, indeed, much of philosophy) can be found in the *Stanford Encyclopedia of Philosophy*. See Bennett Helm, "Friendship," *The Stanford Encyclopedia of Philosophy* (Fall 2009 Edition), Edward N. Zalta (ed.), <http://plato.stanford.edu/archives/fall2009/entries/friendship/>.

3. For a discussion of this, see Bennett Helm, *Love, Friendship, and the Self* (Oxford: Oxford University Press, 2010); Sandra Lynch, *Philosophy and Love* (Edinburgh: Edinburgh University Press, 2005); and Dean Cocking and Jeanette Kennett, "Friendship and the Self," *Journal of Philosophy* 108 (1998): 502–527.

4. The first hug and Leonard's acknowledgment of it appear in "The Bath Item Gift Hypothesis." The second hug appears in "The Large Hadron Collision."

5. Todd VanDerWerff of the A.V. Club has noted that Jim Parsons and Kayley Cuoco form one of the standout relationships in the show, that "[Parsons and Cuoco have] a chemistry here that has some of the rattle and rhythm of the great comedic duos, and while I think the people on the Internet who want Sheldon and Penny to get together are pretty much insane, I can see what they're feeding off of." See Todd VanDerWerff, "The Adhesive Duck Deficiency," the A.V. Club, November 17, 2009, <www.avclub.com/articles/the-adhesive-duck-deficiency,35454/>.

6. See, respectively, "The Maternal Congruence" and "The Agreement Dissection."

# DECONSTRUCTING THE WOMEN OF *THE BIG BANG THEORY:* SO MUCH MORE THAN GIRLFRIENDS

*Mark D. White and Maryanne L. Fisher*

Gender is a big deal for *The Big Bang Theory*. At first glance, viewers might see Penny, Bernadette, Amy, and the other women on the show as merely the sidekicks who help flesh out the leading men: Penny is the on-and-off girlfriend of Leonard, Bernadette dates Wolowitz, Amy is "with" Sheldon (at least in some quasi-Vulcan capacity), and Leslie is one of Leonard's earlier and very memorable sexual partners. Yet these women are so much more than just girlfriends and even more than colleagues, friends, or neighbors—they also embody a constellation of feminist issues concerning sex, gender, and behavioral expectations.

In addition to teaching us a little quantum physics, dropping loads of sci-fi and superhero trivia, and giving us lots of laughs, *The Big Bang Theory* can also help us illustrate gender theory, especially in the way the show uses the wide range of characters, female *and* male, to challenge our traditional ideas about what it means to be a man or a woman. More precisely, this chapter will explore, with the help of some major figures in feminist philosophy, the ways in which the female characters push the boundaries of what it means to be "feminine" or "a woman." (And don't worry, we won't leave out the men!)

## The *Big Bang* Gender Theory

Feminist scholars, including philosophers, often make a hard distinction between a person's *sex*, which is biological, and a person's *gender*, which is social or political. By this, we mean that unlike sex, a person's gender is not determined by her or his chromosomes but rather by how other people and society in general choose to categorize her or him, as well as how that person chooses to categorize her- or himself. On one hand, while a person's sex can be fairly easily seen by peeking in her or his undies, that same person's gender is a much more complicated affair. Yet on the other hand, gender is more amenable to change, either by an individual person's changing her or his appearance, mannerisms, or attitudes, or through a broader societal shift (such as women's movements).

The most straightforward example of this in *The Big Bang Theory* is Louis/Louise, Sheldon and Leonard's neighbor in apartment 4B before Penny moved in, whom we see for the first time in one of the flashback scenes from "The Staircase Implementation." Biologically, "Louis" is obviously a very large man, but by dressing as a woman, "Louise" has chosen to adopt the female gender in her outward appearance. Because we don't spend much time with Louis/Louise—do I smell a prequel series, anybody?—it's impossible to know which gender he/she identifies with internally. Nonetheless, the insight of the distinction between sex and gender is that Louis/ Louise does not necessarily have to adopt the male gender simply because of his male biology.

It's not only Louis/Louise, though. Almost all of the characters on *The Big Bang Theory* break stereotypes about how men and women are "supposed" to be or act. Penny is the "normal" one of the bunch, which, ironically, makes her stand out as "abnormal." The men all possess various traits commonly thought of as feminine (such as Leonard's sensitivity), and, aside from Penny, the women possess traditionally male traits (such as Leslie's sexual aggressiveness). None of the men is particularly athletic or "dominant," and most of the women (with the exception of Penny) are very intelligent—portrayals that stand against common perceptions of the "essence" of men and women.[1]

## "It's a Warm Summer Evening in Ancient Greece . . ."

Though the point has been reinforced and refined by modern feminist scholars, the distinction between sex and gender goes back at least as far as Sheldon's proverbial "warm summer evening in ancient Greece" from "The Gorilla Experiment." In *The Republic*, Plato (424–347 BCE) argued that the biological differences between men and women—that "the female bears and the male begets"—are not relevant for the issue of occupation. Indeed, Plato challenges those who think otherwise to provide a valid reason why women (in general) cannot perform the same tasks as men.[2] More directly, the philosopher John Stuart Mill (1806–1873) wrote in *The Subjection of Women* that "Standing on the ground of common sense and the constitution of the human mind, I deny that anyone knows, or can know, the nature of the two sexes. . . . What is now called the nature of women is an eminently artificial thing."[3] Although

Mill noted the potential oppression in defining "women" as men prefer, modern feminists have emphasized the point, arguing that formal equality between the sexes does not guarantee real equality because the common perception of women in society, and even among women themselves, has been formed historically by men and cannot simply be revoked as if it were a law.[4]

In modern times, the most influential philosopher to write on issues of gender has been Simone de Beauvoir (1908–1986), whose 1952 book *The Second Sex* set the tone for feminist philosophy and scholarship from that point on. The most famous line in the book, "One is not born, but rather becomes, a woman," is a memorable and highly influential statement of the distinction between sex and gender.[5] Beauvoir described the status of women in society as "the Other," defined by men in comparison to men, thereby condemned to being the "second sex." In the spirit of *existentialism* and its emphasis on self-creation and radical freedom, Beauvoir called on women to take control of their identities and define themselves as they want to be, not as men have wanted them to be, and not to let their biology determine their destinies.[6]

In her 1989 book *Gender Trouble*, contemporary philosopher and theorist Judith Butler built on Beauvoir's description of the sex/gender distinction and added her own unique twist.[7] Butler's chief contribution was the concept of *performativity*: gender is merely a matter of performance, in which the categories of "woman" and "man" are defined only by how people behave (or "perform" them), without any prior foundation. Like Beauvoir, Butler's position is *antiessentialist*: there are no essentially female or male characteristics, but instead, men and women are expected to behave in certain ways, deeply rooted in historical inequality and promoted by those in power—men—in order to maintain that power over others (or the Other), namely, women. By "following the script" laid out by men, women only perpetuate these patterns of discrimination and oppression. Furthermore, not only is there no essential difference between the female and male genders, there is, in fact, no "female gender" (or "male gender") at all. Each person is unique, and it is up to each person to choose how to live her or his life, following the performance of any gender (which, Butler also argues, is not necessarily limited to the familiar two).[8]

## *The Big Bang* Performativity

Now let's look at how the women of *The Big Bang Theory* "perform" their "roles," starting with Penny. Penny is pretty, sweet, perky, and all things we traditionally think of as feminine: the perfect California girl (just by way of Nebraska). Though she is very funny, both clever and quick (especially when knocking Sheldon down a few pegs), she isn't particularly bright in the same way as Leonard or Sheldon. Consider her job as a waitress at the Cheesecake Factory. In "The Maternal Congruence," she had to (gasp) memorize the menu: "Hey, it's a big menu. There's two pages just for desserts." Her unlikely relationship with Leonard shows that she can see beneath the geeky surface. Yet as she did in "The Precious Fragmentation," she sometimes doubts herself, quipping, "I need to go back to dating dumb guys from the gym."

Her portrayal is achingly stereotypical, but perhaps that's the point. Her femininity—or, to be more precise, her performance of femininity, in literal terms, as well as Butler's—can be seen as satirical.[9] Compared with Beauvoir, Butler was very pessimistic about the prospects for self-creation and eventual freedom from the chains of patriarchal oppression. She wrote that it is impossible to escape gender altogether, but one can satirize it, and in that way one can achieve a tiny bit of political change through parody.[10] So Penny's nuanced portrayal of "the girl next door," sweet and pretty, who nonetheless shows glimpses of the traditionally male qualities of wisdom and biting humor, may be seen in the spirit of Butler's call for satirizing gender norms.

As we move to the other women on the show, we can see that as they get smarter, they also become (slightly) less physically attractive. For instance, take Bernadette, Howard's on-and-off girlfriend—and, as of the end of season 4, his fiancée. She's definitely smarter than Penny—so much so that Penny feels threatened and asks Sheldon for physics lessons in "The Gorilla Experiment"—but not too smart, so that she doesn't threaten traditional notions of how being feminine and being intelligent aren't "supposed" to mix. She's also very pretty but in a more subtle way than Penny—rather than wearing tight tank tops and short shorts, Bernadette rocks the sweater vest-eyeglasses combination. She can ask pointed questions about Leonard's physics experiment with big eyes and a girly smile. Just as easily, she can say with wry humor, as she did in "The Boyfriend Complexity": "Oh, I was working with penicillin-resistant gonorrhea in the lab today, and I was just trying to remember if I washed my hands."

One step further to the end of the smarts-looks continuum—that's two blocks over from the spacetime continuum, if you're wondering—and we reach Amy. Her complete lack of glamour, the way she pronounces her multiple-syllable words without the typical default girl smile and fake stumble, and the fact that she is considered Sheldon's "girl-who-is-a-friend," make her the least traditionally feminine of the three women. This is further reinforced by her social awkwardness: she lacks all of Penny's ease; she is unconcerned with her appearance, compared to Penny or Bernadette; and she is roughly Sheldon's intellectual equal.[11] Definitely not what mainstream society expects from a female—in fact, exactly the opposite, highlighting the absurdity of gender expectations that deny a smart but not conventionally attractive female the full status of "woman."

## "Come for the Breasts—Stay for the Brains."

Through these three female characters, we see a range of attractiveness and intelligence but always in inverse proportion: the prettiest is not very smart, and the smartest is not very pretty. Although Penny best fits the traditional notion of femininity—sweet, pretty, and not too smart—more broadly speaking, all three affirm the stereotype that very beautiful, feminine women cannot be smart and very smart women cannot be beautiful or feminine. The best we can hope for, by this logic, is someone like Bernadette, who is smart "enough" and pretty "enough," but not exceedingly one or the other. Nothing against Bernadette, but this expectation of a "trade-off" between beauty and looks (as well as confidence, poise, and so on) is nonetheless a limitation imposed by custom and history on women and represents part of the artificiality of gender.

Luckily, *The Big Bang Theory* also provides us with examples of women who break this pattern. Consider the vivacious Elizabeth Plimpton, who is Sheldon's personal guest, due to her renowned work on cosmological physics. She's drop-dead gorgeous and sexy but at the same time incredibly smart—*and* sexually promiscuous, breaking another traditional feminine stereotype by sleeping with Leonard and Raj in short order (and hoping for a foursome with them and Howard). Like Bernadette, she's a bit scatterbrained: for example, when meeting Sheldon at his apartment in "The Plimpton Stimulation," she says, "I completely forgot your address, but then I remembered that I'd written it on my hand. Lucky for me, I didn't confuse it with what I'd written on my other hand, which are the coordinates for a newly discovered neutron star. 'Cause if I tried to go there, I'd be crushed by hypergravity." In combining amazing looks, intelligence, and sexual appetite with just a side of ditziness for flavor, Dr. Plimpton breaks the broader stereotype that women should be pretty or smart but not both—and *definitely* not sexually aggressive.

Unfortunately, Elizabeth appears in only one episode, but that is more than made up for by Leslie Winkle, a fellow research scientist at the university, Leonard's occasional sex partner, and one of the banes of Sheldon's existence. Like Amy, she's on Sheldon's general level intellectually, but she also has Penny's cleverness in her verbal jousts with him (especially when she deflates his pomposity with a well-placed "dumbass"). Her attractiveness is not overbearing and seems completely casual—her confidence shines through her tossed-together appearance. Although not on the level of Elizabeth Plimpton in her carnal appetites, Leslie is "sexually liberated," perfectly content to have casual encounters with Leonard as well as Howard, who accuses her in "The Cushion Saturation" of using him as a "bought-and-sold sex toy," to which she replies, "No, not at all. You're also arm candy." In "The Hamburger Postulate," she describes her appeal as a smart, attractive woman with the phrase "come for the breasts, stay for the brains."[12] In this sense, Leslie stands as the feminist icon of the show: a very smart, confident, attractive, and sexually assertive woman who constructs her own identity, regardless of what the men around her may think.

### Knock Knock . . . Manhood?
### Knock Knock . . . Manhood?
### Knock Knock . . . Manhood?

Before we wrap this episode and get ready for the production note, let's not forget the men of *The Big Bang Theory*, who challenge traditional ideas about gender no less than the women do. Because scholars such as Beauvoir and Butler focus on women's gender issues and how the term *woman* and everything connected to it is defined in relation to "man," issues concerning the male gender naturally receive less attention. Yet setting aside the topics of power and oppression, men can be subject to the same problems with gender roles and expectations as women (even if the consequences are different).

In fact, not one of the four lead men in the series fits the stereotypical picture of a "man." Although they're all very smart (except in Sheldon's opinion), Leonard is sensitive and short, Sheldon is very thin and persnickety (to put it mildly and pretentiously), Raj is afraid of women (except when inebriated), and Howard lives with his emasculating mother (and is further emasculated by Bernadette . . . and Raj . . . and Sheldon). None of them watch or participate in sports (though Sheldon is an expert in the rules of football, having grown up in Texas), and they all enjoy "juvenile" activities such as playing video games and reading comic books.[13] Their collective failure to meet the standard model of a "man" is reinforced by the men Penny brings home: huge, muscular, ruggedly handsome, albeit usually dumb as rocks (especially Zack from "The Lunar Excitation," who thought the laser the guys were bouncing off the moon would blow it up).[14] The one exception is Dr. David Underhill. Introduced in "The Bath Gift Item Hypothesis," Underhill is a prominent physicist who received a MacArthur Genius Grant but looks as if he jumped out of a "Hot Firemen" calendar. Although this combination definitely confounds Penny's expectations, she later decides he's not that smart after all when she discovers the nude pictures of his wife on his cell phone (which only confirms yet another male stereotype: infidelity).

Just as women such as Amy and Leslie may be seen as less than "real women" because they don't conform to society's standard of femininity, many people would view our four male friends as less than "real men," despite their Ph.D.s (and a master's degree from the Massachusetts Institute of Technology, thank you very much), simply because they don't exhibit the "typical" behavior and appearance that society expects from those of the male gender. On the bright side, there are signs that these stereotypes may be diminishing, given the heightened respect and admiration for men such as Bill Gates and Mark Zuckerberg—not to mention the fact that Peter Orzsag seems to be as popular with women as Robert Pattinson is.[15] Yet this does not negate the fact that men are subject to same socially constructed preconceptions of behaviors as women are, even if the ramifications are different.[16]

## White and Fisher Productions #1

A sitcom about four young, socially awkward scientists and the "normal" girl who hangs out with them may not seem like the most obvious source material for an exploration of gender theory and feminist philosophy, but in a way it's ideal. There are plenty of shows on TV—not to mention movies, especially romantic comedies—that feature only "pretty people" whom casting directors discover in modeling agencies, chosen to fulfill viewers' fantasies about what the perfect woman or man looks like, with scripts designed by committee to deliver socially idealized behavior. And that's just wonderful. (Yes, Sheldon, that was sarcasm.)

Yet deviations from the norm are often much more interesting. Penny's a great character, but we wouldn't want everyone on the show to be just like her—as the solitary "normal" person, she becomes interesting when in the company of Leonard and the gang, and the guys are even more interesting in contrast to her, as well as to one another. Not only do almost all of the characters challenge gender expectations, but they each do so in their own unique ways. Does it make them any more interesting to label them male or female as well? Ultimately, that's what Butler is getting at: gender is artificial, a label that unnecessarily limits and constrains us. If *The Big Bang Theory* can help us see that, it would be the ultimate act of change through parody—and one hell of a bazinga!

# NOTES

1. We don't have space to talk about this at length, but issues of sexuality are also relevant here, because a man with "feminine" characteristics or a woman with "male" characteristics is often perceived as homosexual. That perceptions of gender and sexuality are so tightly intertwined is one reason that queer studies is a close descendant of gender studies.

2. Plato, *The Republic*, trans. Desmond Lee (London: Penguin Classics, 2007), 451b–457b. Plato's claims to proto-feminism are widely challenged, given statements such as "it is natural of women to take part in all occupations as well as men, though in all women will be the weaker partners" (ibid., 455d); on this controversy, see Steven Forde, "Gender and Justice in Plato," *American Political Science Review* 92, no. 3: 657–670.

3. John Stuart Mill, *The Subjection of Women*, ed. Susan M. Okin (Indianapolis: Hackett, 1988), 22.

4. For a brief history of work on the social construction of gender, see Martha Nussbaum, "The Professor of Parody," *New Republic*, February 22, 1999, <http://www.akad.se/Nussbaum.pdf>.

5. Simone de Beauvoir, *The Second Sex* (New York: Vintage Books, 1952), 267.

6. Self-creation and radical freedom are also key insights of the existentialist philosopher Jean-Paul Sartre (1905–1980), who was Beauvoir's lifelong partner.

7. Judith Butler, *Gender Trouble*, 2nd ed. (Abingdon, UK: Routledge, 1999).

8. Butler takes the argument even one step further, claiming that sex, as well as gender, is socially constructed because of the arbitrary "decision" to assign sex based on reproductive organs; see *Gender Trouble*, chap. 3.

9. Of course, if we are going to call Penny a parody of traditional femininity, what do we call her friend Christy, "the whore of Omaha," who in "The Dumpling Paradox" makes Penny seem like Marie Curie?

10. Hence the title of Nussbaum's article cited earlier, "The Professor of Parody," which is a critique of Butler's work, especially what Nussbaum sees as a relatively weak form of protest compared to other political action, even by scholars, which advanced the actual status of women and improved their well-being. See Butler, *Gender Trouble*, 187–189 (using cross-dressing as the main example of parodying traditional gender roles).

11. Leonard's mother seems to be between Bernadette and Amy—wicked smart, with a staid but not unattractive fashion sense and is incredibly awkward and formal. (While sober, that is.)

12. As longtime sitcom fans, we find it wonderful to see Sara Gilbert (Leslie) and Johnny Galecki (Leonard) reprise their pairing from *Roseanne*, which also challenged traditional gender roles by portraying Gilbert's Darlene as dominant over Galecki's David (while Becky and Mark were very stereotypical—oh, don't get us started . . .).

13. Your humble authors just read comics for the profound insights into gender theory. (Bazinga.)

14. Everyone knows they'd have to bounce the laser off the moon at least a couple of times to blow it up. Duh.

15. We wish this was a bazinga, we truly do.

16. As above, sexuality often enters into this as well, because a man who fails to conform to the stereotype will often be regarded as homosexual. For instance, Ryan Pacifico, a currency trader (and a heterosexual), was a victim of gay-bashing at work because he was a vegetarian and therefore not seen by his boss as a "real man". See Zachary A. Kramer, "Of Meat and Manhood," *Washington University Law Review* 89 (2011): 287–322, discussed in Mark D. White, "Can a Vegetarian Sue for Employment Discrimination?" *Psychology Today*, March 28, 2011, <www.psychologytoday.com/blog/maybe-its-just-me/201103/can-vegetarian-sue-employment-discrimination>.

# THE EPISODE COMPENDIUM

"Hey, It's a Big Menu—There's Two
Pages Just for Desserts"

| Season/# | Episode | Air date |
|----------|---------|----------|
| 1.01 | Pilot | 09.24.07 |
| 1.02 | The Big Bran Hypothesis | 10.01.07 |
| 1.03 | The Fuzzy Boots Corollary | 10.08.07 |
| 1.04 | The Luminous Fish Effect | 10.15.07 |
| 1.05 | The Hamburger Postulate | 10.22.07 |
| 1.06 | The Middle-Earth Paradigm | 10.29.07 |
| 1.07 | The Dumpling Paradox | 11.05.07 |
| 1.08 | The Grasshopper Experiment | 11.12.07 |
| 1.09 | The Cooper-Hofstadter Polarization | 03.17.08 |
| 1.10 | The Loobenfeld Decay | 03.24.08 |
| 1.11 | The Pancake Batter Anomaly | 03.31.08 |
| 1.12 | The Jerusalem Duality | 04.14.08 |
| 1.13 | The Bat Jar Conjecture | 04.21.08 |
| 1.14 | The Nerdvana Annihilation | 04.28.08 |

*(continued)*

| Season/# | Episode | Air date |
|---|---|---|
| 1.15 | The Pork Chop Indeterminacy | 05.05.08 |
| 1.16 | The Peanut Reaction | 05.12.08 |
| 1.17 | The Tangerine Factor | 05.19.08 |
| 2.01 | The Bad Fish Paradigm | 09.22.08 |
| 2.02 | The Codpiece Topology | 09.29.08 |
| 2.03 | The Barbarian Sublimation | 10.06.08 |
| 2.04 | The Griffin Equivalency | 10.13.08 |
| 2.05 | The Euclid Alternative | 10.20.08 |
| 2.06 | The Cooper-Nowitzki Theorem | 11.03.08 |
| 2.07 | The Panty Piñata Polarization | 11.10.08 |
| 2.08 | The Lizard-Spock Expansion | 11.17.08 |
| 2.09 | The White Asparagus Triangulation | 11.24.08 |
| 2.10 | The Vartabedian Conundrum | 12.08.08 |
| 2.11 | The Bath Item Gift Hypothesis | 12.15.08 |
| 2.12 | The Killer Robot Instability | 01.12.09 |
| 2.13 | The Friendship Algorithm | 01.19.09 |
| 2.14 | The Financial Permeability | 02.02.09 |
| 2.15 | The Maternal Capacitance | 02.09.09 |
| 2.16 | The Cushion Saturation | 03.02.09 |
| 2.17 | The Terminator Decoupling | 03.09.09 |
| 2.18 | The Work Song Nanocluster | 03.16.09 |
| 2.19 | The Dead Hooker Juxtaposition | 03.30.09 |
| 2.20 | The Hofstadter Isotope | 04.13.09 |
| 2.21 | The Vegas Renormalization | 04.27.09 |
| 2.22 | The Classified Materials Turbulence | 05.04.09 |
| 2.23 | The Monopolar Expedition | 05.11.09 |

*(continued)*

| Season/# | Episode | Air date |
| --- | --- | --- |
| 3.01 | The Electric Can Opener Fluctuation | 09.21.09 |
| 3.02 | The Jiminy Conjecture | 09.28.09 |
| 3.03 | The Gothowitz Deviation | 10.05.09 |
| 3.04 | The Pirate Solution | 10.12.09 |
| 3.05 | The Creepy Candy Coating Corollary | 10.19.09 |
| 3.06 | The Cornhusker Vortex | 11.02.09 |
| 3.07 | The Guitarist Amplification | 11.09.09 |
| 3.08 | The Adhesive Duck Deficiency | 11.16.09 |
| 3.09 | The Vengeance Formulation | 11.23.09 |
| 3.10 | The Gorilla Experiment | 12.07.09 |
| 3.11 | The Maternal Congruence | 12.14.09 |
| 3.12 | The Psychic Vortex | 01.11.10 |
| 3.13 | The Bozeman Reaction | 01.18.10 |
| 3.14 | The Einstein Approximation | 02.01.10 |
| 3.15 | The Large Hadron Collision | 02.08.10 |
| 3.16 | The Excelsior Acquisition | 03.01.10 |
| 3.17 | The Precious Fragmentation | 03.08.10 |
| 3.18 | The Pants Alternative | 03.22.10 |
| 3.19 | The Wheaton Recurrence | 04.12.10 |
| 3.20 | The Spaghetti Catalyst | 05.03.10 |
| 3.21 | The Plimpton Stimulation | 05.10.10 |
| 3.22 | The Staircase Implementation | 05.17.10 |
| 3.23 | The Lunar Excitation | 05.24.10 |
| 4.01 | The Robotic Manipulation | 09.23.10 |
| 4.02 | The Cruciferous Vegetable Amplification | 09.30.10 |
| 4.03 | The Zazzy Substitution | 10.07.10 |

*(continued)*

| Season/# | Episode | Air date |
|---|---|---|
| 4.04 | The Hot Troll Deviation | 10.14.10 |
| 4.05 | The Desperation Emanation | 10.21.10 |
| 4.06 | The Irish Pub Formulation | 10.28.10 |
| 4.07 | The Apology Insufficiency | 11.04.10 |
| 4.08 | The 21-Second Excitation | 11.11.10 |
| 4.09 | The Boyfriend Complexity | 11.18.10 |
| 4.10 | The Alien Parasite Hypothesis | 12.09.10 |
| 4.11 | The Justice League Recombination | 12.16.10 |
| 4.12 | The Bus Pants Utilization | 01.06.11 |
| 4.13 | The Love Car Displacement | 01.20.11 |
| 4.14 | The Thespian Catalyst | 02.03.11 |
| 4.15 | The Benefactor Factor | 02.10.11 |
| 4.16 | The Cohabitation Formulation | 02.17.11 |
| 4.17 | The Toast Derivation | 02.24.11 |
| 4.18 | The Prestidigitation Approximation | 03.10.11 |
| 4.19 | The Zarnecki Incursion | 03.31.11 |
| 4.20 | The Herb Garden Germination | 04.07.11 |
| 4.21 | The Agreement Dissection | 04.28.11 |
| 4.22 | The Wildebeest Implementation | 05.05.11 |
| 4.23 | The Engagement Reaction | 05.12.11 |
| 4.24 | The Roommate Transmogrification | 05.19.11 |

# CONTRIBUTORS

But If We Were Part of the Team . . .
We Could Drink for Free in Any Bar
in Any College Town

**Adam Barkman** (Ph.D., Free University of Amsterdam) is an assistant professor of philosophy at Redeemer University College. He is the author of *C. S. Lewis and Philosophy as a Way of Life*, *Through Common Things*, and *Above All Things* and is the coeditor of *Manga and Philosophy* and *The Philosophy of Ang Lee*. Although he doesn't have a pair of Incredible Hulk hands or a Green Lantern lantern, he does have a nice collection of Superman T-shirts.

**Ashley Barkman** is a professor at Redeemer University College. Her recent publications include several contributions to the Pop Culture and Philosophy series, including *Mad Men*, *30 Rock*, and *Manga*. As a mom of two toddlers and one more on the way, she expects to be sassed in Eskimo talk in due time.

**Gregory L. Bock** is currently an assistant professor of philosophy at Walters State Community College in Morristown, Tennessee and a Ph.D. candidate at the University of Tennessee,

Knoxville. His interests include ethics, philosophy of religion, and Secret Agent Laser Obstacle Chess.

**Jeffrey L. Bock** is currently working as the operations manager for a small web marketing firm in his hometown of Longview, Texas. He has an intense interest in all things pop culture and consumes entertainment in many forms like popcorn. He writes fiction in his spare time. As for education, he easily identifies with and sympathizes with Howard Wolowitz's master's degree. Jeff's "lowly" master's degree is in history, which he received from the University of Texas at Tyler.

**W. Scott Clifton** is currently a philosophy graduate student at the University of Washington-Seattle, working in the areas of aesthetics, philosophy of mind, and ethics. When he's not working on his dissertation, he sits at the feet of Sheldon, Leonard, Howard, and Raj, learning how to live the life of the mind. Bazinga!

**Nicholas G. Evans** is a doctoral candidate at the Centre for Applied Philosophy and Public Ethics, the Australian National University, Canberra. His research interests include biosecurity and freedom of speech and the ethics of futuristic military technology. He has published in *New Wars and New Soldiers: Military Ethics in the Contemporary World* (Ashgate, 2011), *Nanoethics*, and TheConversation.edu.au. When he isn't strapped to his desk trying to convince people the world is about to end, he's to be found riding his bicycle at unsafe speeds down mountains. He also did an honors degree in physics once, which means he occasionally tears up with nostalgia while watching *The Big Bang Theory*.

**Don Fallis** is an associate professor of information resources and an adjunct associate professor of philosophy at the University of Arizona. He has written several philosophy articles on lying and deception, including "What Is Lying?"

in the *Journal of Philosophy* and "The Most Terrific Liar You Ever Saw in Your Life," in the forthcoming *The Catcher in the Rye and Philosophy*. He is actually a math nerd, rather than a physics nerd. (His Erdös number is 5.) But having enjoyed living in Tucson, Arizona, for more than ten years, he agrees with Sheldon: "Why wouldn't the Sonoran Desert make a perfectly good promised land?"

**Maryanne L. Fisher** is an associate professor in the Department of Psychology at Saint Mary's University and a member of the interuniversity Women and Gender Studies Program. As a psychological researcher who uses an evolutionary perspective, she has focused on "unraveling the mysteries" of interpersonal relationships "that all started with a Big Bang" and has published approximately sixty peer-reviewed articles on this topic. She is an editor of an upcoming book, *Evolution's Empress: Darwinian Perspectives on the Nature of Women* (Oxford University Press). Her main research topic is women's intrasexual competition for mates. She thinks Penny should be happy to have someone like Amy for a friend because who else would "commence operation 'Priya Wouldn't Wanna Be-ya'" to get rid of one's mating rival?

**Andrew Zimmerman Jones** attended Wabash College, where he majored in physics and minored in philosophy in an effort to unravel the mysteries of the universe. He now works as a science writer, as the About.com Physics Guide, and is the author of *String Theory for Dummies*. He's contributed to *Heroes and Philosophy*, *Green Lantern and Philosophy*, and the upcoming *Avengers and Philosophy* and *The Girl with the Dragon Tattoo and Philosophy*. Andrew can be found online at http://www.azjones.info/. He lives in central Indiana with his wife, two young sons, and a growing T-shirt collection that would rival a certain CalTech string theorist's in geek-filled splendor.

**Dean A. Kowalski** is an associate professor of philosophy at the University of Wisconsin-Waukesha. He is the author of *Classic Questions and Contemporary Film* (2005) and *Moral Theory at the Movies* (2012). He is the editor of *Steven Spielberg and Philosophy* (2008) and *The Philosophy of The X-Files* (2009) and the coeditor of *The Philosophy of Joss Whedon* (2011). Every December since 2002, he has sent Rupert Murdoch thirty pieces of silverware. He now eats with plastic forks, yet his Fridays remain *Firefly*-less. Murdoch! . . . Murrr-doch!!

**Jon Lawhead** received his B.A. in philosophy from the University of California, Berkeley, in 2007, and is currently a doctoral candidate in philosophy at Columbia University. He works mainly in the foundations of the natural sciences, with a special interest in problems at the foundations of fundamental physics, complex systems theory, climatology, and information theory. When he is not banging his head against big scientific questions, he enjoys juggling a variety of nontraditional objects and participating in amateur locksmithing events. He lives in a secret underground lair with his Siamese cat Cerebro.

**Greg Littmann** Around fourteen billion years ago, Greg Littmann was in a hot, dense state. He expanded along with the rest of the universe and has been, among other things, hydrogen and helium gas, interstellar dust, beautiful sinewy cephalopods, and ferocious dinosaurs. In the late twentieth century, the parts of Greg Littmann came together for the first time, in the form of a simian primate. In this form, he is seized by a desire to understand the universe around him. He has a Ph.D. in philosophy from UNC-CH and teaches at SIUE. He has published in evolutionary epistemology and the philosophy of logic and has written book chapters relating philosophy to *Doctor Who, Dune, Final Fantasy, Game of Thrones, The Onion, Sherlock Holmes, The Terminator,* and *The Walking Dead.* In two billion years' time, he will become part of a huge new galaxy when our Milky Way smashes spectacularly into Andromeda, which is a cool way to go if you have to go.

**Ruth E. Lowe** is a Ph.D. candidate at the University of St. Andrews, Scotland. She is currently working on paradoxes in political dialogues about minority rights, ethnicity, and culture in modern liberal democracies. Other philosophical interests include law, mind, history, aesthetics, and rhetoric. One day, she hopes to be an actual real philosopher.

**Adolfas Mackonis** has just recently entered the glorious social strata of Sheldon, Leonard, and Raj as a doctor of philosophy from Vilnius University in Lithuania. He has a spot on his couch where he thinks about logic, philosophy of science, and methodology of science. In other words, Adolfas studies how people reason, how people should reason, and whether people should reason at all. The requirement of being as empathic as Sheldon comes with the territory.

**Massimo Pigliucci** is a professor of philosophy at the City University of New York's Lehman College and Graduate Center. In his previous (academic) life, he was an evolutionary biologist. He is the author of *Nonsense on Stilts: How to Tell Science from Bunk* and of the forthcoming *The Intelligent Person's Guide to the Meaning of Life*. He has contributed to *The Philosophy of the Daily Show* (he thinks Jon Stewart is a modern Socrates but funnier) and to the forthcoming *The Philosophy of Sherlock Holmes*. His musings can be regularly found at rationallyspeaking.org. Whenever he watches the *Big Bang Theory*, he can't avoid the strong feeling that he might have ended up like Sheldon if philosophy had not come to his rescue.

**Janelle Pötzsch** is a research assistant at the Ruhr-University of Bochum, Germany. When not writing her Ph.D. thesis on business ethics (yes, there is such a thing!) or essays about nerds, she, an avid jogger, seeks a runner's high that will "tear the mask off nature," having her "stare at the face of God."

**Kenneth Wayne Sayles III** earned his M.S. in computer science in 2004 from the University of Texas at El Paso (UTEP) investigating the effects of computer personalities on users. He has worked in information security since 2006 and holds the following certifications: CISSP, CIEH, CEPT, CISA, and CISM. He completed a M.A. in philosophy in 2010, also from UTEP, after demonstrating how classical social contract theory can be used to better understand the Internet. His essay in this book is his first contribution to the popular culture and philosophy genre. In his free time he debates which is better, *Star Trek IV* or *Star Trek V*, and he often wonders what Penny's last name is.

**Donna Marie Smith** works with some of the best geeks in "the whole universe" at the Palm Beach County Library System in Florida. She has contributed essays to *Doctor Who and Philosophy* and *The Catcher in the Rye and Philosophy* and reviews books on media studies for *Library Journal*. Unlike Dr. Sheldon Cooper, she doesn't consider the adorably geeky actor Wil Wheaton to be "Evil Wil." In fact, she hopes to *someday*—like Sheldon—be lucky enough to have Wil sign her *Star Trek: The Next Generation* Ensign Wesley Crusher action figure, which she's kept mint-in-box for fifteen years.

**Mark D. White** is a professor and the chair of the Department of Political Science, Economics, and Philosophy at the College of Staten Island/CUNY, where he teaches courses that combine economics, philosophy, and law. He is the author of *Kantian Ethics and Economics: Autonomy, Dignity, and Character* (Stanford, 2011) and has edited (or coedited) books for the present series on Batman, Watchmen, Iron Man, Green Lantern, and the Avengers. He suspects he may share Raj's pathological fear of talking to women, but strangely enough he's never had a chance to find out.

# INDEX

## Cornucopia . . . Let's Make That Our Word of the Day